# Read & Think 2019
# SPANISH

# Read & Think
# SPANISH

Learn the language and discover
the culture of the Spanish-speaking
world through reading

## The Editors of
## *Think Spanish!* Magazine

New York   Chicago   San Francisco   Lisbon   London   Madrid   Mexico City
Milan   New Delhi   San Juan   Seoul   Singapore   Sydney   Toronto

# Essex County Council Libraries

**Library of Congress Cataloging-in-Publication Data**

Read & think Spanish : learn the language and discover the culture of the Spanish-
speaking world through reading / the editors of Think Spanish! Magazine.
    xiv, 206 p. : ill. ; 23 cm.
    ISBN 0-07-146033-0
    1. Spanish language—Readers.
PC4117 .R33    2006
468.6'421—dc22                   2005053117

3  4  5  6  7  8  9  10  11  12  13  14   DOC/DOC   0  9  8  7  6  (0-07-146033-0)
3  4  5  6  7  8  9  10  11  12  13  14   DOC/DOC   0  9  8  7  6  (0-07-147492-7)

ISBN-13: 978-0-07-146033-0 (book alone)
ISBN-10:     0-07-146033-0 (book alone)
ISBN-13: 978-0-07-147492-4 (book for set)
ISBN-10:     0-07-147492-7 (book for set)
ISBN-13: 978-0-07-146034-7 (book and CD set)
ISBN-10:     0-07-146034-9 (book and CD set)

McGraw-Hill books are available at special quantity discounts to use as premiums and
sales promotions, or for use in corporate training programs. For more information, please
write to the Director of Special Sales, Professional Publishing, McGraw-Hill, Two Penn
Plaza, New York, NY 10121-2298. Or contact your local bookstore.

This book is printed on acid-free paper.

# Contents

## Cultura

## Viaje

# Tradición

# Celebración

# Personas

# Deportes

# Música

# Historia

# Geografía

# Gastronomía

# Introduction

*Read & Think Spanish!* is an engaging and non-intimidating approach to language learning. A dynamic, at-home language immersion, *Read & Think Spanish!* is intended to increase Spanish fluency while teaching you about life and culture in Spanish-speaking countries.

This language learning tool is designed to build on and expand your confidence with Spanish, presenting vocabulary and phrases in meaningful and motivating content emphasizing all four language skills: reading, writing, speaking, and understanding the spoken language.

*Read & Think Spanish!* brings the Spanish language to life! Our diverse team of international writers is excited about sharing their language and culture with you. Read a travel narrative from Spain and a documentary on Colombian folk music. Explore the geography of the Amazon and the jungles of Costa Rica. And don't forget, while you are enjoying these intriguing articles, you are learning Spanish.

*Read & Think Spanish!* is used by educators and students of all ages to increase Spanish fluency naturally and effectively. Using this as a complement to classroom study or as a self-study guide, you will actively build grammar and develop vocabulary.

The cultural information provided in each chapter creates a deeper understanding of the traditions and cultures in Spanish-speaking countries and in turn fosters greater interest and success with learning Spanish. Each article is accompanied by a bilingual glossary. You can read and learn without stopping to look up words in a dictionary or phrase book.

*Read & Think Spanish!* **accommodates a range of skill sets from beginning to advanced:**

• **Beginning:** We recommend that the student have the equivalent of one semester of college- or high-school-level Spanish. Your previous experience with Spanish may have been through studies at a private or public school, self-study programs, or immersion programs. *Read & Think Spanish!* will allow you to immerse yourself in the language and the culture; and your understanding of sentence structure and use of verbs will be reinforced.

• **Intermediate:** As an intermediate student, you will learn new vocabulary and phrases. You will notice increased fluency and comprehension. You will also learn nuances about the language and the culture as you experience the authentic writing styles of authors from different countries.

• **Advanced:** The advanced student will continue to gain valuable information, as language acquisition is a life-long endeavor. The diverse topics from a team of international writers offer you the opportunity to learn new vocabulary and gain new insight into the language and the people.

Whatever your current skill level, *Read & Think Spanish!* is an effective, fun, and accessible way to learn Spanish.

Experience the enthusiasm that comes with learning a new language and discovering a new culture. Read, speak, enjoy—Think Spanish!

# Guidelines for Success

*Read & Think Spanish!* is divided into chapters guiding you through the cultures and traditions of different Spanish-speaking countries. At the end of each chapter is a "Test your comprehension" section. This section encourages development of reading comprehension and the understanding of written Spanish in different voices.

It is not necessary for you to read *Read & Think Spanish!* from start to finish or in any certain order. You can read one chapter at a time or pick an article or chapter that is of particular interest to you. You can complete the test questions by article or by chapter. This flexibility allows you to go at your own pace, reading and re-reading when needed. The high-interest articles encourage enthusiasm as you study and make the material more enjoyable to read.

• Read through the article to get the general idea of the story line. Do not get frustrated if the first time through you do not fully understand the vocabulary.

• After you gain an understanding of the article, read through the story again and focus on vocabulary that is new to you. Notice how the vocabulary is used in context.

• Practice reading the article aloud.

• If you have access to an audio recorder practice recording the articles or ask a fluent speaker to record them for you. Listen to the recording and notice how your listening comprehension improves over time.

**Repeat, Repeat, Repeat!** This is especially important for memorizing important parts and forms of words. Sometimes only active repetition will secure your memory for certain hard-to-retain items. Frequent vocal repetition impresses the forms on your "mental ear." This auditory dimension will help you recognize and recall the words later. With *Read & Think Spanish!* you have the opportunity to repeat different learning processes as often as you like as many times as you want. Repeat reading, repeat listening, and repeat speaking will aid in your overall success mastering the Spanish language.

# Custom Bilingual Glossary

A custom bilingual glossary is provided next to each article to facilitate ease and understanding while reading in Spanish. With uninterrupted reading, comprehension is improved and vocabulary is rapidly absorbed.

Every article contains new grammar, vocabulary, and phrases, as well as repetition of previous vocabulary and phrases. The repetition throughout the articles enhances reading comprehension and encourages memorization. The articles are written in different perspectives. Most articles are written in third person while some are written in first person. This change of voice allows you to recognize verbs as they are conjugated in different tenses.

Spanish instructors often recommend that students "create an image" or associate foreign words with something familiar to enhance memorization of new vocabulary. As you are learning new vocabulary with *Read & Think Spanish!* you will not have to "create" these images. The images will be automatically created for you as the story unfolds. Take your time as you are reading and imagine the story as it is written, absorbing the new vocabulary. If a vocabulary word is particularly difficult, try focusing on an image in the story that the word represents as you say the word or phrase aloud.

Verbs in the glossary are written first in their conjugated form as they appear in the article as well as in their infinitive form.

For example:   **salimos/salir:** we went/to go
**aportaban/aportar:** they carried/to carry

# Test Your Comprehension

The test questions provided at the end of each chapter are designed to further develop your reading comprehension skills and ensure your overall success with Spanish. In addition to determining the general meaning of the article by word formation, grammar, and vocabulary, you will also learn how to use context to determine meaning. Understanding context allows you to make educated "guesses" about the meaning of unfamiliar words based on the context of a sentence, paragraph, or article. Answers are provided at the end of the book and within each chapter.

## About the Author

*Read & Think Spanish!* is based on articles from *Think Spanish! Audio Magazine*, a monthly language learning periodical published by Second Language Publishing. The writers for *Think Spanish! Audio Magazine* are native Spanish speakers, including college and high school Spanish instructors, travel experts, and journalists. Articles in this book were coordinated and compiled under the direction of Kelly Garboden, Founder and Editor-in-Chief of Second Language Publishing. For subscription information about *Think Spanish! Audio Magazine* visit www.readspanish.com.

# Read & Think
# SPANISH

Los hombres son como los astros,
que unos dan luz de sí y otros brillan con la que reciben.

José Martí

# Cultura

# Los vejigantes
## PUERTO RICO

Loiza es un **pueblo** al noreste de Puerto Rico. Sus **habitantes** son de descendencia africana **ya que muchos** de los **esclavos traídos a la isla** durante **la conquista española se asentaron** allí. Los esclavos no tenían **libertad de religión** y los españoles **se encargaron** de **convertirlos** al **cristianismo**.

Los vejigantes **nacen** como una forma de **mantener** su religión **mezclada** con la religión cristiana. Ellos representan a los **Moros** que **no eran** cristianos.

Durante las fiestas de **Santiago Apóstol** el 25 de julio, los vejigantes **salen a la calle para asustar a los jóvenes**. **Usualmente**, las personas **se visten** con **mamelucos** grandes y de **colores brillantes**.

Las **mangas parecen alas**. **Lo más impresionante** son las **máscaras** que usan. Están **hechas de coco**. El coco **se corta en 45 grados**. Luego **se saca la fruta de adentro** y la parte **mas dura** del interior. En el exterior **se talla** una **cara grotesca**, pintada también de colores brillantes. Los **dientes** se hacen de **bambú** y los **cuernos** del **tallo** de los **racimos** de **guineo**.

Los vejigantes son parte de la tradición puertorriqueña y de la integración de diferentes **razas** en nuestra cultura.

# ¿Quién es el jíbaro?

## PUERTO RICO

El **jíbaro** es el **orgullo** de Puerto Rico. Representa al hombre **trabajador** del **campo**. Su figura simboliza la honestidad y el **sentimiento** de **lucha** del pueblo puertorriqueño.

El jíbaro es **humilde**. **Viste pantalones anchos**, **camisas holgadas a medio abrochar** y un **sombrero de paja**, la pava, sobre su cabeza para **cubrirse del sol candente** del Caribe. La pava también se **ha convertido** en símbolo de nuestro país. El jíbaro es **luchador**, **pobre**, pero **lleno de sueños**. **Contra viento y marea**, **se mantiene fuerte**. Así es el pueblo de Puerto Rico. Así es el puertorriqueño y el jíbaro se mantiene vivo **para recordarnos lo que somos**. Nuestro **famoso compositor**, Rafael Hernández, **supo** de su importancia y le escribió una **canción**: El Jíbaro.

**jíbaro:** Puerto Rican peasant
**orgullo:** pride
**trabajador:** hard worker
**campo:** field/the country
**sentimiento:** feeling
**lucha:** fight/battle
**humilde:** humble
**viste pantalones anchos:** wears wide pants
**camisas holgadas a medio abrochar:** half-buttoned, loose shirts
**sombrero de paja:** straw hat
**cubrirse del sol candente:** to cover himself from the hot sun
**ha convertido/convertir:** has become/ to become
**luchador:** fighter
**pobre:** poor
**lleno de sueños:** filled with dreams
**contra viento y marea:** against all odds (idiom)
**se mantiene fuerte/mantener:** keeps himself strong/to keep
**para recordarnos lo que somos:** to remind us of what we are
**famoso compositor:** famous composer/song writer
**supo/saber:** knew/to know
**canción:** song

## CULTURE NOTE

Traditionally a *jíbaro* was a poor mountain man (as in the American hillbilly)—someone from the mountains, in *el campo* or *"la isla"* as they refer to the heart of the island in Puerto Rico. Not all residents of the interior of the island were *jíbaros*. Some were *hacendados* from well-to-do families. The *hacendados,* who considered themselves *españoles*, were well educated, often completing their education in Europe, and had servants. Music was a major component in the development of the *jíbaro* persona. *Jíbaros* made their own entertainment and most of the time that meant music. With strong Spanish roots, the *jíbaros* became poets, composers, and great story tellers. A variety of instruments contribute to the rich variety of folk music found in Puerto Rico. Some of the most popular include the percussion instruments called *tambours* (hollowed tree trunks covered with stretched-out animal skin), *maracas* (gourds filled with pebbles or dried beans and mounted on handles), and a variety of drums whose original designs were brought from Africa.

| | |
|---|---|
| **ir de tapas:** to go around to the bars eating tapas (popular expression) | |

**ir de tapas:** to go around to the bars eating tapas (popular expression)
**costumbre culinaria:** culinary custom
**amantes del buen comer:** lovers of good food
**se niegan/negarse:** they refuse to do something/to refuse to do something
**vistosos:** colorful, spectacular
**han sobrevivido/sobrevivir:** they have survived/to survive
**a través de los siglos:** throughout the centuries
**aunque:** although
**modalidades:** forms, types
**según:** according to
**normas:** rules
**tapeo:** eating tapas
**son compartidas/compartir:** they are shared/to share
**acudir en grupo:** to go in groups
**pedir:** to ask for
**comerlas con el resto/comer:** eat them with the rest of the group/to eat
**vinillo:** diminutive of vino (wine)
**alegrar el alma:** to cheer up one's soul
**hablar sin parar:** to talk non-stop
**alrededor:** around
**parece que muestren/mostrar:** it seems like they show/to show
**desprecio:** scorn, contempt
**se da prioridad:** priority is given
**gesto:** gesture
**charla:** chat; talk
**se la debemos/deber:** we owe it/to owe
**rey:** king
**bajo sus órdenes:** under his orders
**mesones:** inns
**copas y jarras:** glasses and pitchers
**acompañados con:** with, together with
**pretendía/pretender:** he pretended/to pretend
**se empapara/empaparse:** it got soaked/to get soaked
**no subiese tan rápido a la cabeza:** it didn't go to their heads, to get drunk
**asiduos:** regular customers
**tabernas:** taverns
**evitando/evitar:** avoiding/to avoid
**peleas:** fights
**alborotos:** disturbances

# De tapeo
### ESPAÑA

**Ir de tapas** es una **costumbre culinaria** a la que pocos **amantes del buen comer se niegan**. Estos platos, tan pequeños como **vistosos**, **han sobrevivido a través de los siglos** y son, sin duda, los reyes de la vida social española.

**Aunque** las recetas y **modalidades** varían **según** la región donde las comamos, las **normas** del **tapeo son compartidas** por todos los españoles: **acudir en grupo, pedir** varias tapas para **comerlas con el resto,** beber un **vinillo** para **alegrar el alma** y **hablar sin parar**. De hecho, si se observa a las personas que están **alrededor** de una mesa con tapas **parece que muestren** un elegante **desprecio** hacia la comida y es que, en realidad, **se da prioridad** al **gesto** y a la buena **charla** entre amigos.

La existencia de las tapas **se la debemos** al **rey** Alfonso X ya que fue **bajo sus órdenes** que los **mesones** castellanos empezaron a servir las **copas y jarras** de vino **acompañados con** algo de comida. Con esta nueva norma, el monarca **pretendía** que el alimento **se empapara** del alcohol y el vino **no subiese tan rápido a la cabeza** de los **asiduos** a las **tabernas**, **evitando** así **peleas** y otros **alborotos**.

A pesar de ser un **manjar apto para todos los bolsillos**, las tapas y su relación con la **alta alcurnia** no es poca, pues deben también su nombre a otro monarca. **Cuenta la leyenda** que el rey Alfonso XIII, de visita en la provincia de Cádiz, decidió entrar en el Ventorrillo del Chato—una **venta** que hoy en día aún existe para **refrigerarse** y **descansar un rato.** El **camarero** le llevó una copa de **jerez** al monarca y cuando la depositó en la mesa una **ventisca de arena** entró por la ventana.

Muy **avispado**, el **mozo** tuvo la idea de **tapar** la copa con una **loncha de jamón** para evitar que la arena (o algún **bichito volador**) **arruinara** el vino, **disculpándose** ante el rey por "**colocar** una **tapa**" para proteger el jerez. Le gustó tanto el **ingenioso sobrenombre** a Alfonso XIII que al rato pidió otra copa de jerez "pero con otra tapa igual". Los miembros de la Corte que le **acompañaban** imitaron el **pedido** y, desde entonces, la historia cuenta que la comida que acompaña a la bebida en los **aperitivos** recibe el nombre de tapas.

De las lonchas de jamón o queso que constituían las primeras tapas de la historia se ha pasado a una variedad tal que **supera toda imaginación.** **Chocos, patatas bravas, aceitunas rellenas, boquerones, croquetas, champiñones al ajillo, embutido, pescaíto frito, sepia a la plancha, gambas, tigres, bombas, chistorra** o **pulpo a la gallega**, son algunas de **las más demandadas.** Como **acompañamiento**, no puede faltar el vino o la sangría, aunque cada vez más, se está **imponiendo** la **cerveza.** **¿Alguien se apunta** a unas auténticas tapitas?

**a pesar de:** in spite of
**manjar:** delicacy
**apto para todos los bolsillos:** fit for all pockets (Idiom meaning "cheap")
**alta alcurnia:** high lineage, high
**cuenta la leyenda:** the legend says that
**venta:** country inn
**refrigerarse:** to get chilled
**descansar:** to rest
**un rato:** a (short) while
**camarero:** waiter
**jerez:** sherry
**ventisca de arena:** sand blizzard
**avispado:** sharp, bright
**mozo:** waiter
**tapar:** to cover
**loncha de jamón:** ham slice
**bichito volador:** little flying bug
**arruinara/arruinar:** it would wreck/to wreck, to destroy
**disculpándose/disculparse:** apologizing/ to apologize
**colocar:** to put
**tapa:** cover
**ingenioso sobrenombre:** witty nickname
**acompañaban/acompañar:** they went with him/to go with
**pedido:** order
**aperitivos:** appetizers
**supera toda imaginación:** it goes beyond imagination
**chocos:** squid rings
**patatas bravas:** spicy potatoes
**aceitunas rellenas:** stuffed olives
**boquerones:** fresh anchovies
**croquetas:** croquettes
**champiñones al ajillo:** garlic mushrooms
**embutido:** different pork sausages
**pescaíto frito:** little fried fish
**sepia a la plancha:** grilled cuttlefish
**gambas:** shrimp
**tigres:** stuffed mussels
**bombas:** breaded meat-balls
**chistorra:** a kind of chorizo
**pulpo a la gallega:** Galician octupus
**las más demandadas:** the most requested
**acompañamiento:** accompaniment
**impondiendo/imponer:** imposed/to impose
**cerveza:** beer
**¿Alguien se apunta…?:** Anyone interested…? Anyone up for…?

**me tiraría:** I would lie on (the bed)

**descansar:** to rest

**ratito/rato:** little while/time, while

**modorra:** drowsiness

**sueño:** sleep

**almorzar:** lunch

**extendida:** widespread

**pueblos:** small towns

**aunque:** although

**menos:** less

**palabra:** word

**proviene/provenir:** it came from/ to come from

**correspondía/corresponder:** it corresponded/to correspond

**mediodía:** midday

**relacionamos/relacionar:** we relate/to relate

**en realidad:** in fact, actually

**reposo:** rest

**acompañado/acompañar:** accompanied/to accompany

**suele seguir:** usually follows

**disfruta/disfrutar:** enjoys/to enjoy

**duerme/dormir:** sleeps/to sleep

**se relaja/relajarse:** it relaxes/to relax

**holgazanería:** laziness

**estudios:** studies

**afirman/afirmar:** they affirm/to affirm

**mitad:** middle

**ayudan/ayudar:** they help/to help

**recuperar:** to recover, regain

**descargar ansiedades:** to relieve anxieties

**desbloquear:** to unblock

**mente:** mind

**altas temperaturas:** high temperatures

**agotador:** exhausting

**se convierte/convertir:** it becomes/ to become

**excusa perfecta:** perfect excuse

**resguardarse:** to take shelter

**no perder fuerzas:** not lose strength

# La siesta en Argentina
## ARGENTINA

Zzzzzzzzzzzz..... ¡Cómo **me tiraría** a **descansar** un **ratito**! ¡Qué **modorra**! ¿A quién no le da **sueño** luego de **almorzar**?

La siesta es una costumbre **extendida** en la mayoría de las provincias del interior de Argentina y en muchos **pueblos** de Latinoamérica, **aunque menos** en las grandes ciudades.

La **palabra** siesta **proviene** del latín *sixta*, que significa "la sexta hora del día"; entre los romanos **correspondía** al **mediodía**, las horas comprendidas entre las 13 y las 16 hs. Nosotros **relacionamos** a la siesta con el sueño pero **en realidad**, la siesta es el **reposo** (**acompañado** o no del sueño) que **suele seguir** a la comida del mediodía. El que **disfruta** de una siesta entonces, **duerme** un rato o simplemente **se relaja** unos instantes luego del almuerzo.

Los detractores de esta costumbre la relacionan con **holgazanería** pero, en realidad, existen varios **estudios** que **afirman** que unos minutos de relax en la **mitad** del día **ayudan** a **recuperar** energías, **descargar ansiedades**, **desbloquear** la **mente** y estimular la creatividad. En lugares con **altas temperaturas**, donde el clima del mediodía es **agotador**, la siesta **se convierte** en la **excusa perfecta** para **resguardarse** del calor excesivo y **no perder fuerzas**.

Pero, como en todo en la vida, el **equilibrio** es fundamental, **ya que** el **prolongado descanso vespertino podría alterar** el **ciclo normal** del sueño. Los especialistas recomiendan siestas de entre 15 y 30 minutos **diarios** y **nunca más** de 40.

En las grandes ciudades **suele escucharse** la **queja** famosa de "**no tengo tiempo** para la siesta" porque en la mayoría de los **casos** se la **confunde** con la acción de "**meterse en la cama** a dormir"; **sin embargo**, un simple relax de 20 minutos en algún sofá **basta** para **aliviar** tensiones, **descansar** y seguir con las actividades. Otras investigaciones **aseguran** que el efecto **reparador** de este descanso **previene** el **envejecimiento** y **alarga la vida**. De hecho, los efectos inmediatos de una buena siesta **se reflejan** en la **luminosidad** de la **cara** y en el buen humor. **¿Descansamos** un rato?

**equilibrio:** balance
**ya que:** since
**prolongado/ prolongar:** extended/to extend
**descanso:** break
**vespertino:** evening
**podría alterar:** it could alter, modify
**ciclo normal:** normal cycle
**diarios:** daily
**nunca más:** never more
**suele escucharse/escuchar:** usually hears/to hear
**queja:** complaint
**no tengo tiempo:** I have no time
**casos:** cases
**confunde/confundir:** confuses/ to confuse
**meterse en la cama:** get into bed
**sin embargo:** however
**basta/bastar:** it will be enough/to be enough
**aliviar:** to relieve, soothe
**descansar:** to rest
**aseguran/asegurar:** assured/to assure
**reparador:** restorative, invigorating
**previene/prevenir:** it prevents/to prevent
**envejecimiento:** aging
**alarga la vida:** it prolongs life
**se reflejan/reflejar:** it reflects/to reflect
**luminosidad:** luminosity
**cara:** face
**descansamos/descansar:** we rest/to rest

| | |
|---|---|
| **pescando:** fishing | |

pescando: fishing
se encuentra/encontrarse: there is/
  to be
caleta: small beach
llamada/llamar: called/to call
pescadores: fishermen
siguen/seguir: they keep/to keep
costumbre: custom
antepasados: ancestors
mar: sea
rústicos: rustic
botes: small boat
hechos de: made of
caña: cane
caballitos: little horses
balsilla: small raft
a simple vista: at first sight
resistente: resistant
furia marina: marine fury
herencia: heritage
habitó/habitar: it inhabited/to inhabit
zona costera: coastal area
fecha: date
humildes: humble, poor
se ganan la vida/ganar: they earn their
  living/to earn
sacando/sacar: taking out/to take out
medio de transporte: means of
  transportation
aparecía/aparecer: it appeared/
  to appear
grabado: engraved
lengua: language
llegaron/llegar: they arrived/to arrive
colonizadores: colonists
reino: kingdom
fueron rebautizados/rebautizar: they
  were rebaptized/to rebaptize
se montaban/montar: they got in/
  to get in
miden/medir: they measure/to
  measure
de largo: long
de ancho: width
de forma alargada: elongated shape
materia prima: raw material or matter
embarcación: boat
crece/crecer: it grows/to grow
cerca: near
ha alcanzado/alcanzar: it has reached/
  to reach
desarrollo: development
es cortada/cortar: it is cut/to cut
luego: afterwards
ponerla/poner: put it/to put
secar: to dry
arena: sand

# Pescando con "caballos"
## PERU

A 450 kilómetros al norte de Lima, en el departamento de La Libertad, **se encuentra** una famosa **caleta llamada** Huanchaco donde los **pescadores** del lugar **siguen** la **costumbre** de sus **antepasados** al salir al **mar** en unos **rústicos botes hechos de caña** llamados "**caballitos** de totora". Esta frágil **balsilla a simple vista** pero **resistente** a la **furia marina** es la **herencia** de la cultura mochica, que **habitó** esta **zona costera** del Perú hace más de 1.200 años. Desde esa **fecha**, los **humildes** pescadores de este lugar **se ganan la vida sacando** los frutos del mar de esta forma.

Este **medio de transporte** ya **aparecía grabado** en las cerámicas pre-incas. Se les llamaba *tup* en **lengua** mochica, pero cuando **llegaron** los **colonizadores** españoles a este **reino fueron rebautizados** como "caballitos", por la forma en que los indígenas **se montaban** en ellos para salir al mar. Los caballitos **miden** entre tres y cuatro metros **de largo** por metro o metro y medio **de ancho**, y son **de forma alargada**. La **materia prima** para hacer esta pequeña **embarcación** es la caña de totora que **crece cerca** de esta caleta de pescadores. Una vez que la totora **ha alcanzado** su máximo **desarrollo es cortada** desde su base para **luego ponerla** a **secar** en las **arena** de la playa.

De allí, manos expertas **prensan** los **carrizos tejiendo** una **popa** ancha hasta **finalizar** con una **fina proa arqueada en punta**. Este ritual de construcción **continúa llevándose a cabo** desde hace **siglos**.

**Muy de madrugada**, como **caballeros** en sus **corceles** los *huanchaqueros* o pescadores salen **en busca** del **jurel**, **chita** o **corvina**. Observar a los pescadores **navegando hábilmente** en sus míticos caballitos es un **espectáculo** turístico.

Los **curtidos** hombres regresan del mar antes del **mediodía** con sus **canastillas repletas** de **pescados** cuando la **pesca** es buena. Luego, las embarcaciones **son puestas de pie** en la arena como **vigilantes mirando hacia** el mar.

**Lamentablemente** esta actividad **parece extinguirse** por el **escaso** interés de las nuevas generaciones. Muchos de los **hijos** de los *huanchaqueros* viajan a Lima a **buscar** un futuro mejor. El **desaliento** también **tiene que ver** con la poca pesca **debido a** la actual presencia de **barcos arrastreros** que **arrasan** con todo los peces que **encuentran a su paso**. La dificultad por encontrar los totorales hoy día por la **acelerada** urbanización de Huanchaco también **está actuando en contra** para que, **en un futuro próximo**, esta **milenaria actividad pesquera** pueda quedar sólo en recuerdo.

**prensan/prensar:** they press/to press
**carrizos:** a riverbank plant
**tejiendo/tejer:** weaving/to weave
**popa:** stern
**finalizar:** to finish
**fina:** fine
**proa:** bow (in a boat)
**arqueada:** bent, curved (arch shape)
**en punta:** pointy
**continúa llevándose a cabo:** it continues to be carried out
**siglos:** centuries
**muy de madrugada:** very late in the night or very early in the morning
**caballeros:** knights (horseback riders)
**corceles:** steeds
**en busca:** in search of
**jurel:** scad
**chita, corvina:** types of fish
**navegando/navegar:** sailing/to sail
**hábilmente:** skillfully
**espectáculo:** show
**curtidos:** hardened
**mediodía:** midday, noon
**canastillas:** small baskets
**repletas:** full
**pescados:** fish
**pesca:** fishing
**son puestas de pie:** they are stood up
**vigilantes:** guards, watchmen
**mirando/mirar:** looking at/to look at
**hacia:** towards
**lamentablemente:** unfortunately
**parece/parecer:** it seems/to seem
**extinguirse:** to die out
**escaso:** scarce
**hijos:** children
**buscar:** to look for
**desaliento:** discouragement
**tiene que ver:** it has to do
**debido a:** due to
**barcos arrastreros:** trawling boats, trawlers
**arrasan/arrasar:** they destroy/ to destroy
**encuentran/encontrar:** they find/ to find
**a su paso:** in their way
**acelerada:** accelerated, fast
**está actuando/actuar:** it is acting/ to act
**en contra:** against
**en un futuro próximo:** in the near future
**milenaria:** thousand-year-old
**actividad pesquera:** fishing activity
**pueda quedar sólo en recuerdo:** it can only remain as a part of the past

**último:** last
**volví/volver:** I returned/to return
**querer:** to want
**traerme:** to bring with me
**valija:** valise, bag
**llena de:** full of
**alebrijes:** name of a typical Mexican craft, artisanry
**lindos:** pretty, nice
**parecen salidos de:** they seem to come from
**cuento fantástico:** fantastic story
**aunque:** although
**pueden encontrarse/encontrar:** they can be found/to find
**casi todo el país:** almost all of the country
**madera:** wood
**cartón:** cardboard
**papel maché:** paper mache
**criaturas:** creatures
**suelen mezclarse:** they usually mix
**ejemplares:** copies, examples
**tortugas:** turtles
**mariposas:** butterflies
**sapos:** frogs
**elaborados/elaborar:** made/to make
**manos mágicas:** magic hands
**vivos:** lively
**llamativos:** bright, colorful
**leyendas:** legends
**se disputan/disputar:** they dispute/ to dispute, to compete for
**dicen/decir:** they say/to say
**salen/salir:** they go out/to go out
**árboles:** trees
**cuevas:** caves
**nubes:** clouds
**sostienen/sostener:** they hold, maintain/to hold, to maintain
**derivan/derivar:** they derive/to derive
**enfermó/enfermar:** he fell ill/to fall ill
**extraña:** strange
**afección:** condition
**lo dejó inconsciente:** it left him unconscious
**cama:** bed

# Los alebrijes, artesanía mexicana
## MÉXICO

En mi **último** viaje a México, **volví** a entusiasmarme y a **querer traerme** la **valija llena de alebrijes**. ¡Es que son tan **lindos** y tan coloridos que **parecen salidos de** un **cuento fantástico**! Los alebrijes son artesanías características de México, especialmente de Oaxaca **aunque pueden encontrarse** en **casi todo el país**. Los hay de **madera**, de **cartón** y de **papel maché**.

Son figuras de animales o **criaturas** fantásticas. En general **suelen mezclarse** dos o más animales, aunque también existen **ejemplares** de las clásicas **tortugas**, **mariposas**, escorpiones y **sapos**. Parecen **elaborados** por **manos mágicas**, con colores muy **vivos** y **llamativos** y formas que impactan por la perfección de su manufactura.

Existen varias **leyendas** que **se disputan** su invención y origen. Algunos **dicen** que son demonios que **salen de los árboles**, de las **cuevas**, ríos y **nubes**. Otros **sostienen** que **derivan** de las máscaras de animales características de Oaxaca. Pero la leyenda que tiene más adeptos los relaciona con Pedro Linares, un hombre de la ciudad de México, que a los 30 años **enfermó** de una **extraña afección** que **lo dejó inconsciente** en la **cama** durante varios días.

En su agonía **soñaba con** un bosque extraño donde había animales desconocidos y fantásticos: **burros con alas** de mariposa, **gallos** con **cuernos de toro**, leones con **cabezas de águila** y perros con **patas de araña,** entre otros. Un **ruido ensordecedor gritaba** el nombre de "alebrijes" y él en su esfuerzo por **salir de aquella pesadilla despertó** de la enfermedad. Cuando **se repuso** totalmente y recordó su sueño, **quiso** que su familia y todas las personas conocieran a estos animales que lo habían **salvado. Valiéndose de** sus habilidades como **cartonero, moldeó** esas extrañas criaturas que tanto **admiraba.**

**Hoy en día**, los alebrijes **no sólo** forman parte de la cultura popular mexicana **sino también** del arte contemporáneo con **reconocimiento** internacional.

**soñaba con/soñar:** he dreamed of/to dream
**burros con alas:** donkeys with wings
**gallos:** roosters
**cuernos de toro:** bull horns
**cabezas de águila:** eagle heads
**patas de araña:** spider legs
**ruido ensordecedor:** deafening noise
**gritaba/gritar:** screamed/to scream
**salir de aquella:** to get rid of that
**pesadilla:** nightmare, bad dream
**despertó/despertar:** he woke up/to wake up
**se repuso/reponerse:** he recovered/to recover
**quiso/querer:** he wanted/to want
**salvado/salvar:** saved/to save
**valiéndose de:** making use of
**cartonero:** cardboard-maker or seller
**moldeó/moldear:** he molded/to mold
**admiraba/admirar:** he admired/to admire
**hoy en día:** nowadays
**no sólo...sino también:** not only ... but also
**reconocimiento:** recognition

**CULTURE NOTE** To communicate well with people of other countries, you must learn to speak well, right? Yes, but speaking isn't everything. Your gestures and other nonverbal actions matter too. The United States and Mexico are relatively different in nonverbal cues because of historical and cultural differences. Mexico is a high-contact culture. People tend to stand closer, touch frequently, and maintain good eye contact. In Mexico, when greeting someone for the first time the handshake is the customary greeting. Longtime friends may engage in a full embrace, which is called the *abrazo*. Women tend to greet with a kiss on the cheek rather than an *abrazo*. When meeting with someone, eye contact is important in Mexico. Not making eye contact implies boredom or disinterest. Certain gestures in America mean different things in Mexico. In Mexico, placing your hands in your pockets is considered impolite. It suggests that you are keeping a secret or hiding something from the person with whom you are talking. Standing with your hands on your hips is considered challenging and hostile to another Mexican. Understanding even a few key gestures from different cultures can make you a better communicator. So next time you travel, be culturally sensitive. Find out the local gestures, and let your body talk.

**mojito:** a traditional Cuban drink

**pertenencia:** belonging

**vestimentas:** clothing

**trajes típicos:** typical outfits, folk outfits

**sobresale/sobresalir:** she stands out/to stand out

**distinguidos:** distinguished

**la lleva/llevar:** she wears it/to wear

**derrocha/derrochar:** she brims over/to brim over

**gracia:** grace

**andar:** walking

**atrae/atraer:** she attracts/to attract

**miradas:** looks

**se topa/toparse:** she runs into/to run, bump into

**camino:** way

**si bien:** even though

**país:** country

**existen/existir:** there are/to be

**principalmente:** mainly

**tipos:** kinds

**vestir de diario:** everyday dress, everyday clothes

**encajes:** lace

**gala:** full dress

**se usa/usar:** it is used/to use

**festejos:** holidays

**motivos:** reasons

**elaborada:** elaborated

**acompañando:** together with

**según:** depending on

**ancha:** wide

**confeccionada:** made

**tela:** fabric

**algodón:** cotton

**suele usarse:** it is usually used

**ambas:** both

**blusas:** blouses

**pegada:** tight

**suelta:** loose

# La pollera panameña
## PANAMA

La pollera es a Panamá, lo que el **mojito** es a Cuba, el tango a la Argentina, o el carnaval a Brasil: un orgullo, un símbolo de nacionalidad, identidad y **pertenencia.** Entre las **vestimentas** y **trajes típicos** del mundo, la pollera panameña **sobresale** como uno de los más espectaculares y **distinguidos.** La mujer que **la lleva derrocha gracia** en sus movimientos, elegancia en su **andar** y atrae las **miradas** de todo aquel con quien **se topa** en su **camino.**

**Si bien** hay variaciones en todas las regiones del **país,** **existen principalmente** dos **tipos** de polleras: la pollera montuna, que es la de **vestir de diario** o de trabajo; y la pollera de **encajes** o de **gala,** que es la que **se usa** para **festejos** o **motivos** importantes y que es una versión más **elaborada** de este vestido nacional. **Acompañando** a la pollera y, **según** el caso, las mujeres completan la vestimenta con diferentes accesorios.

La pollera montuna, **ancha** y **confeccionada** con **tela** calicó (de **algodón**), **suele usarse** con basquiñas o chambras: **ambas** son **blusas,** **pegada** al cuerpo la primera, y más **suelta** la segunda, que pueden ser blancas o de color.

Este **conjunto puede terminarse** con el **cabello** con **trenzas** y flores naturales, con un **sombrero de paja** o con **peinetas doradas** y algunos trembleques (flores **hechas a mano** que pueden ser de diferentes materiales, desde un **fino alambre enroscado** hasta **escamas** de **pescado** y **seda**).

La pollera de encajes, la más **lujosa** y delicada, ancha y con dos o tres divisiones, está muy decorada con **lanas** y **cintas**. Se usa con una blusa **amplia** de **lino** y también está confeccionada con **bordados** y encajes. Para vestir sus cabellos, las mujeres **lucen** este traje con peinetas importantes que pueden ser de **oro** y tremblecues (generalmente blancos), en el resto de la cabeza.

Este **vestido de gala se adorna** con gran cantidad de **joyas**: **cadenas, aros, pulseras, anillos** y **hebillas** son sólo algunas de ellas, que pueden ser de oro, perlas o **piedras preciosas**. Los **zapatos se llaman** chapines y pueden ser de **satén** o **terciopelo**, en general, muy **planos** y con una hebilla de oro, encajes y cintas.

Históricamente no hay muchos **archivos**, ni **detalles** exactos que **revelen** el origen de la pollera panameña, **aunque** algunos **reconocen** sus **raíces** en España.

---

**conjunto:** ensemble, set
**puede terminarse/terminar** it can end/to end
**cabello:** hair
**trenzas:** braids
**sombrero de paja:** straw hat
**peinetas:** an accessory to hold the hair up. Very traditional in countries like Panamá or Spain but only worn with traditional dresses on special occasions.
**doradas:** golden
**hechas a mano:** handmade
**fino:** thin
**alambre:** wire
**enroscado:** coiled
**escamas:** scales
**pescado:** fish
**seda:** silk
**lujosa:** luxurious
**lanas:** wools
**cintas:** bands, strips
**amplia:** large, wide
**lino:** linen
**bordados:** embroidery
**lucen/lucir:** they wear/to wear with grace
**oro:** gold
**vestido de gala:** full dress
**se adorna/adornar:** it is decorated/to decorate
**joyas:** jewelry
**cadenas:** chains
**aros:** hoops, earrings
**pulseras:** bracelets
**anillos:** rings
**hebillas:** buckles
**piedras preciosas:** gems
**zapatos:** shoes
**se llaman/llamarse:** they are called/to be called
**satén:** satin
**terciopelo:** velvet
**planos:** low, without heel
**archivos:** files
**detalles:** details
**revelen/revelar:** they reveal/to reveal
**aunque:** although
**reconocen/reconocer:** they recognize/to recognize

# El gaucho, habitante del campo
## URUGUAY

**Se lo conoce** como *cowboy* en Norteamérica, como llanero en Venezuela y como gaucho en la pampa argentina y en el Uruguay. Es, simplemente, el habitante típico de las zonas rurales en el continente americano. En Uruguay, el gaucho es una figura importante del folclore nacional **ya que** simboliza la **libertad** y la individualidad. Las representaciones poéticas del gaucho lo describen como el ideal de **valentía** e independencia. Pero **más allá** de cómo lo presenten la música, la literatura, y la **pintura**, este **personaje constituye** un símbolo importante dentro de la cultura uruguaya.

**Si nos acercamos** a la realidad, el gaucho es el **hombre de campo** que trabaja **principalmente arreando ganado**. En su imagen **estereotípica**, siempre **está acompañado** de un **caballo** que, además de servirle de transporte, es una de las pocas posesiones materiales que **se asocian** con el **modo de vida** gauchesco. **En la actualidad**, el caballo **sigue siendo** una pieza fundamental de las actividades que el gaucho **realiza** en el campo.

Tradicionalmente, el gaucho **contaba** también entre sus posesiones con el **facón** y las boleadoras, que le servían como **arma** y como **herramienta** de trabajo. El facón es un **cuchillo** largo que los gauchos **llevan** en la **espalda**, **colgando** del **cinturón**, para múltiples usos, ya sea para defensa personal, para comer, o para **cuerear** las **vacas**. Hoy en día siguen usándolo, principalmente, a la hora de trabajar. Las boleadoras son dos **piedras redondeadas** unidas por una **cuerda hecha** con **cuero trenzado**.

Una **hendidura** que **recorre** el exterior de las piedras **permite atar** la cuerda **de forma que** las piedras estén bien **aseguradas** y **no se escapen**. Los gauchos las **utilizaban** para **atrapar** al ganado **cimarrón** o salvaje y para **cazar ñandúes**. Actualmente las boleadoras ya no se usan porque el ganado es doméstico con lo cual este instrumento resulta innecesario.

El gaucho sigue siendo fácilmente **distinguible** por sus **vestimentas**. Usa bombachas o chiripá (un **pantalón de pierna ancha ajustado a la cintura** con una **faja** o **cinto**) que puede ser de **tela** o cuero con decoraciones en **plata** u otros metales. El **atuendo** se complementa con una **camisa** y **pañuelo al cuello**. Lleva también un **sombrero de ala ancha sujetado** al **mentón** con una **cinta** que le permite **cabalgar sin temor** a **perderlo**. El **abrigo** tradicional es el poncho, que resulta ideal para **mantener** el **calor** en las **madrugadas** frías en las que sale a cabalgar. En los pies usa **botas** de cuero, también **pensadas** para las **cabalgatas**, ya que debe **proteger** los pies y **piernas** del continuo **roce** con los **estribos**. Cuando no está encima de su caballo, el gaucho **puede verse** usando **alpargatas,** un tipo de calzado **llegado** de Europa.

En Montevideo, un museo **rinde homenaje** a la figura del gaucho. Allí se pueden **apreciar** representaciones tradicionales de este personaje durante sus **horas de ocio,** ya sea jugando a la taba (un juego típico del campo), tomando mate, o **fumando** un **cigarro armado** por él mismo.

En Tacuarembó, uno de los departamentos norteños del país se conmemoran las **costumbres** gauchescas con la Fiesta de la Patria Gaucha en el mes de febrero o de marzo. Durante su celebración, a la que muchos de sus **asistentes concurren a caballo**, se realizan actividades tradicionalmente asociadas con las **tareas** del campo. Está presente la música folclórica con sus guitarras, así como el **asado con cuero,** y varias **pruebas de destreza** como las **jineteadas**, las domas y las cabalgatas. Este tipo de fiestas contribuye a **fomentar** la identidad nacional uruguaya, dentro de la que el gaucho conserva, aún hoy, un lugar **destacado**.

**distinguible:** easy to distinguish
**vestimentas::** clothing
**pantalón:** pants
**de pierna ancha:** wide leg
**ajustado:** tight
**cintura:** waist
**faja:** girdle
**cinto:** belt
**tela:** fabric
**plata:** silver
**atuendo:** attire
**camisa:** shirt
**pañuelo:** handkerchief
**al cuello:** around the neck
**sombrero de ala ancha:** wide-brimmed hat
**sujetado:** fixed
**mentón:** chin
**cinta:** lace
**cabalgar:** to ride
**sin temor:** without fear
**perderlo/perder:** losing it/to lose
**abrigo:** coat
**mantener:** to keep
**calor:** heat
**madrugadas:** early mornings
**botas:** boots
**pensadas:** thought, intended
**cabalgatas:** horseback rides
**proteger:** to protect
**piernas:** legs
**roce:** rubbing, friction
**estribos:** stirrups
**puede verse:** it can be seen
**alpargatas:** canvas sandals, espadrilles
**llegado/llegar:** arrived/to arrive
**rinde homenaje/rendir homenaje:** they pay homage/to pay homage
**apreciar:** to appreciate
**horas de ocio:** spare time
**fumando/fumar:** smoking/to smoke
**cigarro:** cigarrette
**armado/armar:** assembled/to assemble
**costumbres:** customs
**asistentes:** the public
**concurren/concurrir:** they converge/to converge, to meet
**a caballo:** riding a horse
**tareas:** tasks
**asado con cuero:** beef that is roasted in its hide over an open fire
**pruebas de destreza:** skill contests
**jineteadas:** breaking-in (horses and/or bulls, as in cowboy rodeos)
**fomentar:** to promote
**destacado:** outstanding

# La carretanagua
## NICARAGUA

Nicaragua es un país **muy arraigado** a tradiciones ancestrales, las cuales están presentes en **casi todas** sus costumbres y cultura. Muchas de estas tradiciones **encierran profundas creencias** en **personajes fantasmagóricos** o **brujas**, como La Mocuana, La Llorona y La Cegua. Pero **quizás** el **más conocido** y **temido** es el fantasma de La Carretanagua: una **desvencijada carreta tirada por flaquísimos** y **viejos bueyes** y **conducida** por La Muerte misma. La "Muerte Quirina", un terrorífico **esqueleto envuelto** en un **sudario** de **sábanas blancas**, cargando su guadaña **amenazadora** y **rodeada de calaveras**.

Algunos **aseguran** haber **padecido** una horrible **fiebre** luego de haberla visto, otros el haber perdido el habla por varios días. Dicen que **recorre** las **calles oscuras**, alrededor de la una de la **madrugada**, haciendo mucho **ruido** a su paso ya que **se trata de** una **carreta vieja** y **destartalada**. Los que la **oyen** pasar temen **asomarse** por las ventanas y **encontrarla** es que según la superstición, el día siguiente de haberla visto, está marcado con la muerte de alguno de los de su pueblo. La misteriosa carreta **se mueve** muy rápido y al llegar a las **esquinas desaparece**, **reapareciendo** sobre otra calle atemorizando a animales y creando **desasosiego** y **mucho miedo** entre la gente.

La Carretanagua (o Carreta Nagua) es un símbolo muy fuerte en la mitología y folklore nicaragüense, en la que **se amalgama** un **pasado doloroso** y una imaginación creativa y supersticiosa. Con ella **se recuerda** a las persecuciones y torturas que sufrían los indios a manos de los conquistadores. Dicen que en los tiempos de la colonia, en el Siglo XVI, los españoles llegaban a medianoche en carretas **buscando** oro y **riquezas** y **sacando** a los indios de sus **caseríos**; se los llevaban como esclavos **encadenados** a sus carretas. El mito de la Carretanagua **parece** haber nacido también de la necesidad de los nicaragüenses de **darle** forma material y concreta a un fenómeno tan incontrolable como la muerte.

---

**muy arraigado:** deeply rooted
**casi todas:** almost all
**encierran:** they hold; contain
**profundas creencias:** profound beliefs
**personajes fantasmagóricos:** ghostly characters
**brujas:** witches
**quizás:** perhaps
**más conocido:** famous, more well-known
**temido/temer:** feared/to fear
**desvencijada carreta:** rickety cart
**tirada por:** drawn by
**flaquísimos:** skinny
**viejos bueyes:** old oxen
**conducida/conducir:** driven/to drive
**esqueleto:** skeleton
**envuelto:** wrapped
**sudario:** shroud; winding sheet
**sábanas blancas:** white sheets
**cargando/cargar:** carrying/to carry
**guadaña amenazadora:** threatening scythe
**rodeada de calaveras:** surrounded by skulls
**aseguran/asegurar:** they assure/ to assure
**padecido/padecer:** suffered from/to suffer from
**fiebre:** fever
**recorre:** go over or through
**calles oscuras:** dark streets
**madrugada:** early morning
**ruido:** noise
**se trata de:** it is about
**carreta vieja:** old cart
**destartalada:** shabby
**oyen/oír:** they hear/to hear
**asomarse:** to lean out (of the window)
**encontrarla/encontrar:** find it/to find
**se mueve/mover:** it moves/to move
**esquinas:** corners
**desaparece:** disappear
**reapareciendo:** reappearing
**desasosiego:** anxiety; restlessness
**mucho miedo:** much fear
**se amalgama:** amalgamate; mix
**pasado doloroso:** painful past
**se recuerda/recordar:** remember/to remember
**buscando/buscar:** looking for/to look
**riquezas:** riches, wealth
**sacando/sacar:** taking out/to take out
**caseríos:** country houses
**encadenados/encadenar:** chained/ to chain
**parece/parecer:** it seems/to seem
**darle/dar:** give/to give

# El rodeo y los "huasos"
## CHILE

"¡¡Arre!!" Entre todas las fiestas y **juegos** tradicionales, el rodeo es uno de los más **emocionantes**, **alegres** y **coloridos** de Chile. **Se originó** hace muchos años como consecuencia del **duro trabajo** de los **campesinos** y su necesidad de **ordenar** el **ganado**. Cada **primavera** los animales son **traídos** desde los **cerros**, donde pasan el **invierno**. Este trabajo debe ser realizado por los hombres más **fuertes** y **hábiles** en el **manejo del caballo** y del **lazo**: los huasos. Viven principalmente en valles fértiles o en **granjas** con tierras cultivadas y su **tarea** es **conducir** a los animales **bordeando** precipicios, cruzando ríos, **bajando y subiendo pendientes** hasta llegar al corral. En esta **travesía** muchos **vacunos se espantan** y **descarrían** por lo que los huasos tienen que correr **velozmente** tras ellos, **atajarlos** con sus lazos y **unirlos** otra vez al grupo.

Cada año se celebra en Chile el Campeonato Nacional de Rodeo. Este juego ha **ganado** mucha fama (algunas rivalidades) ya que aquí se **pone a prueba** la capacidad, **fortaleza física** y **destreza** de estos *cowboys* chilenos, que se caracterizan por su **orgullo**, **seguridad** y **picardía**. El colorido de sus **vestimentas** y la de sus caballos reflejan el espíritu de tradición: sombreros, pantalones generalmente **rayados**, **botas de cuero**, **espuelas adornadas** y **mantas** o ponchos de colores vistosos. El rodeo consiste básicamente en imitar el trabajo de estos campesinos: atajar y controlar al ganado. Los **jinetes** corren de a pares. El **novillo** que va a ser corrido se lleva a una **pista circular** con **portones** que permiten su entrada y salida. Para comenzar, un arreador con grito **estridente** provoca la **carrera** del animal que busca la salida del corral. Entonces, los huasos deben tratar de alcanzarlo y detenerlo en un punto determinado, **señalado** con una **bandera**. Con espíritu deportivo, el **fallo del jurado** es riguroso y estricto. Este paisaje de fiesta se completa con la música, los bailes tradicionales y **por supuesto**, con una gastronomía especial típica del lugar.

---

**juegos:** games
**emocionantes:** exciting
**alegres:** joyful
**coloridos:** colorful
**se originó/originar:** it started, it began /to start, to begin
**duro trabajo:** hard work
**campesinos:** country men, farmers
**ordenar:** to arrange, put in order
**ganado:** livestock
**primavera:** spring
**traídos/traer:** brought/to bring
**cerros:** hills
**invierno:** winter
**fuertes:** strong
**hábiles:** skillful
**manejo del caballo/manejar:** handling the horses/manejar
**lazo:** whip
**granjas:** farms
**tarea:** task
**conducir:** to take
**bordeando/bordear:** going round/to go round
**bajando y subiendo:** going down and going up
**pendientes:** slopes, inclines
**travesía:** trip
**vacunos:** cattle
**se espantan/espantar:** they get scared/to scare, to frighten
**descarrían/descarriar:** they go astray/to separate, to go astray
**velozmente:** quickly
**atajarlos/atajar:** intercept them, stop them/to intercept, to stop
**unirlos/unir:** join them/to join
**ganado/ganar:** it gained/to gain
**pone a prueba:** put to the test
**fortaleza física:** physical strength
**destreza:** skill
**orgullo:** pride
**seguridad:** confidence
**picardía:** craftiness
**vestimentas:** clothing
**rayados:** striped
**botas de cuero:** leather boots
**espuelas adornadas:** decorated spurs
**mantas:** blankets
**jinetes:** rider, horsemen
**novillo:** young bull
**pista circular:** circular court
**portones:** big gates
**estridente:** noisy, strident
**carrera:** race
**señalado/señalar:** marked/to mark
**bandera:** flag
**fallo del jurado:** verdict of the jury
**por supuesto:** of course

# Examina tu comprensión

## Los vejigantes, page 4

**1.** What is the country of origin of the people of the city of Loiza?

**2.** The festival on July 25 represents the mixtures of what groups?

**3.** Of what material are the *Vejigantes* masks made?

## De tapeo, page 6

**1.** Besides eating, what is involved with, and an important part of, the *tapas* tradition?

**2.** In what province does the legend of the *tapa* take place?

**3.** When the sand storm hit what great idea did the waiter have and why?

**4.** Describe or list different types of *tapas*.

## La siesta en Argentina, page 8

**1.** What is the origin of the word *siesta*?

**2.** A *siesta* is a time not only to sleep but do what?

**3.** What are some of the health benefits of the *siesta*?

**4.** Experts recommend a *siesta* of how many minutes per day?

## Pescando con "caballos", page 10

**1.** In Huanchco the fishermen keep the pre-Incan custom of their ancestors by making what?

**2.** For how many years has this ancient fishing vessel been used?

**3.** This valuable custom is in danger of extinction because of what three things?

# Test your comprehension

## Los alebrijes, page 12

**1.** *Alebrijes* are Mexican art objects made of what material?

**2.** What types of figures are depicted in *alebrijes* art?

**3.** There are various legends regarding the origin of *Alebrijes*. What legend has the most followers? Tell this legend in your own words.

## La pollera, page 14

**1.** What are the two different types of *polleras* and when are they worn?

**2.** What materials are used to make the flowers worn on the straw hat?

**3.** What are the shoes called that are worn with the *pollera* and what fabric are they made of?

**4.** What is the origin of the *pollera*?

## El gaucho, page 16

**1.** What does the "*gaucho*" symbolize?

**2.** What is the *boleadoras* made of and what purpose does it serve?

**3.** Describe traditional *gaucho* clothing.

## El rodeo y los "huasos", page 19

**1.** Why did the rodeo begin?

**2.** What three things are put to the test during the rodeo games?

Viajar es imprescindible y la sed de viaje,
un síntoma neto de inteligencia.

Enrique Jardiel Poncela

# Viaje

# El barrio gótico de Barcelona
## ESPAÑA

Barcelona es una **ciudad** de **contrastes.** Y **después de** visitar la ciudad moderna, un **paseo** por su Barrio Gótico **nos hace olvidar** los **altos edificios** y el **ruido** de los **coches.** El nombre de esta zona **es debido a** los monumentos góticos que **posee.** Pero es interesante **saber** que este barrio **ocupa lo que** fue, **hace siglos,** una **antigua ciudad romana.** Aquí, podemos visitar la "Plaza Nova", con dos **torres semicirculares** de la antigua **muralla** romana.

**Podemos continuar** nuestro paseo con una visita a la Catedral. **Su construcción comenzó** en el **siglo XIII**, y su **fachada** es del siglo XIX. **El complejo de la Catedral comprende** tres **palacios medievales**: Cases dels Canonges, Casa del Degà y Casa de l'Ardiaca. **Desde allí**, tenemos un bonito **recorrido**: después del Cloister, un **agradable paseo cubierto, llegaremos** al **Puente de los Suspiros** y a la Plaza de San Jaume. **A continuación, veremos**, en esta plaza, dos edificios: el "Palau de la Generalitat" o "**Palacio** de la Generalidad" y el **Ayuntamiento**. La Plaza de San Jaume **está rodeada** de estrechas calles, **ideales** para **pasear.** A continuación, **seguiremos** una **estrecha** calle **llena de tiendas,** para **llegar** a la Plaza del Rey. Esta plaza es **una de las más nobles** de Barcelona. Aquí, podemos visitar el Museo de Historia y también el Mirador del Rei Martí, **para aquellos que quieran ver** una **vista panorámica** del Barrio Gótico.

Y un **consejo**: ¡el **calzado cómodo** es esencial!

# Humacao, la perla de Puerto Rico
## PUERTO RICO

"La perla del oriente" o "La ciudad gris" son algunos de los nombres con los que se conoce el pueblo de Humacao, Puerto Rico. Esta pequeña localidad, ubicada en la costa este de la isla, toma su nombre del indio taino que la gobernaba en tiempos de la conquista española. Los nativos de este pueblo se denominan humacaenos.

Humacao tiene cerca de 59.000 habitantes repartidos por sus 15 vecindarios. Este pueblo es rico en playas hermosas. Uno de los hoteles más famosos y exclusivos de la isla se encuentra allí, el Hotel Palmas del Mar. Humacao también posee museos y un enorme observatorio desde donde se pueden ver las galaxias más lejanas. En Humacao se produce café, arroz, tabaco y aceite de castor pero su mayor industria, evidentemente, es el turismo.

El 8 de diciembre se celebran las fiestas a la Santa Patrona: La Inmaculada Concepción de Maria. El primer fin de semana de septiembre todos los humacaenos y visitantes disfrutan del Festival de la Pana durante el que se organizan eventos musicales, deportivos y culturales, y durante el que se cocinan muchas recetas típicas. ¿Hechas con que? Con pana, por supuesto. La próxima vez que vengan a Puerto Rico, visiten nuestra "perla del oriente".

la perla del oriente: the pearl of the orient (east)
gris: gray
se conoce/conocerse: it's known/to be known
localidad: locality, town
ubicada: located
costa este: east coast
toma su nombre: it takes its name
taino: natives from the island of Puerto Rico
en tiempos de la conquista española: in times of the Spanish conquest
humacaenos: natives from Humacao
cerca de: close to
repartidos por: spread about
vecindarios: neighborhoods
rico: rich
playas hermosas: beautiful beaches
se encuentra/encontrarse: it is located/to be located
enorme: huge
desde: from
galaxias más lejanas: farthest galaxies
arroz: rice
aceite de castor: castor oil
mayor industria: main industry
fiestas a la Santa Patrona: Patron Saint celebrations. Each town in Puerto Rico has its patron saint and festivities are celebrated every month in different towns to honor them.
primer fin de semana: first weekend
visitantes: visitors
disfrutan/disfrutar: enjoy/to enjoy
Festival de la Pana: The Breadfruit Festival
se organizan/organizar: they are organized/to organize
deportivos: sports
se cocinan/cocinar: they are cooked/to cook
recetas típicas: typical recipes
hechas: made
pana: breadfruit—a tropical fruit with green colored rind. The flesh is sweet, reminiscent of a sweet potato.
por supuesto: of course
próxima vez: next time

# Colonia del Sacramento
## URUGUAY

**Pasear** por las **calles empedradas** del barrio viejo de Colonia del Sacramento es un **placer** del que **disfrutan tanto lugareños como** turistas en **cualquier estación** del año.

Los **fines de semana**, Colonia **se llena** de argentinos que **cruzan** en barco desde la cercana Buenos Aires a disfrutar el ritmo tranquilo de sus calles y plazas. Los turistas recorren las tiendas de productos típicos, generalmente **ropa confeccionada** con **lana** o **cuero. Asimismo**, visitan los **puestos** de **artesanía** que **se ubican alrededor** de las plazas, en los que es difícil decidirse: ¿Unos **posavasos** de cuero **repujado** o una **caja** de **alfajores**? ¿Unos **pendientes** en **amatista** o unos **guantes** y **gorro** de lana **hechos a mano**? **Quizás incluso** unos **juguetes de madera** para los niños, hechos por artesanos locales. Hay para **todos los gustos**.

Después de las **compras** de la mañana, **lo mejor** es **hacer una parada** en alguno de los restaurantes locales. **Aunque** son pequeños preparan deliciosos platos típicos, **tales como** pastas **caseras, carne asada**, pescados y otros productos del mar, en **cazuelas** y **ensopados** o **empanados** y **fritos**. Para los **postres**, uno puede **elegir** flan con dulce de leche o ensalada de frutas con helado. Si bien estos dos postres son sólo dos de las opciones disponibles, son también, sin lugar a dudas, los más **solicitados**. Después de la **caminata** y el **almuerzo**, nada mejor que una siesta para **recuperar fuerzas**.

Por la tarde, los que **gustan de** la historia **están de suerte**. Colonia del Sacramento **fue fundada** por los portugueses en 1680 como forma de **ganar** territorio americano a los españoles.

Colonia es, pues, la ciudad más **antigua** del Uruguay **actual** y **ha sido nombrada** como *Patrimonio Histórico de la Humanidad* por la UNESCO gracias a su valor cultural. Como tal, **cuenta con** varios museos. Uno de los mejores es el Museo de los **Azulejos,** que **posee** una hermosa colección de *azulejos* portugueses. Uno de los aspectos más interesantes del museo es el **edificio** en el que **está alojado:** una casa antigua y bien preservada, de **paredes anchísimas** y **puertas** y **techos bajos,** característicos de la **época.**

Colonia tiene también algo que **ofrecer** a los **enamorados.** Muchas parejas de novios eligen celebrar aquí su **boda** por la belleza de su **iglesia principal,** la Iglesia Matriz, la más antigua del país. **Si bien** es pequeña y simple, el **entorno** de las calles empedradas y los siglos de historia que **la rodean le dan un aire especial.** No es raro **toparse,** al **pasar** cerca de la iglesia, con un grupo de **festejantes tirando arroz** a los **novios.** Quienes quieran **pasar** la **luna de miel** en Colonia tienen una buena opción en los hoteles antiguos de la ciudad que, con sus patios internos y sus **fuentes,** sus **portones** de **hierro forjado** y sus **enredaderas, proporcionan** un **ambiente** romántico único.

Al **atardecer,** la opción más popular es ir a comprar unos **bizcochos** en la **panadería** y salir, con el mate **bajo el brazo,** a caminar por el **puerto** en compañía de amigos o familia. Situado sobre el Río de la Plata, el pequeño puerto **alberga botes** y **barcos veleros,** turistas que deciden **llegar por mar** con su propio transporte, o lugareños que disfrutan **saliendo** a **pescar río arriba.** El puerto es también el sitio ideal para ir a pescar y son muchos los que **aprovechan** la oportunidad. Pero tanto para navegantes como para pescadores y turistas, **deleitarse** con la **puesta del sol** sobre el río, entre los barcos, es siempre el **cierre** perfecto para un fin de semana en Colonia de Sacramento.

**antigua:** old
**actual:** nowadays
**ha sido nombrada/nombrar:** it has been nominated/to nominate
**cuenta con/contar con:** it has/to have
**azulejos:** tiles
**posee/poseer:** it has/to have
**edificio:** building
**está alojado:** it is housed
**paredes:** walls
**anchísimas:** very wide
**puertas:** doors
**techos:** ceilings
**bajos:** low
**época:** period, time
**ofrecer:** to offer
**enamorados:** lovers
**boda:** wedding
**iglesia principal:** main church
**si bien:** although
**entorno:** environment
**la rodean/rodear:** they surround it/ to surround
**le dan un aire especial:** they make it special
**toparse:** to bump into
**pasar:** to walk by
**festejantes:** the people celebrating
**tirando/tirar:** throwing/to throw
**arroz:** rice
**novios:** the bride and groom
**pasar:** to spend
**luna de miel:** honeymoon
**fuentes:** fountains
**portones:** hall doors
**hierro forjado:** wrought iron
**enredaderas:** creeper, climbing plant
**proporcionan/proporcionar:** they provide/to provide
**ambiente:** atmosphere
**atardecer:** evening, dusk, sunset
**bizcochos:** cake
**panadería:** bakery
**bajo el brazo:** under one's arm
**puerto:** harbor
**alberga/albergar:** it harbors/to harbor
**botes:** small boats
**barcos veleros:** sailing boats
**llegar por mar:** to arrive by sea
**saliendo/salir:** leaving/to leave
**pescar:** to fish
**río arriba:** up the river
**aprovechan/aprovechar:** they take advantage of/to take advantage of
**deleitarse:** to take delight
**puesta del sol:** sunset
**cierre:** close

| Glossary | |
|---|---|
| **verano:** summer | |
| **explotó/explotar:** it explodes/ to explode | |
| **calor:** heat | |
| **días son mucho más largos:** days are longer | |
| **calle:** street | |
| **minifaldas:** mini skirts | |
| **escotes:** décolleté (low-cut, low-necked garment) | |
| **bermudas:** Bermuda (shorts) | |
| **temporada alta estival:** high summer season | |
| **alegría:** joy | |
| **miles de familias:** thousands of families | |
| **equipaje:** luggage | |
| **nunca falta:** is never missing | |
| **traje de baño:** bathing suit | |
| **toalla:** towel | |
| **bronceador:** suntan oil | |
| **listos:** ready | |
| **playa:** beach | |
| **ofrece/ofrecer:** it offers/to offer | |
| **opciones:** options | |
| **arena:** sand | |
| **a no más de:** not more than | |
| **principales ciudades balnearias:** main city spas, resorts | |
| **son algunas:** are some | |
| **concurridas:** crowded | |
| **mar con temperature:** sea with temperatures | |
| **valientes:** brave, courageous | |
| **anchísimas:** very wide | |
| **no sólo...sino también:** not only... but also | |
| **para disfrutar:** to enjoy | |
| **salidas nocturnas:** night life (outing) | |
| **la más grande:** the greatest | |
| **desarrollo:** development | |
| **caminar:** to walk | |
| **rambla:** boulevard | |
| **vera del mar:** beside the sea | |
| **sentarse a mirar:** to sit down to watch | |
| **destrezas:** skills | |
| **surfistas:** surfers | |
| **tirarse:** to throw or hurl oneself | |
| **lagarto al sol:** lizard in the sun | |
| **actividades diurnas:** daytime activities | |

# Verano en enero y febrero
## ARGENTINA

**Explotó** el **calor**, los **días son mucho más largos** y en la **calle** se ven **minifaldas, escotes** y **bermudas**. La **temporada alta estival** en Argentina se vive con **alegría** y con la mirada puesta en el mar. **Miles de familias** preparan su **equipaje** en el que **nunca falta** el **traje de baño**, la **toalla** y el **bronceador, listos** para unas vacaciones en la **playa**.

La provincia de Buenos Aires **ofrece** múltiples **opciones** para los turistas decididos a pasar unos días sobre la **arena**. **A no más de** 400 kilómetros de la capital, se encuentran las **principales ciudades balnearias**. Mar del Plata, Pinamar, Cariló o Villa Gessell **son algunas** de las más **concurridas**.

Con un **mar con temperatura** para **valientes**, pero con playas **anchísimas** y largas, estas ciudades se caracterizan **no sólo** por una costa generosa **para disfrutar** durante el día, **sino también** por una gran diversidad de entretenimiento y **salidas nocturnas**.

Mar del Plata es **la más grande** y la que cuenta con más **desarrollo. Caminar** o hacer *footing* por la **rambla** a la **vera del mar, sentarse a mirar** las **destrezas** de los **surfistas** o **tirarse** como un **lagarto al sol** son algunas de las **actividades diurnas**.

Por las noches, puede verse a **gente colorada por el sol**, **probando suerte** en el casino, **haciendo cola para entrar** en alguno de los **espectáculos teatrales** o **disfrutando de un café** en algunas del las **terrazas al aire libre**, siempre y cuando el **viento marino** lo permita. Pinamar y Cariló con un aire más señorial, combinan la playa con el **bosque**, la **arena amarilla** con la **madera oscura** de los **árboles**. Una **mezcla mágica** para quienes buscan **relajarse** y **pasar unos días** al lado del mar **en plena naturaleza**.

Y para los **adolescentes** que quieren divertirse, las playas ventosas pero **menos frías** de Villa Gessell son la mejor opción. **Allí**, durante el día, se pueden realizar todo tipo de actividades y **deportes** playeros, **mientras** que por la noche es el momento de **acudir** a recitales, **espectáculos callejeros** y **discotecas** para **bailar hasta el amanecer**.

## CULTURE NOTE

More and more people have realized that you do not have to be in college to "study abroad." People of all ages and all walks of life are discovering the benefits and enjoyment of turning a vacation into an opportunity to study Spanish. Learning Spanish is more than learning the world's second most-used language. It can also turn an average vacation into an extraordinary one, making friends from all over the world while truly immersing yourself in another culture. The global boom in cultural tourism has resulted in a vast selection of language schools and tour packages. The company we turn to again and again is AmeriSpan. They customize each program to fit your needs. They have various language programs all around the world, for all ages and all Spanish levels, from beginning to advanced. You can read about their programs and in-depth destination reviews at: www.amerispan.com. *¡Buen Viaje!*

# Mallorca y sus castillos
## ESPAÑA

Las **Islas Baleares**, archipiélago **situado** en el Mar Mediterráneo, **son conocidas** por su **belleza** pero, **sobre todo**, por ser un **destino** turístico de **interés** internacional. Sus **instalaciones** hoteleras y sus playas son el primer objetivo **para aquellos que buscan sol** y **diversión**. Pero en estas islas y, especialmente en Mallorca, existen **antiguos** monumentos y castillos, **cuya** visita es **de obligado cumplimiento**.

**Comenzando** desde el Castillo de Alaró, situado en la **cumbre de la montaña** que lleva el **mismo nombre**, en la **Sierra** Tramuntana, hasta castillos como el del Rey o el de Santueri, Mallorca tiene una **variada** oferta turística y cultural.

A tres kilómetros de Palma de Mallorca (**principal ciudad** de la isla de Mallorca) y a unos 140 metros de **altitud**, **rodeado** por un **bosque de pinos**, está el **castillo gótico** de Bellver (significa "buena **vista**"), muy peculiar **debido a** su forma totalmente circular. **Fue construido** en el año 1300, aproximadamente. El rey Jaime I, **aquejado** de tuberculosis, **quiso** construir este castillo para **descansar** en un **entorno sano**. El **corto periodo** de **tiempo empleado** para la construcción de este castillo (40 años), dio **como resultado** su peculiar **estilo arquitectónico**.

---

**castillos:** castles
**Islas Baleares:** Balearic Islands
**situado:** located
**son conocidas/ser conocido:** they are known/to be known
**belleza:** beauty
**sobre todo:** especially
**destino:** destination
**interés:** interest
**instalaciones:** facilities
**para aquellos que buscan sol:** for those looking for the sun
**diversión:** fun
**antiguos:** old, ancient
**cuya:** which
**de obligado cumplimiento:** a must
**comenzando/comenzar:** starting/to start
**cumbre de la montaña:** summit, peak of the mountain
**mismo nombre:** same name
**sierra:** mountain range
**variada:** assorted
**principal ciudad:** main city
**altitud:** altitude
**rodeado/rodear:** surrounded/ to surround
**bosque de pinos:** pine forest
**castillo gótico:** gothic castle
**vista:** view
**debido a:** due to
**fue construido/construir:** it was built/to build
**aquejado:** sick, suffering from
**quiso/querer:** he wanted/to want
**descansar:** to rest
**entorno:** environment
**sano:** healthy
**corto periodo:** short period
**tiempo:** time
**empleado/emplear:** used/to used
**como resultado:** as a result
**estilo arquitectónico:** architectural style

Un gran patio circular forma el centro del castillo, **alrededor del que se encuentran habitaciones** y **salas**. Tiene cuatro **torres**, **la mayor** y con base circular, **se llama** la Torre del **Homenaje**; el resto tienen forma de **herradura**. **De hecho**, este es el **único** castillo de planta circular de toda Europa. **Actualmente**, las **piedras** de este castillo son muy blancas. El motivo de tan peculiar aspecto es que en el **pasado**, **concretamente** en el siglo XIX, **tuvieron que limpiar** la **fachada** del castillo, pues **había sido quemado** como **método de desinfección** para **acabar** con una **plaga de peste**.

Este castillo ha tenido múltiples usos. **En un principio**, fue la residencia de Jaime II de Mallorca, pero **poster-iormente fue utilizado** como **refugio** contra la plaga de peste; como **puesto de defensa** contra los ataques del **ejér-cito** turco; como escenario para fiestas y representaciones teatrales, o incluso como **cárcel** hasta el siglo XX. **Pasear** sobre la **ancha** circunferencia de la **parte superior** del castillo y **mirar hacia abajo**, hacia el patio interior, es realmente espectacular.

En el interior del Castillo de Bellver interior se encuentra el Museo de la Ciudad, que **abarca** la historia de esta isla desde la Prehistoria hasta la **Edad Media**. Sin duda, lo que más **vale la pena** es la espectacular panorámica que **nos ofrece**.

alrededor del que: around which
se encuentran/encontrarse: there are/to be
habitaciones: rooms
salas: halls
torres: towers
la mayor: the biggest
se llama/llamarse: it is called/to call
homenaje: tribute
herradura: horseshoe
de hecho: in fact
único: unique
actualmente: nowadays
piedras: stones, rocks
pasado: past
concretamente: specifically
tuvieron que/tener que: they had to/to have to
limpiar: to clean
fachada: facade
había sido quemado/quemar: it had been burnt/to burn
método de desinfección: method of disinfection
acabar: to finish
plaga de peste: bubonic plague
en un principio: at first
posteriormente: later
fue utilizado/utilizar: it was used/to use
refugio: refuge, shelter
puesto de defensa: place of defense
ejército: army
cárcel: prison, jail
pasear: to walk, to go for a walk
ancha: wide
parte superior: top
mirar hacia abajo: to look downwards
abarca/abarcar: it includes/to include
Edad Media: Middle Ages
vale la pena: it is worth it
nos ofrece/ofrecer: it offers us/to offer

# Un paraíso en el Caribe
## DOMINICAN REPUBLIC

**En los últimos años**, la República Dominicana **se ha convertido** en uno de los **principales destinos** del Caribe, **tanto** para los turistas **procedentes de** América **como** para los europeos. Y **no es de extrañar**, pues cuenta con su exotismo caribeño, con el carácter **abierto** y **acogedor** de sus **gentes** y con un **entorno** natural de increíble **belleza**.

La isla española, que **pertenece** a las Grandes Antillas, está dividida en dos zonas: la República Dominicana y Haití. La República Dominicana ocupa **dos tercios** de la **superficie** de la isla, la cual está **formada** en un 80 **por ciento** por **montañas**. La montaña más alta es Pico Duarte, con unos 3.170 metros. La geografía de este país es muy diversa: **desde planicies** semidesérticas **a** valles con **bosques tropicales**. **Así**, algunos turistas **prefieren** las playas de **arena dorada** que **se extienden** sobre un tercio de la costa dominicana. Es en esta zona donde **se encuentran** los principales centros turísticos. La provincia de Barahona **incluye** cascadas, montañas y unas extensas playas de agua **cristalina**. **Entre** sus hábitats naturales está el Lago Enriquillo, el más grande de las Antillas.

La Romana fue un gran **puerto azucarero** hasta los años 70. Allí **encontraremos** Casa de Campo, uno de los **balnearios** más famosos del mundo. Y si **queremos** visitar Altos de Chavón, el pueblo de los artistas, **disfrutaremos** de un entorno similar a los pequeños pueblos del sur de Francia, a la **orilla del río** Chavón.

Para los **amantes** de la costa, Playa Grande pone a su disposición unas 300 hectáreas de vegetación de 1.500 metros de playa. También pueden disfrutar de su campo de golf a **orillas del mar**. Pero no debemos **olvidar** Punta Cana, con sus playas de agua **azulada**, y **muy próxima** a Playa Grande está Bávaro, con sus hoteles, a pocos minutos del aeropuerto de Punta Cana.

Otro tipo de visitantes prefiere visitar el interior, pues **piensan** que aquí pueden encontrar el **verdadero encanto** de la República Dominicana. La isla **está atravesada** por tres impresionantes **cordilleras, paralelas** en **sentido** Este-Oeste. Por un lado, está la Cordillera Central, que se extiende desde Haití hasta San Cristóbal, cerca de Santo Domingo. En esta cordillera se encuentra el Pico Duarte. Por otro lado, más al norte, se encuentra la Cordillera Septentrional, que atraviesa el valle de Cibao, donde están las **antiguas minas de oro**. Por último, la Cordillera Oriental se encuentra en el Este y es la más pequeña. Un **dato reconfortante** es que en **la mayoría de** las islas caribeñas no hay **serpientes venenosas** ni insectos **cuya picadura** o agujón sean una **amenaza** vital. Si usted planea visitar la República Dominicana, **tenga en cuenta** que, aunque su lengua oficial es el español, en las principales zonas turísticas muchos dominicanos hablan inglés y **alemán**, y **algunos** conocen también el francés y el italiano. Pero si usted decide visitar la zona interior, allí los residentes solamente hablan español, así que es conveniente que usted tenga unos **conocimientos** básicos de este idioma.

Entre los principales atractivos de la República Dominicana destacan su clima subtropical, con una **temperatura media** de 28 **grados centígrados** y sus playas de agua azul turquesa, con palmeras que ofrecen una reconfortante **sombra**. **Además de** su **envidiable entorno natural**, en los últimos años el Departamento de Turismo dominicano **ha incrementado** la **oferta** de nuevas formas de turismo.

**amantes:** lovers
**orillas del mar:** seashore
**olvidar:** to forget
**azulada:** bluish
**muy próxima:** very close
**piensan/pensar:** they think/to think
**verdadero:** true
**encanto:** charm
**está atravesada/atravesar:** it is crossed/to cross
**cordilleras:** mountain ranges
**paralelas:** parallel
**sentido:** sense
**antiguas minas de oro:** ancient gold mines
**dato:** piece of information
**reconfortante:** comforting
**la mayoría de:** most of
**serpientes venenosas:** poisonous snakes
**cuya:** whose
**picadura:** bite
**agujón:** sting
**amenaza:** threat
**tenga en cuenta/tener en cuenta:** take into account/to take into account
**alemán:** German
**algunos:** some of them
**conocimientos:** knowledge
**temperatura media:** average temperature
**grados centígrados:** degrees Celsius
**sombra:** shade
**además de:** as well as
**envidiable:** enviable
**entorno natural:** natural environment
**ha incrementado/incrementar:** it has increased/to increase
**oferta:** offer

| | |
|---|---|
| **privilegiada:** privileged | |
| **ubicación:** location | |
| **playas:** beaches | |
| **cálidas:** warm | |
| **todo el mundo:** all around the world | |
| **conocida como:** known as | |
| **se encuentra/encontrarse:** it is located/to locate | |
| **descansan/descansar:** they rest/ to rest | |
| **ilumina/iluminar:** it illuminates/ to illuminate | |
| **arena:** sand | |
| **grados centígrados:** degrees Celsius | |
| **al oeste:** to the west | |
| **orillas cubanas:** Cuban shores | |
| **fondos marinos:** sea beds | |
| **poseen/poseer:** they have/to have | |
| **peces:** fish | |
| **langostas:** lobsters | |
| **camarones:** prawns | |
| **cangrejos:** crabs | |
| **centenar de moluscos:** one hundred mollusks | |
| **paraíso:** paradise | |
| **fina:** fine, very thin | |
| **despliega/desplegar:** it shows/ to show | |
| **paleta de azules:** palette of blues | |
| **distinguen/distinguir:** they distinguish/to distinguish | |
| **nos ofrece/ofrecer:** it offers us/ to offer | |
| **podemos encontrar/poder:** we can find/can | |
| **estalactitas y estalagmitas:** stalactites and stalagmites | |
| **fauna marina:** marine fauna | |
| **abundan/abundar:** there are plentiful/to be plentiful | |
| **morenas:** morays | |
| **meros:** groupers | |
| **nos invita/invitar:** it invites us/ to invite | |
| **antiguo barco alemán:** old German ship | |
| **naufragó/naufragar:** it was wrecked/to wreck | |
| **se ubica/ubicarse:** it is located/ to be located | |
| **Bahía de Cochinos:** Bay of Pigs | |

# Varadero, arenas blancas
## CUBA

La **privilegiada ubicación** de Cuba hace que sus **playas** transparentes y **cálidas** sean una atracción para turistas de **todo el mundo** durante los 365 días del año. Varadero, **conocida como** "la playa preferida por su sol", **se encuentra** en Matanzas, provincia cuyas costas **descansan** en el océano Atlántico y el Mar Caribe. En Varadero, el sol **ilumina** la **arena** durante unas 12 horas diarias y la temperatura es de, aproximadamente, 25 **grados centígrados**. **Al oeste**, esta provincia limita con La Habana; al este, con Villa Clara, y al sudeste, con Cienfuegos.

¿Por qué son tan especiales las playas de Varadero? ¿Qué las diferencia de las otras **orillas cubanas**? Sus **fondos marinos**. **Poseen** más de 40 clases de corales, una increíble diversidad de **peces**, **langostas**, **camarones**, **cangrejos**, tortugas y casi un **centenar de moluscos**. En este pequeño **paraíso** cubano, la arena es blanca y **fina** y la costa, de 22 kilómetros de longitud, **despliega** una **paleta de azules** inimaginables en el horizonte. Aunque en Varadero la belleza del Caribe se despliega a cada paso, cada una de sus playas ofrece particularidades que las **distinguen**. Playa Coral **nos ofrece** más de 30 especies de corales, mientras que Cueva de Saturno es una caverna en la que **podemos encontrar estalactitas y estalagmitas**. Las Mandarinas posee una variada **fauna marina** en la que **abundan** los peces coralinos, las **morenas** y los **meros**.

Playa Caribe **nos invita** a la aventura ya que en ella se encuentran los secretos y misterios de un **antiguo barco alemán** que **naufragó** en la costa cubana. Por su parte, Punta Perdiz posee uno de los ecosistemas más diversificados del Mar Caribe y **se ubica** en la popular **Bahía de Cochinos**.

**Por último,** El Cenote tiene un gran **lago y grietas** en las que es posible **sumergirse** hasta 25 metros. Es importante **destacar** que esta playa se encuentra en la Ciénaga de Zapata, uno de los mayores y mejor preservados **humedales** de la región.

Pero Varadero no es sólo sus playas. A aquellos interesados en **tomar contacto** con las **raíces populares** de la región, posiblemente les interesará visitar la Cueva de Ambrosio en la que se encuentran **dibujos rupestres realizados** por aborígenes y, **se supone,** también por **esclavos.** La Casa de la Cultura Los Corales también **nos permite aproximarnos** a la cultura popular cubana ya que es allí donde los artistas locales **exponen** sus **mejores obras.** Además, los **fines de semana** es posible ver **obras de teatro** y **espectáculos. Y si** de **aprender** a bailar **se trata,** este centro cultural ofrece **clases de baile** dictadas por profesores que **brindan** sus servicios a los turistas.

En el Museo Municipal de Varadero la ciudad **guarda viejos secretos.** Allí **se exhiben piezas claves** de la cultura y la historia. La arquitectura del museo **rescata** el **estilo** tradicional de muchas construcciones de la zona **combinando** la textura de la **madera** con colores vibrantes. **Sin lugar a dudas,** Varadero, este pequeño paraíso cubano, nos ofrece la posibilidad de **disfrutar** de unas de las playas **más hermosas** del mundo y de la **riqueza** y **encanto** de la cultura del Caribe.

---

cadena: chain
rodeada/rodear: surrounded/
  to surround
parte nórdica: Nordic part
ha distribuido/distribuir: it has
  distributed/to distribute
cordilleras: mountain ranges
mundialmente: worldwide
hacia: towards
este: east
sur: south
carreteras: roads
se originan/originar: they start/
  to start
cuyo: whose
se encuentra/encontrar: it is located/
  to be located
playas: beaches
siendo/ser: being/to be
todos los gustos: all tastes
específicamente: especially
deportes acuáticos: water sports
por ejemplo: for example
llena de: full of
tortugas: turtles
escala: scale
no deja/dejar: it doesn't leave/to leave
espacio libre: free space
selva: jungle
estilo amazónico: Amazon style
repleta de: full of
estilo de vida: lifestyle
secos: dry
carretas de maderas: wooden oxcarts
perdido/perder: lost/to lose
vigencia: relevance
se destacan/destacar: they stand out/
  to stand out
afamados: famous, well known
anfitrión: host
últimas: last
ya sea: whether it is
relajarse: to relax
amabilidad: kindness
disfrutar: to enjoy
única: unique
sabor: flavor
todos lados del mundo: all over
  the world

# Un paraíso exótico
## COSTA RICA

Costa Rica es parte de la gran **cadena** andina Sierra Madre, **rodeada** de volcanes y montañas: en la **parte nórdica** de la región la actividad volcánica **ha distribuido** la zona en **cordilleras**: en el noroeste la Cordillera de Guanacaste; en el sureste, la Cordillera de Tilarán, dominada por el Arenal, uno de los volcanes más activos **mundialmente**; **hacia** el **este**, la Cordillera Central, y hacia el **sur** la Cordillera Salamanca. Todas las **carreteras** y rutas **se originan** en la Meseta Central, el corazón de la nación en **cuyo** centro **se encuentra** San José, la capital de Costa Rica. En esta parte, la temperatura general durante el año es de 23 grados centígrados.

Las **playas** son unas de las atracciones más populares de este país **siendo** predominante la costa del Pacífico. La costa tiene una longitud de más de 1.800 kilómetros y una colección de playas atractivas para **todos los gustos**, y **específicamente** para los **deportes acuáticos** como el surf. En Nancite, **por ejemplo**, la playa se **llena de tortugas** durante meses a una **escala** tan grande que **no deja espacio libre**. En el Atlántico está Tortuguero, una **selva** al **estilo amazónico**, **repleta de** vida animal y flora de abundancia paradisíaca. Al sur del Atlántico están las playas más populares de esta zona, Cahuita y Puerto Viejo, con el aroma caribeño en las comidas, vegetación y **estilo de vida**. Los meses más **secos** en San José son desde diciembre hasta abril.

El símbolo de Costa Rica son las **carretas de maderas** decoradas, que ya han **perdido vigencia** pero **se destacan** en la zona de Sarchí. Cerca de San José en Santa Ana y Escazú se encuentran **afamados** artistas contemporáneos. Costa Rica, país rico en cultura, es también **anfitrión** del Festival Internacional de Música durante las **últimas** semanas de agosto. **Ya sea** para **relajarse** con la **amabilidad** de su gente, **disfrutar** de la vegetación **única** de playas y selva, o experimentar el **sabor** de la cultura de este país centroamericano, Costa Rica es un lugar paradisíaco para turistas llegados de **todos lados del mundo**.

# El turismo rural
## ESPAÑA

**Durante los últimos años**, el turismo rural **ha llegado a ser** en España una alternativa al turismo convencional. Pero, ¿Cuál es la **principal** característica del turismo rural? El **entorno**, la **ausencia** de **multitudes**, el relax y la posibilidad de practicar actividades como hacer **rutas en bicicleta**, **colaborar** en las **tareas** de una **granja** o en los **cultivos**, o simplemente hacer **senderismo**.

**Hablando de** España, **hay dos tipos de alojamientos rurales**: las casas rurales y los hoteles rurales. **En cuanto a** las casas rurales, es posible **alquilar toda la casa**, normalmente **durante un fin de semana como mínimo**, o alquilar una **habitación los días que queramos**. **Tanto** las casas **como** los hoteles rurales son **antiguos edificios reconstruidos**, **viejas casas de pueblo** e **incluso pequeños castillos**.

El **ambiente** de las casas rurales es **amigable**. Normalmente existe la posibilidad de **degustar** la gastronomía típica **de cada lugar**. Muchas casas rurales tienen **piscina**, principalmente en la zona mediterránea y sur de la península.

**Hoy en día**, **podemos encontrar** mucha información en internet, simplemente **escribiendo** en un **buscador** las palabras "casa rural" o "turismo rural", **debido a** la gran oferta existente.

¡Esta es **una de las mejores formas de olvidar** el **estrés** y el teléfono móvil! Aunque sólo sea durante dos días, **respirar aire puro** y **ver preciosos paisajes nos ayuda**, **no sólo física**, **sino mentalmente**.

---

**durante los últimos años**: during the last years
**ha llegado a ser**: has become
**principal**: main
**entorno**: environment, scene
**ausencia**: absence
**multitudes**: crowds, multitudes
**rutas en bicicleta**: bicycle routes
**colaborar**: to collaborate, to help
**tareas**: jobs, tasks
**granja**: farm
**cultivos**: crops
**senderismo**: hiking
**hablando de/hablar**: talking about/ to talk
**hay dos tipos de alojamientos rurales**: there are two types of rural lodging
**en cuanto a**: as for, with regard to
**alquilar**: to rent
**toda la casa**: the entire house
**durante un fin de semana**: for a weekend
**como mínimo**: as a minimum
**habitación**: room
**los días que queramos**: as many days as we want
**tanto ...como**: both ...and
**antiguos edificios**: old buildings
**reconstruidos**: reconstructed
**viejas casas de pueblo**: old village houses
**incluso**: even
**pequeños castillos**: small castles
**ambiente**: atmosphere
**amigable**: friendly
**degustar**: to taste
**de cada lugar**: from every place
**piscina**: swimming pool
**hoy en día**: nowadays
**podemos encontrar**: we can find
**escribiendo/escribir**: writing/to write
**buscador**: search engine
**debido a**: due to
**una de las mejores formas de olvidar**: one of the best ways to forget
**estrés**: stress
**respirar aire puro**: to breathe clean air
**ver preciosos paisajes**: to see wonderful landscapes
**nos ayuda/ayudar**: helps us/to help
**no sólo física(mente), sino**
**mentalmente**: not only physically, but mentally

<table>
<tr><td>

**pequeña ciudad mexicana:** small
  Mexican city
**carretera:** road
**clima:** climate
**moderado:** moderate
**no muy fríos:** not very cold
**no alcanzan/alcanzar:** they do not
  reach/to reach
**extremadamente altas:** extremely
  high
**localidad:** locality, city
**atmósfera colonial:** colonial
  atmosphere
**agradable:** pleasant
**jubilados:** retired people
**hoy en día:** nowadays
**acoge/acoger:** it welcomes/
  to welcome
**estudiantes:** students
**visitan/visitar:** they visit/to visit
**personas jubiladas:** retired people
**siguen sintiéndose atraídas:** keep on
  feeling attracted
**expatriados:** expatriates
**viviendo/vivir:** living/to live
**podemos/poder:** we can/can
**encontrar:** to find
**mercados:** markets
**deseemos/desear:** we wish/to wish
**mercadillo al aire libre:** open air
  market
**reúne/reunir:** it gathers/to gather
**alrededores:** surrounding areas
**asistir:** to attend
**hay infinidad:** there are a great
  number, many
**piezas artesanales:** handmade pieces
**procedentes de:** coming from
**cualquier lugar:** any place
**se reúnen/reunirse:** they gather/
  to gather
**mejores aspectos:** best aspects
**junto con:** together with
**comodidades:** comforts
**grandes urbes:** big cities
**invitan/invitar:** they invite/to invite
**visitarla:** to visit it
**sin importar:** it doesn't matter
**época del año:** time of year
**elijamos/elegir:** we choose/to choose
**estancia:** stay
**inolvidable:** unforgettable

</td></tr>
</table>

# San Miguel de Allende
## MÉXICO

San Miguel de Allende es una **pequeña ciudad mexicana** situada, por **carretera**, a poco más de una hora del aeropuerto de León, y a unas cuatro horas al norte de la ciudad de México. Su altitud es de 1.908 metros y su **clima** es **moderado**: inviernos **no muy fríos** y veranos que **no alcanzan** temperaturas **extremadamente altas**.

Esta bonita **localidad**, de **atmósfera colonial** y **agradable** temperatura, fue durante los años 70 el lugar ideal para los **jubilados** de Estados Unidos y Canadá. **Hoy en día** San Miguel **acoge** a numerosos **estudiantes** que **visitan** la ciudad para estudiar español y arte. Las **personas jubiladas siguen sintiéndose atraídas** por esta ciudad y, de hecho, hay unos 2.000 **expatriados viviendo** aquí.

Es fácil vivir en San Miguel. Aquí, **podemos encontrar** excelentes **mercados** en los que comprar todo aquello que **deseemos**. Cada martes, un gran **mercadillo al aire libre reúne** a muchos vendedores de los **alrededores**. La ciudad ofrece variadas actividades culturales. En agosto podemos **asistir** al festival de música de cámara y en invierno al festival de jazz, entre otros muchos. **Hay infinidad** de galerías de arte y probablemente las mejores tiendas de artesanía de México, con **piezas artesanales procedentes de cualquier lugar** del país.

En San Miguel **se reúnen** los **mejores aspectos** de la pequeña ciudad **junto con** las **comodidades** de las **grandes urbes**. Sus variados restaurantes, sus mercados, el teatro y sus exposiciones de arte nos **invitan** a **visitarla sin importar** la **época del año** que **elijamos**. ¡Nuestra **estancia** aquí será **inolvidable**!

# Tulum, la ciudad sobre el mar
## MÉXICO

**Hace muchísimos años**, los mayas **descubrieron** un **paraíso a orillas de** las **aguas azules y cristalinas** del mar Caribe y allí, sobre un **acantilado** de doce metros de altura sobre el **nivel del mar**, **construyeron** una gran ciudad **amurallada**, una **fortaleza rodeada** por una enorme **pared**. **La llamaron** Tulum, que en su **lengua** quiere decir: **muro, cerco, muralla**.

**Alcanzó** su **esplendor alrededor** del año 1200 DC y hasta la llegada de los conquistadores españoles fue un **puerto mercante** próspero y eficiente, **basado** principalmente en el **trueque**. La **gente común vivía** fuera de esta ciudad **sagrada** y sólo algunos privilegiados como **sacerdotes**, matemáticos, **ingenieros** o astrónomos vivían **dentro** de ella ya que **se los consideraba seres superdotados**. Uno de los mayores **legados** de estos **eruditos** fue el Calendario maya.

LA CIUDAD POR DENTRO
Toda la ciudad **se extiende** a lo largo de seis kilómetros sobre la costa. Existen muchas construcciones de las cuales algunas fueron **dedicadas** a la **veneración**, y otras fueron **edificios administrativos** o **lugares de residencia**.

El edificio más importante es llamado el Castillo: **edificado** sobre rocas es el más alto de la ciudad y fue construido durante diferentes **etapas** de la civilización maya. Fue principalmente utilizado para rituales religiosos y, por su **grandeza**, hacía las veces de faro para los **barcos mercantes** que **navegaban** a lo largo de la costa. Otras de las construcciones relevantes son el Templo de los Frescos, el cual tuvo una gran importancia social y religiosa, y el Gran Palacio o Casa de las Columnas, una estructura de tres **niveles** que **contaba** con numerosas **cámaras pequeñas** y fue habitado por los nobles superiores de la sociedad.

Tulum **deslumbra** por su **belleza, tamaño, fuerza** e historia. Es un lugar para **no perderse**.

---

**hace muchísimos años:** many years ago
**descubrieron/descubrir:** they discovered/to discover
**paraíso:** paradise
**a orillas de:** on the banks of
**aguas azules y cristalinas:** blue and crystalline waters
**acantilado:** cliff
**nivel del mar:** sea level
**construyeron/construir:** they built/ to build
**amurallada:** walled
**fortaleza:** fortress
**rodeada:** surrounded
**pared:** wall
**la llamaron/llamar:** they named it/ to name
**lengua:** language
**muro, cerco, muralla:** wall
**alcanzó/alcanzar:** it reached/to reach
**esplendor:** magnificent
**alrededor:** around
**puerto mercante:** merchant port
**basado:** based
**trueque:** barter
**gente común:** common people
**vivía/vivir:** they lived/to live
**sagrada:** sacred
**sacerdotes:** priests
**ingenieros:** engineers
**dentro:** inside
**se los consideraba/considerar:** they were considered/to consider
**seres superdotados:** gifted beings
**legados:** legacies
**eruditos:** erudite
**se extiende/extenderse:** it extends/ to extend
**dedicadas:** dedicated, devoted
**veneración:** veneration
**edificios administrativos:** administration buildings
**lugares de residencia:** places of residence
**edificado:** built up
**etapas:** stages
**grandeza:** greatness
**barcos mercantes:** merchant boats
**navegaban/navegar:** they sailed/ to sail
**niveles:** levels
**contaba/contar:** it counted/to count
**cámaras pequeñas:** small chambers
**deslumbra/deslumbrar:** it dazzles/ to dazzle
**belleza, tamaño, fuerza:** beauty, size, strength
**no perderse/perder:** not to miss/ to miss

# Examina tu comprensión

## El barrio gótico, page 24

**1.** Centuries ago the Gothic Quarter was what?

**2.** What is the name of the bridge located here?

**3.** What advice is given at the end of the article?

## Colonia del Sacramento, page 26

**1.** What might you find to buy or eat in Colonia del Sacramento?

**2.** What should you do after buying a "*bizcocho*"?

## Verano en enero y febrero, page 28

**1.** As the days get hotter what do you see on the streets of Argentina?

**2.** Describe some favorite daytime activities and nightime activities.

**3.** What city is the biggest and most developed?

**4.** What two cities create a magical place to relax and why?

## Mallorca y sus castillos, page 30

**1.** Why are the Balearic Islands a popular tourist desitination? Where are they located?

**2.** What makes the Bellver Castle so unique and why was it built?

**3.** The stones of the castle are now "very white." Why?

# Test your comprehension

## Un paraíso en el Caribe, page 32

**1.** Name four geographic environments in this country.

**2.** La Ramona has one of the most famous resorts. Name the resort and describe the amenities.

**3.** A comforting aspect about most of the Caribbean islands is the lack of certain creatures. What are they?

## Varadero arenas blancas, page 34

**1.** What makes the beaches of Varadero so special?

**2.** What famous historical sight can you visit at Punta Perdiz?

**3.** Besides the beautiful beaches what else can you enjoy or disover, and where?

## El turismo rural, page 37

**1.** What is the main attraction or appeal of "rural tourism"?

**2.** There are two types of rural lodging. What are they?

**3.** What is recommended as the best way to find information on this type of travel in Spain?

## San Miguel de Allende, page 38

**1.** Tourists from what country are particularly drawn to San Miguel de Allende?

**2.** Students also come to San Miguel de Allende to study what?

## Tulum, page 39

**1.** Only certain people lived inside this walled city. Who were they and why?

Un pueblo sin tradición es un pueblo sin porvenir.

Alberto Lleras Camargo

Tradición

# La quinceañera
## MÉXICO

**Cumplir 15 años** es muy importante para las mujeres mexicanas. **Si bien** en otros países la transición de las adolescentes que **se convierten** en mujeres también se celebra a esta **edad**, en México tiene una **relevancia** y un **festejo** particular.

**Se da por sentado** que fueron los conquistadores españoles los que **trajeron** esta costumbre a México, **tomando** la tradición de la mujer azteca y **adaptándola** al cristianismo. Los aztecas celebraban la **llegada** de las niñas a la **madurez** con una ceremonia religiosa y un banquete. Los conquistadores tomaron la celebración pagana y la **convirtieron** a la Iglesia católica. Así, **hoy en día**, la chica que cumple 15 años **se adentra** en el mundo de la **adultez femenina** con una **misa de acción de gracias**, donde **agradece** y se prepara para los nuevos **retos** por vivir. **Posteriormente**, se celebra una gran fiesta con baile incluido, donde **comparte** su alegría con sus **seres queridos**.

La quinceañera, **vestida de gala** en colores pastel, con **ramo de flores**, **anillo** y **a veces** hasta **corona**, recibe la misa acompañada por familiares, amigos y sobre todo por 14 chicas (representando sus primeros 14 años) y sus **chambelanes** (acompañantes masculinos o **caballeros de honor**). La misa **culmina** con una **oración**, la bendición de los **dones** y la **entrega** del ramo de flores que hace la del cumpleaños a la Virgen María.

Después de la misa, la fiesta es pura **alegría**, baile, comida y **regalos**. Algunas hasta cuentan con la famosa piñata. El momento del **vals** también es **esperado** por todos. La quinceañera baila su primer vals con su padre y luego con todo el que quiera **acercarse a la pista de baile**. Así **sigue** la **diversión** y el festejo, entre más bailes y, **por supuesto**, el **pastel**, especialmente preparado para la ocasión.

# Chichicastenango
## GUATEMALA

Guatemala, **ubicada** en el centro del continente americano, fue, **antes** de la conquista, **núcleo** del Imperio Maya (en **lengua** de los mayas, su nombre quiere decir "tierra de árboles"). Es **precisamente** por esta historia que **se caracteriza** por una gran **diversidad** étnica y cultural. Los grupos principales que hoy la **habitan** son: los indígenas, descendientes de los mayas, subdivididos a su vez en varios grupos que **forman** la familia maya-quiché; y los mestizos y europeos. **Afortunadamente**, estas culturas mantienen todavía sus costumbres celebrando en **casi todos** los pueblos su **propia** fiesta, con bailes y eventos sociales, culturales y deportivos, haciendo de Guatemala un **paraíso** de tradición y color.

Una de las celebraciones más importantes es la que conmemora el pueblo maya-quiché de Chichicastenango en honor a su patrón, Santo Tomás. En la catedral que lleva su nombre y que fue **construida** en 1540, los descendientes de este pueblo **elevan** sus **plegarias** entre **velas**, **pino** y flores, **esparcidas** en el **suelo**, y **queman copal**, un **incienso** típico del país. En la fiesta, que se celebra del 14 al 21 de diciembre, **se llevan a cabo** procesiones y se bailan danzas autóctonas acompañadas por la marimba, un instrumento tradicional y característico de Guatemala. Sin embargo, una de las actividades más curiosas en esta fiesta **gira en torno al** famoso "Palo Volador". En la plaza central, instalan un **palo** o poste muy alto, desde el que varios **jóvenes se lanzan** hacia el suelo, sostenidos por un **lazo** o **soga**, como si **volaran**. ¡Sólo para **valientes**!

Chichicastenango es **conocida**, también, por ser **cuna** de uno de los **legados culturales** más **preciados**: el manuscrito del Popol Vuh, el **libro sagrado** de los maya-quichés. Se dice que este manuscrito, escrito en el siglo XVI por un indígena maya **anónimo**, fue **reescrito** por un religioso de esta localidad **alrededor** del 1700. El Popol Vuh es una **obra literaria única** en la que **se cuenta** la historia y las **leyendas** de los que habitaron, y **aún** habitan, el área de Chichicastenango.

---

**ubicada/ubicar**: located/to locate
**antes**: before
**núcleo**: nucleus, core
**lengua**: language
**precisamente**: precisely
**se caracteriza/caracterizarse**: it characterizes/to characterize
**diversidad**: diversity
**habitan/habitar**: they live/to live
**forman/formar**: they form/to form
**afortunadamente**: fortunately
**casi todos**: almost all
**propia**: own
**paraíso**: paradise
**construida/construir**: built/to build
**elevan/elevar**: they raise/to raise
**plegarias**: prayers
**velas**: candles
**pino**: pine
**esparcidas/esparcir**: spread/to spread
**suelo**: ground
**queman/quemar**: they burn/to burn
**copal**: a typical incense of the country
**incienso**: incense
**se llevan a cabo**: they carry out
**gira en torno al**: revolve around
**palo**: pole, stick
**jóvenes**: young people
**se lanzan/lanzar**: they throw themselves, they jump/to jump
**lazo**: bow
**soga**: rope
**volaran/volar**: they fly/to fly
**valientes**: brave
**conocida/conocer**: known/to know
**cuna**: origin; birthplace
**legados culturales**: cultural legacy
**preciados**: prized, valued
**libro sagrado**: sacred book
**anónimo**: anonymous
**reescrito/reescribir**: re-written/to re-write
**alrededor**: around
**obra literaria única**: unique literary work
**se cuenta/contar**: it is told/to tell
**leyendas**: legends
**aún**: still

**tribu indígena:** indigenous tribe
**noreste:** northeast
**veneraban/venerar:** they worship/to worship
**la llamaban/llamar:** they called her/to call
**proviene/provenir:** it comes from/to come from
**ofrecían/ofrecer:** they offered/to offer
**le agradecían/agradecer:** they thank her/to thank
**les daba/dar:** she gave them/to give
**engendraba/engendrar:** it causes/to cause
**daba vida/dar vida:** it gave life/to give life
**sigue/seguir:** it keeps/to keep
**andina:** Andean
**año tras año:** year after year
**se le rinde tributo a:** they pay tribute to
**naturaleza:** nature
**hace germinar:** it makes germinate
**semillas:** seeds
**madurar:** to ripen
**jóvenes:** young people
**viejos:** old people
**cumplen/cumplir:** they keep/to keep
**pidiendo/pedir:** asking for/to ask for
**fecundidad:** fertility
**terrenos:** pieces of land
**felicidad:** happiness
**festejo:** celebration
**ofrendas:** presents, gifts
**demanda/demandar:** it requires/to require
**mazorcas de maíz:** corn cobs
**habas:** broad beans
**hojas de coca:** coca leaves
**se junta/juntar:** it is put together/to put together
**alimentar:** to feed
**devolverle/devolver:** giving her back/to give back
**así:** this way
**se decoran/decorar:** they are decorated/to decorate
**globos:** balloons
**serpentinas:** streamers
**platos:** dishes
**a base:** using
**se degusta/degustar:** it is sampled/to sample

# La Pachamama
## ARGENTINA

Los incas, **tribu indígena** de la zona de Perú, Bolivia y **noreste** argentino, **veneraban** a la Madre Tierra. **La llamaban** Pachamama, nombre que **proviene** de "pacha" (universo, mundo, tiempo, lugar) y de "mama" (madre). En su honor **ofrecían** una ceremonia en la que **le agradecían** por todo los que **les daba**. Según ellos, la Pachamama producía, **engendraba** y **daba vida**.

Afortunadamente esta tradición **sigue** celebrándose entre la población **andina**, **año tras año**, cada 1 de agosto. **Se le rinde tributo a** la Madre Tierra, la **naturaleza** que **hace germinar** las **semillas** y **madurar** los frutos. **Jóvenes**, **viejos** y niños **cumplen** este homenaje **pidiendo** por la **fecundidad** de sus **terrenos** y la **felicidad** en sus vidas.

Para el **festejo** se preparan durante varias semanas, ya que buscar y preparar las **ofrendas demanda** un gran trabajo: **mazorcas de maíz, habas**, chicha (bebida que se prepara a base de harina de maíz), cigarrillos, **hojas de coca**, alcohol, cerveza y vino, todo **se junta** para **alimentar** a la tierra y **devolverle así** algo de lo que ella da. Las casas

**se decoran** con **globos**, **serpentinas** y flores. Se preparan **platos** típicos y el *yerbiao*, una infusión **a base** de hierbas aromáticas, azúcar, yerba, agua y alcohol, que luego **se degusta** entre todos.

Cuando todo está listo se procede a la ceremonia que puede oficiarse en cualquier momento del día. Se cava un pozo en la tierra, se colocan brazos y sahumerios en su interior para sahumarla y se tapa con un poncho o manta.

Mientras tanto, la tierra que se saca se coloca a un costado y allí se depositan los cigarrillos encendidos por cada uno de los presentes. La tradición dice que de acuerdo a cómo la tierra vaya fumando, así será la suerte de cada uno en ese año.

Una vez sahumada, se destapa el pozo y se da de comer a la Tierra con las ofrendas preparadas: se entierran las hojas de coca, las bebidas y las comidas. También se coloca papel picado (que simboliza la alegría) y artesanías hechas con retazos de lana de oveja (que simbolizan los deseos e intenciones de cada asistente). Luego se tapa la boca de la tierra, se deja caer abundante papel picado y se coloca una piedra grande sobre todo.

Entonando lindas coplas, todos los presentes se preparan para degustar la comida, la bebida y el yerbiao hecho para la ocasión.

# El uso de las plantas medicinales
## ARGENTINA

**En pleno siglo XXI**, donde la tecnología, la **ciencia** y la medicina tradicional dan **muestra** de increíbles **avances** con el objetivo de mejorar la **calidad de vida**, una **corriente de volver** a las **fuentes** y a la naturaleza también está en **auge**. Porque, **si bien** los avances tecnológicos y la globalización **trajeron aparejados** enormes **ventajas**, también **separaron** al hombre de su sensibilidad **innata** y del contacto con la naturaleza: cuestiones fundamentales para **entender** y acompañar el **crecimiento** del ser humano y los ciclos de la vida.

Si, como **alguien dijo alguna vez**, la naturaleza es **sabia**, **bastaría imitarla u observarla** más detenidamente para volvernos, también, un poco más eruditos, inteligentes y seguramente más felices. En Argentina, el uso de las plantas medicinales como remedios naturales contra algunas afecciones o como ayuda preventiva para **mantenerse saludable se ha vuelto popular**, y sus enormes ventajas y benéficos efectos **pueden comprobarse** en poco tiempo. En forma de **té** o de **tinturas**, **junto a** cremas y lociones o simplemente con el contacto de ellas, todo es válido a la hora de **curar**, **calmar o relajar**.

Una **hoja abierta** de aloe vera, por ejemplo, **desinflama** y **cicatriza cualquier quemadura**; un té de **hojas de tilo** calma los nervios y una infusión de valeriana **manda a dormir** al insomnio más **estresado**. A las depresiones leves y la **ansiedad** se puede **hacer frente** con **tisanas de hipérico**, una planta de **hojas amarillas** con pétalos **alargados** en forma de **estrella**; y el aromático té de **menta**, además de ayudar a una buena digestión tiene **propiedades expectorantes** y **carminativas**.

Están **al alcance de la mano**. Y son mucho más económicas, **sanas** y naturales que los medicamentos tradicionales.

# Una Navidad en Paraguay
## PARAGUAY

En todos los países de Sudamérica, la **llegada** de la Navidad **coincide con** la llegada del **verano** y el tiempo cálido. Por eso, la mayoría de los niños **se preguntan** porqué Papa Noel está **vestido** con un **traje** tan **abrigado** y el **arbolito** está **lleno de nieve**.

**Una de las tantas** versiones que **circulan sobre** su origen **se basa en** las raíces de la **mitología nórdica**, según la cual existía un **dios** que **vivía** en una **estrella**, tenía una **larga barba blanca** y **cabalgaba** por el **cielo** llevando **regalos**.

En Paraguay, el **festejo** de la navidad no es muy diferente a cómo se celebra en otros países del **Cono Sur,** ya que no sólo **comparten** proximidad sino también un **clima** similar. En Paraguay la **gente** es muy **creyente** de la religión católica. **En casi todos** los **hogares**, **además de armar** el arbolito, se arma un **pesebre** que **se adorna** con una **flor típica** del lugar: la flor del **cocotero**, cuyo perfume es muy dulce.

En la Nochebuena (24 de diciembre por la noche) las familias van a la Misa del Gallo y luego comparten en la mesa familiar la **cena preparada** con comidas y bebidas típicas: **no pueden faltar** la sopa paraguaya, que se prepara a base de harina de maíz y es más **espesa** que un caldo tradicional, ó el **chipa guasu**, como la sopa paraguaya pero con **maíz fresco** en lugar de **harina**. Todo se acompaña con un **refrescante clericó**: bebida hecha con vino tinto o blanco, frutas de estación, un poco de azúcar y abundante hielo. Los niños visitan los pesebres de las casas **vecinas** del **barrio**, **cantan villancicos** y en **agradecimiento**, los **dueños** de las casas les dan **golosinas** y refrescos. El 25 al mediodía, esto **se repite** en la mayoría de las casas: las familias, amigos y vecinos comparten **almuerzos** y **estadías juntos**.

---

**llegada:** arrival
**coincide con:** coincides with
**verano:** summer
**se preguntan:** they ask themselves
**vestido:** dressed
**traje:** suit
**abrigado:** warm
**arbolito/árbol:** small tree/tree
**lleno de:** full of
**nieve:** snow
**una de las tantas:** one of many
**circulan:** circulate
**sobre:** about
**se basa en:** is based on
**mitología nórdica:** Nordic mythology
**dios:** god
**vivía/vivir:** lived/to live
**estrella:** star
**larga barba blanca:** long white beard
**cabalgaba/cabalgar:** he used to ride/ to ride
**cielo:** sky
**regalos:** presents
**festejo:** celebration
**Cono Sur:** South America (southern part)
**comparten/compatir:** they share/ to share
**clima:** weather
**gente:** people
**creyente:** believer
**en casi todos:** in almost all
**hogares:** homes
**además de:** besides
**armar:** to assemble, put together
**pesebre:** manger
**se adorna/adornar:** it is decorated/ to decorate
**flor típica:** typical flower
**cocotero:** coconut tree
**cena:** dinner
**preparada/preparar:** prepared/ to prepare
**no pueden faltar:** they cannot miss
**espesa:** thick
**chipa guasu:** typical Paraguayan dish
**maíz fresco:** fresh corn
**harina:** flour
**refrescante:** refreshing
**clericó:** a typical drink made with wine and fruits
**vecinas:** neighboring
**barrio:** neighborhood
**cantan/cantar:** they sing/to sing
**villancicos:** Christmas Carols
**agradecimiento:** gratitude
**dueños:** owners
**golosinas:** candies
**se repite/repetir:** it repeats/to repeat
**almuerzos:** lunch
**estadías juntos:** stays together

## La gritería
### NICARAGUA

| Vocabulary | |
|---|---|
| **la gritería:** | The Shouting |
| **viaje de vuelta:** | return trip |
| **estancia:** | stay |
| **tuvimos la oportunidad:** | we had the opportunity |
| **disfrutar:** | to enjoy |
| **mariano:** | relating to the virgin Mary |
| **vida cotidiana:** | daily life |
| **está sufriendo/sufrir:** | it is suffering/to suffer |
| **se olvidan/olvidarse:** | they forget/to forget |
| **sufrimiento:** | suffering |
| **se unen/unirse:** | they join/to join |
| **van de casa en casa:** | they go from house to house |
| **en punto:** | o'clock |
| **cohetes:** | fireworks |
| **revientan/reventar:** | they burst/to burst |
| **por unos instantes:** | for a few moments |
| **cielo:** | sky |
| **brilla/brillar:** | it shines/to shine, to glitter |
| **fuegos artificiales:** | fireworks |
| **se oyen/oír:** | they are heard/to hear |
| **empieza/empezar:** | it begins/to begin |
| **así:** | this way |
| **únicamente:** | only, solely |
| **nicaragüense:** | Nicaraguan |
| **ningún:** | no (other country) |
| **pólvora:** | gunpowder |
| **anuncia/anunciar:** | it announces/to announce |
| **comienzo:** | beginning |
| **dura/durar:** | it lasts/to last |
| **medianoche:** | midnight |
| **incluyen/incluir:** | included/to include |
| **gritando/gritar:** | shouting/to shout |
| **se conoce/conocerse:** | it is known/to be known |
| **¿Quién causa tanta alegría?:** | Who causes so much joy? |
| **respuesta:** | answer |
| **enfrente de:** | in front of |
| **erigidos/erigir:** | erected, built/to build |
| **inquilinos:** | tenants |

Después de 19 años, decidimos hacer un **viaje de vuelta** a Nicaragua. Durante nuestra **estancia** allá, también **tuvimos la oportunidad** de **disfrutar** de una tradición propia de Nicaragua: la gritería. Este estado centroamericano es un país muy religioso y durante el mes de diciembre se celebra el fervor **mariano** en todos los aspectos de la **vida cotidiana**.

Nicaragua **está sufriendo** severos problemas económicos; sin embargo, el 7 de diciembre todos sus habitantes **se olvidan** de su **sufrimiento** y **se unen** a los diversos grupos que **van de casa en casa**. A las seis **en punto** de la tarde los **cohetes revientan** y, **por unos instantes**, el **cielo** del país **brilla**. Durante las próximas seis horas, los cohetes esporádicos y los **fuegos artificiales se oyen** por todas las calles de las ciudades de Nicaragua. **Empieza así** la gritería.

Esta tradición es **únicamente nicaragüense**. **Ningún** otro país celebra de esta manera la festividad de la Purísima. La **pólvora anuncia** el **comienzo** de la gritería a las seis de la tarde y **dura** hasta la **medianoche**. Los grupos que **incluyen** adultos y niños, van de casa en casa **gritando** lo que **se conoce** como "la gritería": *"¿Quién causa tanta alegría?"* Y la **respuesta** es: *"La concepción de María"*. Todo esto se hace **enfrente de** los altares a la virgen **erigidos** por los **inquilinos** de las casas.

Después los grupos **cantan canciones** a la Virgen María que van **leyendo** de unos **libritos** que se compran por dos o tres **córdobas** cada uno. Los inquilinos **regalan** a los cantantes productos típicos como **matracas**, **indios**, **cañas**, limones, **pitos** y otras **cositas**.

Según la tradición, la gritería tiene su origen en León, pueblo que **se caracteriza** por sus celebraciones religiosas, **siendo** la más **alegre** y **grandiosa** la gritería. El creador de la gritería fue monseñor Giordano Carranza en el año 1857 quien **tenía como propósito** tocar los corazones espirituales del pueblo nicaragüense, a quienes **animaba** a gritar a **la Purísima** y a **construir** altares con sus **propias manos**. **Posteriormente** esta tradición **se trasladó** a Masaya y a Granada para luego **iniciarse** en todos los **barrios** de Monimbó y otras ciudades del país hasta llegar a todos sus **rincones.**

En la casa en donde nosotros estábamos se hicieron hasta 900 regalos, es decir, que allí había más de 900 personas **reunidas**, gritando y cantando **delante del** altar. Yo nunca **había visto tanta** gente **como vi** esa noche. Era realmente un **espectáculo**. Muchos de esos altares fueron elaboradamente construidos y era evidente también que **se gastó** mucho dinero en comida y **chunches** para regalar. **Ni siquiera** la crisis económica que **atraviesa** el país **conseguirá menguar** la fiesta de la gritería.

**cantan/cantar:** they sing/to sing
**canciones:** songs
**leyendo/leer:** reading/to read
**libritos:** little books
**córdobas:** the Nicaraguan currency
**regalan/regalar:** they give as a present/to give as a present
**matracas:** rattles
**indios:** clay dolls of the indigenous people in Nicaragua
**cañas:** sugar canes
**pitos:** whistles
**cositas:** little things
**se caracteriza/caracterizarse:** is characterized/to be characterized
**siendo/ser:** being/to be
**alegre:** merry, lively
**grandiosa:** impressive
**tenía como propósito:** he had as his goal
**animaba/animar:** he encouraged/to encourage
**la Purísima:** the immaculate conception
**construir:** to build
**propias manos:** own hands
**posteriormente:** subsequently, later
**se trasladó/trasladarse:** it went/to go
**iniciarse:** to be started
**barrios:** neighboorhoods
**rincones:** corners
**reunidas:** gathered
**delante del:** in front of
**había visto/ver:** I had seen/to see
**tanta:** so many
**como vi/ver:** as I saw/to see
**espectáculo:** show
**se gastó/gastarse:** was spent/to be spent
**chunches:** things (slang word referring to anything with no sepecific name)
**ni siquiera:** not even
**atraviesa/atravesar:** it crosses/to cross
**conseguirá/conseguir:** it will succeed/to succeed
**menguar:** to diminish

**los tiempos:** the times
**abuelo:** grandfather
**me llevaba/llevar:** he would take me/to take
**recoger:** to gather, pick up
**pasto:** grass
**camellos:** camels
**íbamos/ir:** we went/to go
**ponía/poner:** I would put/to put
**hierba:** grass
**caja:** box
**nervios:** excitement
**no me dejaban/dejar:** they would not let me/to let
**se aseguraba/asegurar:** she assured me/to assure
**sobre todo:** above all
**no saliera/salir:** she did not leave/ to leave
**habitación:** room
**esperan/esperar:** they wait/to wait
**viejo gordo:** fat old man
**le decimos/decir:** we call him/to say
**aunque:** although
**madrugada:** dawn
**debajo:** under
**cama:** bed
**traen/traer:** they take/to take
**Tres Reyes Magos:** Three Kings, Three Wise Men
**lejanas:** distant, far off
**encuentran/encontrar:** they find/ to find
**tanta:** so much
**cariño:** affection
**obsequios:** gifts
**largo y ancho:** long and wide
**leerse/leer:** they read/to read
**cartas:** letters
**escritas:** written
**pidiendo/pedir:** asking/to ask
**juguete:** toy
**deseo:** wish
**verdaderos:** true, real
**Navidad boricua:** Puerto Rican Christmas
**remonta/remontar:** goes back to/ to go back
**nacimiento:** birth
**humilde:** humble
**pesebre:** manger

# Gaspar, Melchor y Baltasar
## PUERTO RICO

Eran **los tiempos** en que mi **abuelo me llevaba** a **recoger pasto** para los **camellos**. **Íbamos** al patio y yo **ponía** toda la **hierba** en una **caja** grande. Los **nervios no me dejaban** dormir esa noche pero mi abuela **se aseguraba** de que, **sobre todo**, **no saliera** de mi **habitación**.

La noche del 24 de diciembre todos los niños puertorriqueños **esperan** a Santa Claus o al **viejo gordo** como también **le decimos** en la isla. Esta es una tradición adoptada de los Estados Unidos, **aunque** la celebración más importante de Puerto Rico tiene lugar en la **madrugada** del día 6 de enero. La noche del día 5 todos los pequeños salen a recoger hierba fresca que dejan en una caja **debajo** de la **cama** para los camellos que **traen** a los **Tres Reyes Magos** desde tierras **lejanas**. Hierba fresca y agua es lo que **encuentran** los reyes quienes, a cambio de **tanta** demostración de **cariño**, dejan **obsequios** a los niños a lo **largo y ancho** de todo el país.

Días antes pueden **leerse** miles de **cartas escritas** por los más pequeños **pidiendo** su **juguete** favorito, un **deseo** feliz para su familia o simplemente deseando que los reyes visiten su casa. Gaspar, Melchor y Baltasar son los **verdaderos** reyes de nuestra **Navidad boricua**. La historia de los Tres Reyes Magos se **remonta** al **nacimiento** del niño Jesús en un **humilde pesebre** en Belén.

Fueron ellos quienes, **guiados** por la **Estrella de Belén**, llegaron hasta el **recién nacido** para **ofrecerle oro**, mirra e incienso. Desde entonces, cada diciembre muchas personas miran al cielo por la noche buscando la estrella que guió a estos **entrañables personajes**. **Asimismo**, el día 5 de enero el **primer mandatario** del país **abre** las puertas de la Fortaleza y, entre música y comida típica, honra a todos los niños quienes con su inocencia **devuelven** la **esperanza** y **alegría**. Se trata de una fiesta familiar y de pueblo que se extiende hasta el **anochecer**.

En Puerto Rico el periodo navideño **comienza** después de la celebración del **Día de Acción de Gracias** y se extiende hasta la segunda semana de enero cuando nos **deleitamos** con las **octavitas**, los últimos ocho días de fiesta donde aún puede **sentirse** el aire festivo. Yo no escapo a esta tradición. **Lo mismo que hice** de niña lo **hago de adulta**. Todos los años **espero** a los Tres Reyes Magos **junto** a mis hijos con la misma emoción que sentía cuando era pequeña. Nuestras tradiciones **nunca deben morir**.

**guiados:** guided
**Estrella de Belén:** Star of Bethlehem
**recién nacido:** newborn
**ofrecerle:** to offer him
**oro:** gold
**entrañables personajes:** deeply important figures
**asimismo:** also, as well
**primer mandatario:** president
**abre/abrir:** it opens/to open
**devuelven/devolver:** they give back/ to give back
**esperanza:** hope
**alegría:** happiness
**anochecer:** dark, nightfall
**comienza:** begins, starts
**Día de Acción de Gracias:** Thanksgiving
**deleitamos/deleitar:** we enjoy ourselves/to enjoy oneself
**octavitas:** 8 day period of celebration after the Epiphany (little octaves)
**sentirse/sentir:** you can feel/to feel
**lo mismo que hice:** the same as I did
**hago de adulta:** I do it as an adult
**espero/esperar:** I wait/to wait
**junto:** together with
**nunca deben morir:** must never die

**CULTURE NOTE** In Spain, Christmas Eve is known as *Nochebuena* or "the Good Night." Family members gather together to rejoice and feast around the Nativity scenes that are present in nearly every home. A traditional Christmas treat is *turrón*, an almond candy. The *Magi* are also revered in Spain. Children leave their shoes on the windowsills and fill them with straw, carrots, and barley for the horses of the Wise Men. Their favorite is *Baltasar,* who rides a donkey and is the one believed to leave the gifts.

The main Christmas celebration in Mexico is called *las posadas*, which refers to processions reenacting Joseph and Mary's search for a place to stay in Bethlehem. The pilgrims travel from house to house asking for shelter and are refused until they finally reach the house where an altar and nativity scene have been set up. Here they are admitted with great rejoicing, a traditional prayer is spoken, and the celebration begins. The holiday flower, the poinsettia, is native to Mexico. The enchanting legend of the poinsettia dates back several centuries to a Christmas Eve in Mexico when a small child had no gift to present to the Christ child. On the way to church the child gathered some branches found along the road. The legend tells that the branches were laid by the the altar and a miracle happened. The branches blossomed with brilliant red flowers. At that time they were called *Flores de Noche Buena;* today they are called poinsettias.

# 7 de julio San Fermín
## ESPAÑA

La revolución llega a Pamplona cada 7 de julio. Ese día empiezan las fiestas de **San Fermín, sin duda,** una de las más famosas de España. Durante una semana, el **desenfreno inunda** las calles de la ciudad y **ríos de** vino **corren de boca en boca,** entre bailes y **canciones populares,** que **no dan tregua** al **descanso.** Las imágenes de jóvenes vestidos de blanco con sus **fajas y pañuelos** rojos corriendo delante de **inmensos toros bravos** dan la vuelta al mundo cada año, **mostrando** así una tradición ancestral que **encoge el corazón** de los telespectadores. La **fama** internacional de que **gozan** estas fiestas pamplonesas **debe agradecerse, en gran medida,** al escritor norteamericano Ernest Hemingway, quien en su novela *The sun also rises* **ensalzaba** estas celebraciones.

TRADICIÓN ANCESTRAL

**No obstante,** las fiestas de San Fermín se celebran desde hace más de 400 años. **Cuentan** los historiadores que los **Sanfermines surgieron** de la unión de tres fiestas diferentes: las de carácter religioso en honor al santo y que existen desde la **época de los romanos,** las **ferias comerciales** y las **taurinas,** organizadas **ambas** a partir del siglo XIV. En 1591 nacieron los Sanfermines, que en su primera edición **se prolongaron** durante dos días y **contaron** con **pregón,** actuaciones musicales, **torneo,** teatro y **corrida de toros.** En **años sucesivos, mientras las fiestas crecían en días, se fueron intercalando** nuevas diversiones como los **fuegos artificiales** y las danzas.

Desde 1941 el **pistoletazo de salida** lo da el **chupinazo,** un **cohete** de gran potencia que **se lanza** el 6 de julio a las 12 del **mediodía** desde el **balcón** del **Ayuntamiento.** En ese momento los pamplonicas **se duchan,** literalmente, con litros y litros de **vino tinto,** bebida también preferida durante toda la semana.

---

**San Fermín:** Pamplona's patron saint
**sin duda:** undoubtedly, without doubt
**desenfreno:** wild abandon, debauchery
**inunda/inundar:** it swamps/to flood
**ríos de:** floods of (literally "rivers of")
**corren/correr:** they run/to run
**de boca en boca:** to do the rounds (literally from mouth to mouth)
**canciones populares:** folk songs
**no dan tregua/no dar tregua:** they give no respite/to give no respite
**descanso:** rest, break
**fajas y pañuelos:** sashes and scarves
**inmensos:** enormous
**toros bravos:** fierce bulls
**mostrando/mostrar:** showing/to show
**encoge el corazón:** it makes their heart miss a beat
**fama:** fame
**gozan/gozar:** they enjoy/to enjoy
**debe agradecerse:** is due
**en gran medida:** to a great extent
**ensalzaba/ensalzar:** praised/to praise
**no obstante:** nevertheless
**cuentan/contar:** they tell/to tell
**Sanfermines:** popular name for the feast of San Fermín
**surgieron/surgir:** they appeared/to appear; to emerge
**época de los romanos:** Roman times
**ferias comerciales:** commercial show
**taurinas:** bullfighting (adjective)
**ambas:** both
**se prolongaron/prolongarse:** they went on/to go on
**contaron/contar:** they had/ to have
**pregón:** local festival opening speech
**torneo:** tournament, competition
**corrida de toros:** bullfight
**años sucesivos:** consecutive years
**mientras las fiestas crecían en días:** while the feast grew in days
**se fueron intercalando/intercalar:** they were placed in/to put in
**fuegos artificiales:** fireworks
**pistoletazo de salida:** starting signal
**chupinazo:** fierce shot
**cohete:** rocket
**se lanza/lanzar:** it is launched/ to launch
**mediodía:** midday, noon
**balcón:** balcony
**ayuntamiento:** city hall
**se duchan/ducharse:** they take a shower/to take a shower
**vino tino:** red wine

En los bares y los **chiringuitos**, el alcohol se vende **en cantidades industriales** que ayudan a **mantener los ojos abiertos** durante tantos días. Las **sanfermineras**, con **letras mordaces** y divertidas, son escuchadas por todas las **esquinas**.

## El encierro

El encierro es el **momento estrella** de las fiestas de San Fermín. Antes de las ocho de la mañana, hora puntual del inicio, las bandas musicales **tocan** por las calles para despertar a los que quieran correr o ver el emocionante espectáculo. Aunque en televisión parecen **interminables**, los encierros son **carreras** muy cortas, de unos tres minutos de duración que se corren a gran velocidad a lo largo de unos 800 metros. Para este **reto** hay que estar preparado. **De hecho**, los auténticos **pamplonicas** que **se plantan delante de** las **bestias entrenan** durante todo el año para ser **capaces** de **aguantar** la velocidad y la resistencia necesarias para estar delante de seis toros, ocho **cabestros** y tres **mansos sueltos** que les persiguen. **Acabada la carrera**, los toros llegan a la plaza para morir en **apasionantes** corridas.

**Por desgracia**, cada año hay varios **heridos**, e incluso muertos en algunas ocasiones, **como resultado de** las heridas o contusiones que **sufren** durante los encierros. La **falta de sueño** y la **valentía inconsciente** que da el exceso de alcohol son **malos compañeros** para las decenas de jóvenes que se ponen a correr delante del toro por las **estrechas** calles del **casco antiguo** de Pamplona. Los **extranjeros** suelen ser los peor parados posiblemente porque la falta de información y el **desconocimiento** del español les hacen no prestar atención a las indicaciones y **advertencias** que los organizadores **transmiten** a **los asistentes**.

Y así, entre **cabezadas** en parques, plazas y **portales**, **borracheras** y mucha, mucha **juerga transcurren** los sanfermines hasta que el día 14, a las 12 de la **medianoche**, llegan oficialmente a su fin. Es el momento de cantar el **¡Pobre de mí!**, **quitarse** el pañuelo del cuello y **encender velas** en **señal de tristeza**, **no sin antes alegrarse de** que ya falta menos para las fiestas del **año que viene**.

**chiringuitos:** refreshment stands
**en cantidades industriales:** in huge amounts
**mantener los ojos abiertos:** to keep one's eyes opened
**sanfermineras:** songs sung during the Sanfermines
**letras mordaces:** sharp, caustic lyrics
**esquinas:** corners
**el encierro:** the running of the bulls
**momento estrella:** star moment
**tocan/tocar:** they play/to play
**interminables:** never-ending
**carreras:** races
**reto:** challenge
**de hecho:** in fact
**pamplonicas:** noun to refer to the locals
**se plantan:** they plant themselves
**delante de:** in front of
**bestias:** beasts
**entrenan/entrenar:** they train/to train
**capaces:** capable; able
**aguantar:** to cope with; to stand
**cabestros:** leading-bull
**mansos:** tame
**sueltos:** loose
**acabada la carrera:** once the race is over
**apasionantes:** thrilling
**por desgracia:** unfortunately
**heridos:** wounded
**como resultado de:** as a result of
**sufren/sufrir:** they suffer/to suffer
**falta de sueño:** lack of sleep
**valentía inconsciente:** thoughtless courage
**malos compañeros:** bad partners
**estrechas:** narrow
**casco antiguo:** old quarter
**extranjeros:** foreigners
**desconocimiento:** ignorance
**advertencias:** warnings
**transmiten/transmitir:** they pass on/to pass on
**los asistentes:** those present
**cabezadas:** nods, dozes
**portales:** front door
**borracheras:** drunkenness
**juerga:** binge
**transcurren/transcurrir:** they pass/to pass
**medianoche:** midnight
**¡Pobre de mí!:** Poor me! The last popular song the Pamplonicas sing.
**quitarse:** to take off
**encender velas:** to light candles
**señal de tristeza:** sign of sadness
**no sin antes alegrarse de:** not without being happy that
**año que viene:** next year

# ¡Viva el novio! ¡Viva la novia!
## ESPAÑA

**Hace pocos meses** tuve la ocasión de **asistir** la **boda** de mi **sobrina**. Aunque la costumbre española es celebrar la boda en la ciudad de la novia, mi sobrina **decidió casarase** en Burgos, **a pesar de que** ella es de Madrid. ¿Por qué? La **razón** es muy **sencilla**: **sus padres se casaron** en esa **iglesia**. **Además**, es un **escenario** extraordinario, **debido al retablo** del **siglo** XVI. ¡Marvilloso!

**Hablando** de la celebración, **pocas cosas** han cambiado. En España, es tradicion que la novia **llegue tarde** a la iglesia. Pero en esta boda, **tuvimos que esperar**...¡**casi media hora**! Mientras, el novio tiene que esperar, muy nervioso, **hasta que llegue el coche** con la novia y el **padrino** (normalmente el padre de la futura **esposa**).

**Durante** la celebración, la **misa sigue su curso normal, mientras que fuera de** la iglesia, los amigos de los novics **preparan una broma**. En este caso, cuando los novios **salieron** de la iglesia, **encontraron** su coche **lleno de globos**. Esta es una broma muy popular, pero hay bromas más originales, como por ejemplo, **alquilar** un **carro** un **burro**, y **pasear a los novios** por el centro de la ciudad.

---

**¡Viva!:** Long live! Hurray!
**novio:** bridegroom
**novia:** bride
**hace pocos meses:** few months ago
**asistir:** to attend
**boda:** wedding
**sobrina:** niece
**decidió casarse:** she decided to get married
**a pesar de que:** in spite of the fact that
**razón:** reason
**sencilla:** simple
**sus padres se casaron:** her parents got married
**iglesia:** church
**además:** also
**escenario:** scene
**debido al retablo:** due to the altarpiece
**siglo:** century
**hablando/hablar:** talking/to talk
**pocas cosas:** few things
**llegue tarde:** she is late
**tuvimos que:** we had to
**esperar:** wait
**casi media hora:** nearly half an hour
**hasta que llegue el coche:** until the car arrives
**padrino:** best man
**esposa:** wife
**durante:** during
**misa:** mass
**sigue su curso normal:** it takes its normal course
**mientras que:** whereas
**fuera de:** outside of
**preparan una broma:** they prepare a joke
**salieron/salir:** they went out/to go out
**encontraron/encontrar:** they found/ to find
**lleno de globos:** full of balloons
**alquilar:** to rent; to hire
**carro:** cart
**burro:** donkey
**pasear a los novios:** to take the bride and bridegroom for a ride

**Seguidamente**, los novios van a **hacer las fotos**, mientras que los **invitados** vamos a "tomar algo", **como se dice usualmente**. "¿Tomar algo"? Sí, Es simplemente ir a algún bar o cafetería cerca de la iglesia y **hacer tiempo hasta la hora de ir** al restaurante para comer o cenar.

En este caso, ya que la boda **se celebró** a las 5:30 de la tarde, todos los invitados **nos encontramos** en el hotel para cenar. Primero, un "lunch", y seguidamente fuimos al **comedor. Concretamente**, este hotel us un **antiguo convento rehabilitado**, y el comedor se encuentra en **el que antes era** al **claustro**. ¡Es **agradable** cenar **rodeado por** columnas con **tantos siglos** de historia!

Y finalmente, después de la cena...¡**fuimos a bailar**! Pero primero tienen que bailar los novios, y **por supuesto**, un **vals**. El baile **suele durar** unas 3 o 4 horas. **Poco a poco**, los invitados **nos iremos, deseando** a los **recién casados** mucha felicidad. ¡Y una preciosa **luna de miel**!

**seguidamente:** next
**hacer las fotos:** take the pictures
**invitados:** guests
**como se dice usualmente:** as it is usually said
**hacer tiempo:** to kill time
**hasta la hora de ir:** until its time to go
**se celebró/celebrar:** it was celebrated/ to celebrate
**nos encontramos/encontrarse:** we met/to meet
**comedor:** dining room
**concretamente:** particularly
**antiguo convento rehabilitado:** old restored convent
**el que antes era:** what previously was
**claustro:** cloister
**agradable:** nice
**rodeado por:** surrounded by
**tantos siglos:** so many centuries
**fuimos a bailar:** we went to dance
**por supuesto:** of course
**vals:** waltz
**suele durar:** usually lasts
**poco a poco:** little by little
**nos iremos:** we will leave
**deseando/desear:** wishing/to wish
**recién casados:** newlyweds
**luna de miel:** honeymoon

## CULTURE NOTE

It has been a long-standing tradition for Spanish brides to carry orange blossoms in their bouquet. The orange blossom symbolizes chastity and purity; because the orange tree is an evergreen, it also represents everlasting love. It is also said that since the orange tree bears fruit and blossoms at the same time, its flowers represent happiness and fulfillment. Before getting married in Spain, the groom gives his bride a wedding present of thirteen coins. This gift is a symbol of his commitment to support her and a symbol of sharing everything together. The bride-to-be then carries these coins, in a small bag, to her wedding ceremony. After the wedding the bride tosses her bouquet into the air similar to American weddings. In addition the bride may have a basket of pins. The pins, often resembling lilies or orchids, are given to all the ladies at the reception. They wear them upside down while dancing. If the pin falls out, the girl will marry!

| | |
|---|---|
| **hay un lugar:** there is a place | |
| **construir castillos en el aire:** to build castles in the air | |
| **se trata de:** it is about | |
| **desde hace más de dos siglos:** since more than two centuries ago | |
| **se levantan/levantar:** they built; erected/to build; erect | |
| **torres humanas:** human towers | |
| **ya que:** since, because | |
| **las palabras no suelen hacer justicia:** words don't usually do justice | |
| **espectáculo:** show; spectacle | |
| **suscita/suscitar:** provokes/to provoke | |
| **en directo:** live | |
| **parece ser que:** it seems that | |
| **dio sus primeros pasos:** it took its first steps | |
| **acababa elevando a algunos de sus bailarines:** it ended up raising some of the dancers | |
| **ni mucho menos al nivel de:** far from the level of | |
| **fue evolucionando:** it evolved | |
| **hasta convertirse en:** until they become | |
| **tambor:** drum | |
| **gralla:** oboe-like instrument | |
| **personas de diversas edades y sexos:** people of different ages and genders | |
| **unas sobre de otras:** one on top of the other | |
| **pies en los hombros:** feet on the shoulders | |
| **que está debajo:** that is underneath | |
| **que se van tocando:** that are played | |
| **indican/indicar:** they indicate/to indicate | |
| **de la base:** of the base | |
| **qué altura lleva la torre:** what is the height of the tower at that moment | |
| **puedan calcular:** they can calculate | |
| **tendrán que resistir el peso:** they will have to hold the weight | |
| **puede haber:** there can be | |
| **y hasta:** and up to | |
| **por piso:** in each floor | |
| **dependiendo del tipo de "castell" que se levante:** depending on the kind of "castell" that is being raised | |
| **se corona/coronarse:** it is crowned/to be crowned | |
| **altura maxima:** maximum height | |
| **que se ha conseguido hasta ahora:** that has been reached until now | |
| **que gira entre:** that it is between | |
| **"caps de colla":** Catalan expression to define the "casteller" that leads the "colla" | |
| **con base a:** according to | |
| **reglas arquitectónicas:** architectural rules | |
| **deciden/decidir:** they decide/to decide | |
| **forman/formar:** they form/to form | |
| **en función de:** depending on | |
| **peso:** weight | |
| **altura:** height | |
| **fuerza:** strength | |

# Castillos en el aire
## ESPAÑA

**Hay un lugar** en el mundo donde es posible **construir castillos en el aire**. **Se trata de** Cataluña, una región española en la que **desde hace más de dos siglos se levantan** "castells", unas **torres humanas** de más de 15 metros de altura. Esta es una de las tradiciones catalanas más difíciles de explicar **ya que las palabras no suelen hacer justicia** al **espectáculo** y a la emoción que una actuación de "castellers" **suscita en directo**.

**Parece ser que** esta tradición **dio sus primeros pasos** en Valencia en el siglo XVII, donde una de sus danzas tradicionales **acababa elevando a algunos de sus bailarines**, aunque **ni mucho menos al nivel de** los "castellers". Cuando este baile llegó a las tierras del sur de Cataluña **fue evolucionando hasta convertirse en** auténticas torres humanas.

A ritmo de **tambor** y "gralla", **personas de diversas edades y sexos** se levantan **unas sobre de otras** con los **pies en los hombros** del compañero **que está debajo**. Las diferentes notas musicales **que se van tocando indican** a los "castellers" de la base **qué altura lleva la torre**, para que **puedan calcular** con mejor precisión cuánto tiempo más **tendrán que resistir el peso**. **Puede haber** dos, tres, cuatro **y hasta** cinco personas **por piso, dependiendo del tipo de "castell" que se levante**, aunque siempre **se corona** con un niño o niña. La **altura máxima que se ha conseguido hasta ahora** es de 10 pisos, unos 15 metros aproximadamente, con un número de personas **que gira entre** 50 y 100. Los **"caps de colla", con base a reglas arquitectónicas, deciden** la distribución de los "castellers" que **forman** la torre **en función de** su **peso, altura,** agilidad y **fuerza**.

Una competición de "castellers", **con varias collas participando, puede durar** varias horas, aunque para **levantar** un "castell" no se necesita más de 10 minutos. Unas torres **suben**, otras **caen**, unas son más **anchas**, otras más **altas**, pero en todas se produce una unión intergeneracional perfecta entre abuelos, padres, hijos y nietos. **Los mayores** en la base, los más jóvenes en la **cima**, en una **clara metáfora de la vida misma. A pesar de** que los "castells" **desafían** la **ley de la gravedad** en cada una de sus **actuaciones, no llevan ningún tipo de protección.** El **atuendo** de un "casteller" se compone de unos **pantalones blancos ajustados**, una **faja alrededor del cuerpo** de color negro, una **camisa holgada** del color distintivo de la "colla" y un **pañuelo rojo en la cabeza**. Los **pies están descalzos** para que **se agarren** mejor **sin hacer daño** a los cuerpos de sus compañeros durante la **escalada**.

No es extraño ver caer una de las torres, **como si** de un **castillo de naipes** se tratara. La estructura empieza a tambalearse y la torre **acaba derrumbándose.** La **gran cantidad** de "castellers" que **se concentra** en la base, **a modo de tela de araña, hace que sean las propias personas** las que **amortigüen** las posibles **caídas.** La competitividad entre las diferentes "collas" de Cataluña está presente **en cada** "díada castellera" **por ver quién** levanta la torre más alta, **reuniendo** a **cientos** de personas en un **ambiente** incomparable. Quizás los "castells" sean la tradición que mejor define el carácter de los catalanes: **trabajo en equipo, esfuerzo**, la **capacidad de sufrimiento, afán de superación** y **cordura.**

**con varias collas participando:** with several 'collas' participating
**puede durar:** can last
**levantar:** to raise
**suben/subir:** they go up/to go up
**caen/caer:** they fall down/to fall down
**anchas:** wide
**altas:** tall
**los mayores:** the oldest ones
**cima:** on the top
**clara metáfora de la vida misma:** clear; evident metaphor of life itself
**a pesar de:** in spite of
**desafían/desafiar:** they challenge/to challenge, to defy
**ley de la gravedad:** the law of gravity
**actuaciones:** performances
**no llevan ningún tipo de protección:** they don't wear any kind of protection
**el atuendo:** the attire
**pantalones blancos ajustados:** tight white pants
**faja:** sash
**alrededor del cuerpo:** around their bodies
**camisa holgada:** loose shirt
**pañuelo rojo en la cabeza:** red handkerchief on the head
**pies están descalzos:** feet are bare
**se agarren:** they hold on tightly
**sin hacer daño:** without causing harm
**escalada:** climb
**como si:** as if
**castillo de naipes:** house of cards
**acaba derrumbándose:** it ends up collapsing
**gran cantidad:** great amount
**se concentra:** gathers
**a modo de:** like
**tela de araña:** spider's web
**hace que sean las propias personas:** it makes the people be
**amortigüen:** they break
**caídas:** fall
**en cada:** on each
**por ver quién:** to see who
**reuniendo/reunir:** gathering/to gather
**cientos:** hundreds
**ambiente:** atmosphere
**trabajo en equipo:** teamwork
**esfuerzo:** effort
**capacidad de sufrimiento:** suffering capacity
**afán de superación:** desire for self-improvement
**cordura:** good sense

# Examina tu comprensión

## Chichicastenango, page 45

1. The most important celebration in Guatemala honors what saint?

2. What is the name of the most "curious" activity involving a long pole during the celebration?

3. What manuscript is Chichicastenango famous for?

## La Pachamama, page 46

1. What does the word *pachamama* mean? What is the foundation or purpose of this festival?

2. What kinds of offerings are prepared?

3. The end of the ceremony involves placing offerings in the ground. What do these offerings symbolize?

## Una Navidad en Paraguay, page 49

1. What is the season in South American countries when Christmas is celebrated?

2. In almost every home a place is set aside where something is arranged and decorated. What is this item? How is it decorated?

## La gritería, page 50

1. What signals the beginning of this celebration?

2. What do the Nicaraguans shout? What is the answer?

# Test your comprehension

## Gaspar, Melchor, Baltasar, page 52

**1.** On the 5th of January what are Puerto Rican children likely to leave under their beds?

**2.** What does the president of Puerto Rico do on the 5th of January?

## 7 de Julio, page 54

**1.** To whom do the Spaniards attribute this tradition, as it is practiced today? What book was written about this tradition?

**2.** How long has this tradition been celebrated?

**3.** What was the original reason for this tradition?

## ¡Viva el novio!  page 56

**1.** What was the joke played on the bride and groom after the wedding?

**2.** What type of building was the hotel prior to restoration, where the wedding reception was held?

**3.** What type of dance did the bride and groom dance?

## Castillos en el aire, page 58

**1.** The "Castles in the Air" are a performing team.  What do they do?

**2.** What types of people form the human tower in this competition?

**3.** Describe the clothing the performers wear.

Algún día en cualquier parte, en cualquier lugar
indefectiblemente te encontrarás a ti mismo, y ésa, sólo ésa,
puede ser la más feliz o la más amarga de tus horas.

Pablo Neruda

# Celebración

# La Mamá Negra
## ECUADOR

La Mamá Negra no es una mujer ni tiene la **piel oscura**. Es una gran fiesta local ecuatoriana que **se celebra** en la **localidad** de Latacunga, a poco más de 80 kilómetros de Quito y cuya máxima representación es un hombre disfrazado de mujer y con la **cara pintada** de negro. ¿Quieren saber más? **¡Pues sigan leyendo!** **Existen** varias versiones **acerca** del origen de la fiesta de la Mamá Negra pero la más popular es la que **sostiene** que es la celebración para **venerar** a la Virgen de la Merced o Santísima Tragedia. En 1742 la ciudad quedó **arrasada** por la erupción del Volcán Cotopaxi. Desde entonces su población **empezó** a **rendirle homenaje**, con la **esperanza** de que los **protegiera** de nuevas erupciones. Con esta celebración, los habitantes de la ciudad también **festejan** el aniversario de su independencia. Por el carácter pagano que tiene la tradición, algunos **sacerdotes** de la época **suspendieron** el festejo, pero las autoridades de Latacunga **se encargaron** de **promoverla** y **oficiarla nuevamente** en homenaje a la independencia de la ciudad. Por este motivo, hoy en día **se festeja por partida doble**: el 23 de septiembre, fecha que corresponde al día de la Virgen de la Merced, y el 8 de noviembre por la independencia.

Un mes antes de la fecha, el pueblo entero se prepara y **ensaya** los distintos **papeles** de los personajes que **intervendrán** en la danza y el **desfile**. La figura central es la Mamá Negra que**,** llevando una **muñeca** negra representando a su hija, **cabalga** durante la procesión hasta llegar a la **iglesia** de la Merced. Diferentes personajes la acompañan: su **esposo**, los **huacos**, seres que realizan exorcismos para **limpiar** las **almas** y que **marcan** la presencia de los **chamanes**; el ángel de la estrella que representa al ángel Gabriel; el **rey** moro que simboliza la llegada de los españoles a Ecuador; el capitán símbolo del ejército y muchos más, algunos de los cuales van **repartiendo tragos** a su **paso**. Este **cortejo recorre** las calles **bailando** y **cantando** al **compás** de las bandas que **deleitan incasanbles** con su música.

# El Salvador del Mundo
## SAN SALVADOR

**Cada año**, cuando **comienza** el mes de agosto, los salvadoreños están de fiesta. Del 4 al 6 de ese mes **le rinden homenaje** a su patrono, San Salvador del Mundo, y las **festividades** que **se organizan** en su honor son unas de las más importantes del país.

Durante **toda la semana**, los habitantes **participan** de **desfiles**, procesiones y actos religiosos y culturales. Las actividades culturales y **recreativas** van desde los conciertos de **música folklórica** hasta **espectáculos de fuegos artificiales**. También se organiza una **feria** donde los presentes pueden **comprar recuerdos** de su patrono y otras **artesanías**. **Aunque se trata** de una celebración nacional, los habitantes de la capital son los que **cuentan** con la agenda más **abultada** ya que **casi todas** las actividades **se concentran** allí.

Los actos religiosos **se realizan** en la **Basílica del Sagrado Corazón** y la **atracción principal** es la tradicional "bajada" o **procesión del santo**, la cual hace un **recorrido** por las **calles principales** del centro de San Salvador **representando** la transfiguración de Jesucristo.

**cada año:** each year
**comienza/comenzar:** it starts/to start
**le rinden homenaje:** they pay homage
**festividades:** festivitites
**se organizan/organizarse:** they are organized/to organize
**toda la semana:** all week
**participan/participar:** they participate, take part/to participate
**desfiles:** parades
**recreativas:** recreational
**música folklórica:** folk music
**espectáculos de fuegos artificiales:** fireworks show
**feria:** fair
**comprar:** to buy
**recuerdos:** keepsakes, souvenirs
**artesanías:** crafts
**aunque:** although
**se trata/tratarse:** it is about/to be about
**cuentan/contar:** they have/to have
**abultada:** big
**casi todas:** almost all
**se concentran/concentrarse:** they concentrate/to concentrate
**se realizan/realizarse:** are carried out/ to carry out
**Basílica del Sagrado Corazón:** Basilica of the Sacred Heart
**atracción principal:** main attraction
**procesión del santo:** procession of the saint
**recorrido:** round
**calles principales:** main streets
**representando:** representing

## CULTURE NOTE

Because Spanish was introduced so long ago to Central America, the Spanish spoken in this region has variants and idioms, some regional and others particular to each country. Many *Nahuatl* words are used in El Salvador. Salvadoran Spanish is also more formal than in other countries. People will often address you with a title such as *señor* or *señora* before speaking your name. When entering a shop or café, Salvadorans frequently speak a brief yet polite greeting to everyone in the room. Watching a group of Salvadorans interact is a delight! Gestures, loud voices, and enthusiasm give life to their communication. Greeting by shaking hands and saying *buenos días* or *buenas tardes* is customary. Salvadorans are also very social. Getting together with family and friends is a favorite activity. Dropping in without making prior arrangements is considered acceptable and welcomed.

**muerte:** death
**destino:** destiny
**inexorable:** inexorable
**vida humana:** human life
**asusta/asustar:** it scares/to scare
**angustia:** anguish
**imitar:** to imitate
**vivirla:** to live it
**alegría:** joy
**reconciliarnos:** become reconciled
**enfrentar:** to confront
**miedo:** fear
**burla:** joke
**festejar:** to celebrate
**llorar:** to cry
**espejo:** mirror
**refleja/reflejar:** it reflects/to reflect
**ha vivido:** has lived/ to live
**ilumina/iluminar:** it illuminates/
   to illuminate
**carece de sentido:** it lacks sense
**tampoco:** neither
**hecho de morir:** the fact of dying
**desconocido:** unknown
**comienzo:** beginning
**algo nuevo:** something new
**luto:** mourning
**diversión:** fun
**tristeza:** sadness
**frente:** towards
**burlándose:** mocking
**jugando/jugar:** playing/to play
**conviviendo:** living together
**irónicamente:** ironically
**calaca:** death
**huesuda:** "the bony one" (referring to
   death)
**flaca:** "the thin one" (referring to
   death)
**parca:** death
**se recuerda/recordarse:** it is
   remembered/to remember
**se llenan/llenarse:** they get full of/
   to get full of
**ansiosa:** eager
**compartir:** to share
**fecha:** date
**difuntos:** the dead
**tumba:** grave, tomb
**compañía:** company

# El día de los muertos
## MÉXICO

La **muerte** es el **destino inexorable** de toda **vida humana**. A muchos su sola idea **asusta** y **angustia**. Pero ¿por qué no **imitar** al pueblo mexicano y **vivirla** con **alegría**? Si es inevitable, ¿por qué no **reconciliarnos** con ella? ¿Por qué no **enfrentar** nuestro **miedo** con la **burla**? ¿Por qué no **festejar** en lugar de **llorar**?

Para los mexicanos la muerte es como un **espejo** que **refleja** la forma en que uno **ha vivido**. Cuando la muerte llega, **ilumina** la vida de uno. Para ellos, si la muerte **carece de sentido**, **tampoco** lo tuvo la vida.

Más que el **hecho de morir,** importa lo que sigue al morir. Ese otro mundo **desconocido** y **comienzo** de **algo nuevo**.

**Luto** y alegría, **diversión** y **tristeza**, son los sentimientos del pueblo mexicano **frente** a la muerte: ellos también le tienen miedo pero a diferencia de otros, lo reflejan **burlándose, jugando** y **conviviendo** con ella. **Irónicamente**, la llaman "**calaca**", la "**huesuda**", la "**flaca**", la "**parca**".

El 2 de noviembre **se recuerda** no sólo a los muertos sino a la continuidad de la vida: los cementerios del país **se llenan** de gente **ansiosa** por **compartir** esta **fecha** con sus **difuntos**. Familiares y amigos llegan a la **tumba** de su ser querido, con flores, comida y música para disfrutar en su **compañía**.

En la mayoría de los **casos** la fiesta continúa en la casa de alguno, haciendo honor al célebre **dicho popular**: "El muerto al **cajón** y el **vivo al fiestón**".

En las casas **se improvisan** los famosos altares: **sobre** una mesa **cubierta** con un mantel, **se coloca** una fotografía de la persona **fallecida** y allí se hacen las ofrendas.

El rito de la ofrenda es respetado por toda la familia; todos participan **recordando** a los que se **han ido**, y quienes, según **se cree**, **regresan** este día para **gozar** lo que en vida más **disfrutaban**. Se colocan **velas**, flores, guirnaldas y los objetos personales preferidos del **difunto**. También **se disponen** platos tradicionales de la cocina mexicana y todo **se adorna** con calaveritas de azúcar. Entre las ofrendas más importantes está el "pan de muerto": un **pan dulce** preparado especialmente para la ocasión y el cual se adorna con formas de **huesos** hechos de la **misma masa**.

El aire de la casa **se impregna** con el aroma del **copal** que **se quema** en **sahumadores**, según la **creencia** de que los aromas **atraen** al **alma** que **vaga**.

Con todo esto, **no digo** que uno quiera **morirse** pero finalmente, **¿no estaría tan mal, no?**

**casos:** cases
**dicho popular:** popular saying
**cajón:** big box
**vivo al fiestón:** the living to the big party
**se improvisan/improvisarse:** they are improvised/to improvise
**sobre:** on top of
**cubierta:** covered
**se coloca/colocarse:** it is placed/ to place
**fallecida:** passed away
**recordando/recordar:** remembering/ to remember
**han ido/irse:** are gone/to be gone
**se cree/creerse:** it is believed/to believe
**regresan/regresar:** they return/ to return
**gozar:** to enjoy
**disfrutaban/disfrutar:** they enjoyed/ to enjoy
**velas:** candles
**difunto:** deceased
**se disponen/disponer:** are arranged/ to arrange
**se adorna/adornar:** it is decorated/ to decorate
**calaveritas de azúcar:** little skulls made out of sugar
**pan dulce:** sweet bread
**huesos:** bones
**misma masa:** same dough
**se impregna/impregnarse:** it is infused or filled/to infuse or fill
**copal:** incense
**se quema/quemar:** it is burned/ to burn
**sahumadores:** where you put the incense to burn
**creencia:** belief
**atraen/atraer:** they attract/to attract
**alma:** soul
**vaga/vagar:** it wanders/to wander
**no digo/decir:** I'm not saying/to say
**morirse:** to die
**¿no estaría tan mal, no?:** It wouldn't be that bad, would it?

bastón: baton
disponed/disponer: make use of/
  to make use of
mando: command
palabras: words
Gobernador: Governor
acudieron/acudir: they came/
  to come
vecinos: neighbors
paso: step
unidos: united
tenían/tener: they had/to have
proclamaban/proclamar: they
  proclaimed/to proclaim
aunque: although
tendrían/tener: they would have/
  to have
luchar: to fight
lograr: to obtain
se concretó: it became definite
después: after
conmemora/conmemorar:
  it commemorates/to commemorate
nuevo: new
llamadas: calls
festejan/festejar: they celebrate/
  to celebrate
nacimiento: birth
libre: free
identidad propia: own identity
duran/durar: they last/to last
toda una semana: all week
feriados: holidays
disfrutan/disfrutar: they enjoy/to
  enjoy
desfiles: parades
comidas típicas: typical food
orgullo nacional: national pride
campesinos a caballo: peasants on
  horseback
ataviados: dressed up
vestimentas de gala: festive clothing
participan/participar:
  they participate/to participate
se organizan/organizarse: they are
  organized/to be organized

# Festeja su independencia
## CHILE

"Aquí está el **bastón**, **disponed** de él y del **mando**". Con estas **palabras** inició Mateo de Toro y Zambrano, **Gobernador** de Chile en ese momento, la sesión de Cabildo Abierto a la que **acudieron** los máximos representantes de la ciudad y **vecinos** más importantes. Esta reunión, el 18 de septiembre de 1810, era el primer **paso** hacia la Independencia de su país: los chilenos **unidos** por el amor que **tenían** hacia su tierra, **proclamaban** su independencia de España, **aunque tendrían** que **luchar** un tiempo más para **lograr** su libertad total, ya que ésta **se concretó** 8 años **después** (el 12 de febrero de 1818, luego de la Batalla de Maipú). Cada 18 de septiembre el pueblo chileno **conmemora** un **nuevo** aniversario de la Independencia nacional en las **llamadas** Fiestas Patrias. Cada 18 de septiembre **festejan** el **nacimiento** de Chile como una nación independiente, **libre** y con **identidad propia**.

¡A pura fiesta! Las Fiestas Patrias **duran toda una semana**, comenzando el 18. Estos días en general son **feriados** y los chilenos **disfrutan** de **desfiles**, bailes, juegos, música, **comidas típicas** y otras exhibiciones de **orgullo nacional**. En los desfiles, los "huasos" (**campesinos a caballo**), **ataviados** con sus **vestimentas de gala**, **participan** de los rodeos que **se organizan** para la ocasión.

Muchas de las celebraciones se organizan en "**ramadas**" o "**fondas**"cuyo origen data de **aquella época**: estos eran los lugares de entretenimiento del pueblo, que **se establecían** en **terrenos abiertos** y donde **se reunían** a bailar, comer y **distenderse**.

Los músicos **se instalaban** en carros generalmente **techados** con **caña o paja**, y **tocaban** sus instrumentos para **atraer compradores** a las mesas **cubiertas con tortas**, licores y otras delicias. Hoy en día, **rescatando** la tradición e **imitando** las de entonces, las ramadas **se arman** temporalmente en **fincas**, **predios** o **edificios** abiertos con las terrazas cubiertas con paja y **ramas de árboles** y adornados con **guirnaldas**. Allí **se ubican sillas** y mesas dejando un lugar amplio para el baile: entre **cumbias**, **polcas y cuecas**, se ofrece una gran variedad de comidas típicas que incluye el **asado**, las empanadas y la **chicha**.

¡A jugar! Una de las características de estas fiestas es la **cantidad** de juegos tradicionales que se practican. Para nombrar sólo algunos, "el palo ensebado" es uno de los preferidos: consiste en un **palo de madera** de 5 a 6 metros de alto **enterrado** en la tierra, que **se unta** con grasa y que debe ser **trepado** por los competidores que, resbalando una y otra vez, luchan por **alcanzar** el premio que está en la **cima**. Otro de los juegos tradicionales es la "**carrera de sacos**": los competidores corren **metidos** en bolsas o **sacos de arpillera**.

Otros como el **trompo**, la **rayuela**, la **pallana** y las **bolitas**, también **convocan** a grandes y chicos. Y los juegos no sólo están en la tierra sin también más arriba: durante toda esta semana patria, el **cielo chileno se cubre** de formas y colores en continuo movimiento. Es el **reinado** del "**volantín**" o **barrilete**, una de las actividades más populares.

**ramadas:** festival stall
**fondas:** refreshment stall
**aquella época:** that time
**se establecían/establecerse:** they were set up/ to set up
**terrenos abiertos:** open terrain
**se reunían/reunirse:** they met/to meet
**distenderse:** to relax
**se instalaban/instalarse:** they located themselves/to locate oneself
**techados:** roofed
**caña o paja:** cane or staw
**tocaban/tocar:** they played/to play
**atraer:** to attract
**compradores:** purchasers, buyers
**cubiertas con tortas:** covered with cakes
**rescatando/rescatar:** rescuing/to rescue
**imitando/imitar:** imitating/to imitate
**se arman/armarse:** they are set up/ to be set up
**fincas:** properties
**predios:** premises
**edificios:** buildings
**ramas de árboles:** tree branches
**guirnaldas:** garlands
**se ubican/ubicarse:** they are located/ to be located
**sillas:** chairs
**cumbias, polcas y cuecas:** dance music
**asado:** barbecue
**chicha:** type of alcoholic beverage
**cantidad:** quantity
**palo de madera:** wood pole
**enterrado/enterrar:** buried/to bury
**se unta/untar:** it is smeared/to smear
**trepado:** climbed
**alcanzar:** to reach
**cima:** top
**carrera de sacos:** sack race
**metidos/meter:** put in/to put
**sacos de arpillera:** cloth sacks
**trompo:** top, spinning top
**rayuela:** hopscotch
**pallana:** game played with little stones
**bolitas:** marbles
**convocan/convocar:** they summon/ to summon
**cielo chileno:** Chilean sky
**se cubre/cubrirse:** it is covered/ to cover
**reinado:** reign
**volantín:** kite
**barrilete:** kite

**¡Menudo tomate!:** What a Tomato! The expression is a pun. Tomate means "tomato" but it also means "fight, fuss"

**ríos:** rivers

**salsa roja:** red sauce

**fluyen/fluir:** they flow/to flow

**como si:** as if

**volcán:** volcano

**erupción:** eruption

**protagonizando/protagonizar:** starring/to star

**guerra pacífica:** pacific war

**dando la vuelta al mundo:** going around the world

**allénde las fronteras:** beyond the borders

**como ocurre:** as it happens

**surgió/surgir:** it appeared/to appear

**de forma casual:** in a spontaneous way

**se enzarzó/enzarzarse:** they got involved/to get involved

**pelea:** fight

**a la que cada vez:** to which more and more

**se fue sumando/sumarse:** they started to join/to join

**destino:** destiny

**quiso:** it wanted/to want

**puesto de verduras y frutas:** fruit and vegetable stands

**en los alrededores:** in the surrounding areas

**cajas:** boxes

**expuestas:** displayed

**para su venta:** for sale

**por lo que:** and consequently

**implicados:** the people involved

**tangana:** fight, fuss

**tirárselos unos a otros:** to throw them at one another

**batalla campal:** pitched battle

**mediar:** to intercede

**asunto:** matter, subject

**altercado:** argument, altercation

**pagar:** to pay

**destrozos:** damage, havoc

**tremendo alboroto:** tremendous uproar

**no se olvidó:** it wasn't forgotten

**al llegar el mismo miércoles:** when the same Wednesday arrived

**llevando/llevar:** carrying/to carry

**desde entonces y hasta hoy:** from then until now

# ¡Menudo tomate!
## ESPAÑA

**Ríos** de **salsa roja fluyen** por las calles de Buñol (Valencia) **como si** de lava de un **volcán** en **erupción** se tratara. La imagen de miles de personas **protagonizando** una **guerra "pacífica"** de tomates lleva años **dando la vuelta al mundo** y es que "La Tomatina" es una de las fiestas españolas más conocidas **allénde las fronteras** del país.

**Como ocurre** con muchas otras celebraciones populares, esta tradición **surgió de forma casual.** En agosto de 1945 un grupo de jóvenes **se enzarzó** en una **pelea** en la plaza del pueblo **a la que**

**cada vez se fue sumando** más gente. El **destino quiso** que hubiera cerca un **puesto de verduras y frutas en los alrededores** con las **cajas expuestas** en la calle **para su venta**, **por lo que** los **implicados** en la **tangana** cogieron tomates y empezaron a **tirárselos unos a otros**, empezando una auténtica **batalla campal.** La policía tuvo que **mediar** en el **asunto** y los responsables del **altercado pagar** todos los **destrozos.**

El **tremendo alboroto no se olvidó** y al año siguiente, **al llegar el mismo miércoles** de agosto, los jóvenes de Buñol volvieron a reunirse en la plaza, **llevando** esta vez ellos los tomates. **Desde entonces y hasta hoy**, cada último miércoles del mes de agosto se celebra La Tomatina.

A pesar de la oposición de las autoridades locales durante los primeros años, **lo cierto es que** el **Ayuntamiento** es quien organiza la fiesta y quien compra las más de 120 **toneladas** de tomates que se **lanzan en poco más de** una hora.

El ritual de La Tomatina empieza con la empalmá, que es una **larguísima** noche de fiesta que se "**empalma**" con la mañana. Así, antes del gran momento, los habitantes de Buñol **se reúnen** para **tomar** juntos un gran **desayuno** y **coger fuerzas** para la **lucha**.

**Al punto del mediodía**, cinco grandes **camiones llenos de tomates hasta arriba descargan** su **mercancía** en la plaza del pueblo para **abastecer** las manos de las más de 25.000 personas que cada año **se congregan** en este pueblo valenciano.

El secreto **para que ésta sea una batalla** sin **heridos consiste en aplastar** las **hortalizas** antes de lanzarlas. En los últimos momentos de esta guerra **sin igual**, los tomates están tan **chafados** que pierden su consistencia por lo que a los **combatientes** sólo les queda **restregarlos** contra el vecino o **bañarse** en su salsa.

**Calzadas, paredes, farolas**, coches y árboles **quedan teñidos** de un rojo intenso. Sin embargo, los participantes en la **contienda se ponen manos a la obra** para **limpiarlo** todo y hacer que, en menos de dos horas, no quede **ni rastro** de La Tomatina.

**Exhaustos** por la batalla, los buñolenses **se retiran** a sus casas para **iniciar** una "siesta popular", una tradición **casi tan antigua** como esta guerra de tomates única en el mundo.

**lo cierto es que:** the truth is that
**Ayuntamiento:** Town Hall
**toneladas:** tons
**lanzan/lanzar:** they throw/to throw
**en poco más de:** in a little more than
**larguísima:** very long
**empalma/empalmar:** to join the night with the morning (Expression used when someone stays out all night)
**se reúnen/reunirse:** they gather/ to gather
**tomar:** to have
**desayuno:** breakfast
**coger fuerzas:** to get strength
**lucha:** fight, struggle
**al punto del mediodía:** at 12 pm
**camiones:** trucks
**llenos de tomates hasta arriba:** filled to the top with tomatoes
**descargan/descargar:** they unload/ to unload
**mercancía:** goods
**abastecer:** to supply
**se congregan/congregarse:** they gather/to gather, to concentrate
**para que ésta sea una batalla:** for this one to be a battle
**heridos:** injured people, casualties
**consiste en/consistir en:** it consists of/to consist of
**aplastar:** to smash, to squeeze
**hortalizas:** vegetables
**sin igual:** unrivaled
**chafados:** mashed, crushed
**combatientes:** combatants
**restregarlos/restregar:** rub them/ to rub
**bañarse:** to take a bath
**calzadas:** roads
**paredes:** walls
**farolas:** street lights
**quedan teñidos:** end up dyed
**contienda:** contest, struggle
**se ponen manos a la obra:** they put their hands to work
**limpiarlo/limpiar:** clean it/to clean it
**ni rastro:** without a trace
**exhaustos:** exhausted
**se retiran/retirarse:** they go back/ to go back
**iniciar:** to begin
**casi tan antigua:** almost as old

**"Tulululu pasa, tulululu, pasa…"** empiezan a cantar en **Misquito**, una **mezcla** entre el español y el inglés. Empiezan a bailar **alrededor** de un "Palo" con un ritmo africano y una fusión étnica **que le hacen a uno menearse**. Esta danza **originaria de** la Costa Atlántica de Nicaragua por **los indios misquitos se ha popularizado** por todo el país de Nicaragua.

El baile que tiene su **apogeo a comienzos del** mes de mayo **se ha difundido** por grupos como la Dimensión Costeña. Este **conjunto conmueve** al pueblo nicaragüense con su música **al tocar** sus canciones del Palo de Mayo. **Enfrente del** grupo, **bailan dos mujeres** con **movimientos y meneos** que **jamás se han visto** y uno **no puede quitarse los ojos de ellas** mientras que bailan durante cada **canción cadenciosa**.

Desde el siglo XIX, La Gran Bretaña **había puesto su codiciosa mirada sobre** la Costa Atlántica. **Súbditos ingleses se establecieron** en la región y empezaron a **ubicarse** con los indios. La cultura costeña es el resultado de una confluencia de variadas culturas. Esta convergencia **se llevó a cabo**, principalmente en el siglo del romanticismo. A lo largo de los años, por la Costa Atlántica, como en la región de Bluefields, **acudieron** numerosos personas **oriundas de** Las Islas Antillanas, principalmente de Jamaica. **En aquellos tiempos**, los jóvenes de ambos sexos **salían a coger** flores y **aportaban** un poste que llamaban "el palo de mayo" adornado con frutas y flores en el centro del lugar donde se celebraban las fiestas de ese día. **Lo que se produjo** era una música energética y cultural de los países caribes.

Algunos **lo han llamado el baile prohibido** por sus tonos sexuales, pero como la Marimba de Nicaragua, la Samba de Brasil o la Cumbia de Colombia, el palo de mayo **se ha vuelto** como parte del folklore nicaragüense.

---

**"Tulululu pasa, tulululu, pasa…":** An elementary form of music sung around the May Pole

**empiezan a/empezar:** they start to/ to start

**cantar:** to sing

**Misquito:** language spoken by the Miskito Indians

**mezcla:** mixture

**alrededor:** around

**que le hacen a uno menearse:** that makes one shake

**originaria de:** originating from

**los indios misquitos:** the Miskito Indians

**se ha popularizado:** has been popularized

**apogeo:** peak

**a comienzos del:** in the beginning of

**se ha difundido/difundir:** has been spread/to spread

**conjunto:** group; band

**conmueve/conmover:** move/to move

**al tocar:** upon playing

**enfrente del:** in front of the

**bailan dos mujeres:** two women dance

**movimientos y meneos:** movements and swinging

**jamás se han visto:** have never been seen before

**no puede quitarse los ojos de ellas:** cannot take their eyes off them

**canción cadenciosa:** rhythmical song

**había puesto/poner:** had placed/to put

**su codiciosa mirada sobre:** their covetous look upon

**súbditos ingleses:** English subjects

**se establecieron:** established themselves

**ubicarse:** to situate or locate

**se llevó a cabo:** was carried out

**acudieron/acudir:** came/to come

**oriundas de:** indigenous to; native to

**en aquellos tiempos:** in those days

**salían/salir:** would leave/to leave

**a coger:** to pick

**aportaban/aportar:** carried/to carry

**lo que se produjo:** what was produced

**lo han llamado/llamar:** have called it/ to call

**el baile prohibido:** the forbidden dance

**se ha vuelto:** has become

# Celebración del mercado medieval
## ESPAÑA

Los **pasados** días 30 y 31 de mayo, y el 1 de Junio, los **ciudadanos** de Burgos tuvimos la posibilidad de visitar el Mercado Medieval, situado cerca de la Catedral. Este **acontecimiento** se celebra cada año, y su **principal aliciente** es la maravilloso **ambiente** y la **exposición** de los **oficios** más característicos del Medioevo en Castilla y León, comunidad autónoma española **en la que está incluida** Burgos.

**En realidad**, es **la segunda vez** que **visito** este Mercado, y la experiencia es realmente interesante. **Nosotros llegamos** el día de la inauguración, y aunque **al principio no había mucha gente**, en menos de una hora era difícil **andar entre la multitud**.

**Para empezar**, **compramos** unos **rollos de anís** y otros de chocolate. **Hay que decir** que todos los **alimentos a la venta** eran **artesanales**, al igual que los demás productos: **cestas**, **vidrios**, **collares**, **anillos**. Pudimos ver **cómo se hacía entonces** el pan, el **hojaldre** en **verdaderos hornos**, **al aire libre**. Verdaderos **panaderos cocinaban** sus productos y **cualquier visitante** podía comprarlos **recién hechos**.

También vimos a un **escriba**, a un **artesano del vidrio**, a personas **tejiendo** cestos de **mimbre** e incluso a **cetreros**, haciendo exhibiciones. ¡Las aves **volaban sobre nuestras cabezas**! Y, **por supuesto**, entre la gente estaban los **bufones**, **divirtiendo** al público.

Todo esto, en **un entorno** tan apropiado como las dos plazas de la catedral de Burgos. Al terminar la visita, y **pasar bajo** el Arco de Santa María, **fue como si hubiéramos hecho** un viaje en el tiempo, y **de repente volviéramos** al año 2005.

¡Una experiencia **inolvidable**!

**mercado medieval:** medieval market
**pasados:** last
**ciudadanos:** citizens
**acontecimiento:** event
**principal aliciente:** main incentive
**ambiente:** atmosphere
**exposición:** exhibition
**oficios:** professions
**en la que está incluida/incluir:** in which is included/to include
**en realidad:** actually
**la segunda vez:** the second time
**visito/visitar:** I visit/to visit
**nosotros llegamos/llegar:** we arrived/ to arrive
**al principio:** at the beginning
**no había mucha gente:** there were not many people
**andar entre la multitud:** to walk among the crowd
**para empezar:** to begin
**compramos/comprar:** we bought/ to buy
**rollos de anís:** anise rolls
**hay que decir:** it is necessary to say
**alimentos a la venta:** food on sale
**artesanales:** traditional, handcrafted
**cestas:** baskets
**vidrios:** glass
**collares:** necklaces
**anillos:** rings
**cómo se hacía entonces:** how it was made at that time
**hojaldre:** puff pastry
**verdaderos hornos:** real ovens
**al aire libre:** in the open air
**panaderos:** bakers
**cocinaban/cocinar:** they cooked/ to cook
**cualquier visitante:** any visitor
**recién hechos:** freshly made
**escriba:** scribe
**artesano del vidrio:** glass artisan
**tejiendo/tejer:** weaving/to weave
**mimbre:** wicker
**cetreros:** people who train falcons
**volaban sobre nuestras cabezas:** they flew over our heads
**por supuesto:** of course
**bufones:** jesters
**divirtiendo:** entertaining
**un entorno:** a scene
**pasar bajo:** to go under
**fue como si hubiéramos hecho:** it was as if we had taken
**de repente:** suddenly
**volviéramos/volver:** we came back/ to return, to come back

## La Virgen de la Candelaria
### PERU

En **Puno**, en **pleno altiplano peruano** y **cerca** del **lago** Titicaca, existe una gran celebración donde la **alegría**, la **música andina**, las **danzas incaicas** y la **fe se unen** para **dar honores** a la Virgen de la Candelaria y a la **Madre Tierra**.

La devoción a la **imagen** de esta virgen **se halla** muy **extendida** en Latinoamérica, **ya que se venera** en **casi todos** los países de América donde España **impuso** su religión. La figura de esta **santa madre fue traída** desde España a Puno el 2 de febrero de 1583, momento en el que los **indígenas autóctonos iniciaron** su conversión al catolicismo.

La festividad, que **se desarrolla** en el mes de febrero es una de las más grandes celebraciones de Sudamérica **junto con** el Carnaval de Río de Janeiro en el Brasil y el Carnaval de Oruro, en Bolivia.

Esta fiesta del altiplano andino está **llena de** símbolos y **manifestaciones artístico-culturales** de la cultura quechua, aymara y mestiza. Es por este **motivo** que, en noviembre de 1985, el **gobierno** del Perú **designó** a Puno Capital del Folklore Peruano. La actividad en honor a la Virgen de la Candelaria **se inicia** el 2 de febrero y **se prolonga** durante 15 días.

Es en la **primera semana** donde la fiesta **llega** a su **apogeo**. A la **misa** de la **iglesia** San Juan Bautista y la procesión a la Plaza de Armas, le **sigue** un **desfile** de grupos folklóricos en dirección al **estadio** Enrique Torres Bellón.

---

**Puno:** a city in Peru
**pleno:** full
**altiplano peruano:** Peruvian high plains
**cerca:** near
**lago:** lake
**alegría:** happiness, joy
**música andina:** Andean music
**danzas incaicas:** Incan dances
**fe:** faith
**se unen/unirse:** unites; joins/to unite; to join
**dar honores:** to give honors
**Madre Tierra:** Mother Earth
**imagen:** image
**se halla/hallar:** is found/to find
**extendida:** widespread; spread out
**ya que:** since
**se venera/venerar:** is worshipped/to worship
**casi todos:** almost all
**impuso/imponer:** imposed/to impose
**santa madre:** holy mother
**fue traída/traer:** was brought/to bring
**indígenas autóctonos:** indigenous natives
**iniciaron/iniciar:** they began/to begin
**se desarrolla/desarrollar:** is developed/to develop
**junto con:** together with
**llena de:** full of
**manifestaciones artístico-culturales:** artistic cultural displays
**motivo:** reason
**gobierno:** government
**designó/designar:** designated/to designate
**se inicia/iniciar:** begins/to begin
**se prolonga/prolongar:** it extends/to extend
**primera semana:** first week
**llega/llegar:** it arrives/to arrive
**apogeo:** its height
**misa:** mass
**iglesia:** church
**sigue/seguir:** follows/to follow
**desfile:** parade
**estadio:** stadium

En este **lugar deportivo se congregan** unas 70 bandas musicales, **algunas conformadas** por 300 personas, entre músicos y **bailarines**. Todas estas **agrupaciones esperan ganar** el **concurso** de danzas folklóricas. La música y la danza son **variadas**, **dependiendo** de la región del Perú de dónde **provengan** los danzarines. Los ritmos del huayno y de la saya **colorean** el **ambiente** del **recinto deportivo**. Las bombardas por todo lo alto hacen **vibrar** al **expectante** pueblo puneño.

**Centenares** de **visitantes locales** y **extranjeros** llenan las calles y las **graderías** del estadio, en una **magna** fiesta en la que todos **se contagian**. Música andina, máscaras, **disfraces** de ángeles y demonios **se mezclan** con un **único** objetivo: dar honores a la **querida** imagen de la Virgen de la Candelaria. **Bastarán** sólo ochos minutos de **coreografías** para que los **jueces** decidan qué **banda artística** ganará el **título del año**. Bastarán sólo ocho minutos para **escoger** como ganadora a una banda que **destaque** entre las demás por el ritmo, color, **fuerza** y **sentimiento**.

La tradición incaica y aymara llega a su **plenitud** en esta **festividad**. **No cabe duda** que Puno es la **capital folklórica** del continente.

---

**lugar deportivo:** sports place
**se congregan/congregar:** they congregate/to congregate
**algunas:** some
**conformadas:** made
**bailarines:** dancers
**agrupaciones:** associations
**esperan/esperar:** they wait/to wait
**ganar:** to win
**concurso:** competition, contest
**variadas:** varied, assorted
**dependiendo/depender:** depending/ to depend
**provengan/provenir:** they come from/to come from
**colorean/colorear:** they color/to color
**ambiente:** atmosphere, environment
**recinto deportivo:** sports precinct
**vibrar:** to vibrate
**expectante:** expectant
**centenares:** hundreds
**visitantes locales:** local visitors
**extranjeros:** foreign
**graderías:** stands
**magna:** great
**se contagian/contagiarse:** they spread/ to spread
**disfraces:** disguises, costumes
**se mezclan/mezclar** they get mixed/ to mix
**único:** unique
**querida:** dear, beloved
**bastarán/bastar:** will be enough/to be enough, to suffice
**coreografías:** choreographies
**jueces:** judges
**banda artística:** artistic band
**título del año:** title of the year
**escoger:** to chose
**destaque/destacar:** emphasizes/ to emphasize, stress
**fuerza:** strength
**sentimiento:** feeling
**plenitud:** fullness
**festividad:** festivity
**no cabe duda:** there is no doubt
**capital folklórica:** folklore capital

# La pascua y Semana Santa
## ARGENTINA

La semana Santa **conmemora los últimos días** de la **vida de Cristo**. La Pascua es el **recordatorio** de la muerte y la resurrección de Cristo.

**De hecho**, la palabra "pascua" significa **"paso"** de la **muerte** a la vida. En Argentina, **todos los Jueves Santos** al mediodía se celebra una **misa** en la **catedral** o en las **iglesias**. Por la tarde, se oficia una misa de **la cena** del **Señor** en donde se **rememora** la **última** cena de Cristo con los **doce apóstoles**.

**El viernes Santo** se rememora la cruxificación; en algunas casas católicas se practica el **ayuno**. Algunos también lo **consideran** un día de **silencio** y reflexión. En muchas ciudades, se celebra con **peregrinaciones** que **evocar** el sacrificio de Cristo y también **pasajes bíblicos**.

El sábado está **dedicado** al **lamento** por la muerte de Cristo **mientras que** el **"Domingo de Pascua"** es un día de celebración familiar. Se celebra la **fiesta** de la **Cristiandad**, que es la creencia en la resurrección.

Uno de los **símbolos** que **se utiliza** en la Pascua son los **huevos de Pascua** que se asocian a la fiesta de Pascua aunque tengan un **origen pagano para que los chicos se diviertan**. Muchas familias **acostumbran** hacer una **búsqueda de huevos.** El huevo de Pascua es de chocolate y está **relleno** de **confites** y **sorpresas** que generalmente **consisten de** pequeños **juguetes de plástico**. Los huevos de Pascua tienen diferentes **tamaños**. ¡Los hay **hasta** de dos **kilos**!

# Un lento retorno
## CUBA

En Semana Santa todos **los fieles católicos** del mundo **recuerdan** el **calvario**, la crucifixión, la **muerte** y la resurrección de Cristo. **Y si bien** en todos los países no **se celebra** de la **misma** forma **ni** con el mismo fervor, este tipo de tradiciones católicas son, casi en su **mayoría**, **comunes** con las tradiciones de los pueblos de matriz ibérica y **poseen** características similares a las de estos pueblos. Las celebraciones **incluyen** procesiones y ceremonias religiosas.

En Cuba, este es **apenas** el **octavo** año que **se festeja** la Semana Santa desde que Fidel Castro **asumió** el **poder**, en 1959. El actual **gobierno socialista** había **suprimido** todos los actos en los que **se mezclaba** lo religioso con la fiesta popular, y **se restauraron tras** la visita del Papa Juan Pablo II, en 1998.

**Hoy en día**, en las iglesias se celebran los actos religiosos y en los parques o en **algunas** plazas **se levantan tiendas** que **venden** comidas y bebidas, y se **oye** música y **suele** haber bailes. **Aunque** las procesiones y todos los actos religiosos se organizan todavía **tímidamente ya que** todo necesita contar con las **debidas autorizaciones** del gobierno.

**Luego de tantos** años de **enfrentamientos** entre la Iglesia y el régimen, estos permisos oficiales son vistos como una **señal de apertura**, pero tras varias décadas de **poca enseñanza católica**, son pocos los **jóvenes** que **conocen ritos**, **cánticos** o el **significado real** de las ceremonias.

**los fieles católicos:** catholic congregation
**recuerdan/recordar:** they remember/ to remember
**calvario:** Calvary
**muerte:** death
**y si bien:** and even if
**se celebra/celebrar:** it is celebrated/ to celebrate
**misma:** same
**ni:** nor
**mayoría:** majority
**comunes:** common
**poseen/poseer:** they have/to have
**incluyen/incluir:** they include/ to include
**apenas:** just
**octavo:** eighth
**se festeja/festejar:** it is celebrated/ to celebrate
**asumió/asumir:** he took over/to take over
**poder:** power, authority
**gobierno socialista:** socialist government
**suprimido/suprimir:** supressed/to supress
**se mezclaba/mezclar:** it mixed/to mix
**se restauraron tras/restaurar:** they were reinstated after/to be reinstated
**hoy en día:** nowadays
**algunas:** some
**se levantan/levantar:** they stand up/ to stand up
**tiendas:** stores
**venden/vender:** they sell/to sell
**oye:** listen
**suele/ soler:** it is usual/to be usual
**aunque:** even though
**tímidamente:** timidly
**ya que:** given that
**debidas:** pertinent
**autorizaciones:** authorizations
**luego de tantos:** after so many
**enfrentamientos:** confrontations
**señal de apertura:** sign of opening
**poca enseñanza católica:** little catholic education
**jóvenes:** young people
**conocen/conocer:** they know/ to know
**ritos:** rites
**cánticos:** canticles (a hymn derived from the bible)
**significado real:** real meaning

| | |
|---|---|
| **barrio:** neighborhood | |

barrio: neighborhood
trasladarse: to move
mágico: magic
paseo: walk, stroll
de poco más de una hora: a little
   more than an hour
pasar de: to go from
cielo: heaven
infierno: hell
Lejano Oeste: Far West
fondo del mar: bottom of the sea
y todo gracias a: and all this thanks to
vecinos: neighbors
se remonta/remontarse: it goes back to/
   to go back to
afueras: outskirts
se unió/unirse: it joined/to join
dura/durar: it lasts/to last
justifica/justificar: it accounts for
   it/to account for, to justify
centenares: hundreds
empleadas: used
empiezan ya: they start already
generar: to create, to generate
ornamentación: ornaments
una vez: once
escogido/escoger: chosen/to choose
escenografía: stage design
improvisados artistas: improvised
   artists
deberán/deber: they will have to/
   to have to
llevar a cabo: to carry out
recolectar: to collect
diseñar: design
reciclan/reciclar: they recycle/
   to recycle
envases: containers
vida cotidiana: everyday life
elaborar: to produce, to make
periódicos: newspapers
botellas de plástico: plastic bottles
vasos de yogur: yogurt cups
alambres: wire
cajas de cartón: cardboard boxes
hueveras: egg boxes
resulta: it turns out
asombroso: amazing, astonishing
espectáculo: show
se consigue/conseguir: it is obtained/
   to obtain
una veintena: about twenty
vestidas con sus mejores galas: show-
   ing their best face, best dress
acoge/acoger: it holds/to hold
magos: magicians
orquestas populares: popular dance
   bands

# La fiesta con más Gracia
## ESPAÑA

Visitar el **barrio** de Gracia en Barcelona durante su fiesta mayor es **trasladarse** a un mundo **mágico**. En un **paseo de poco más de una hora** se puede **pasar de cielo** al **infierno**, viajar de la China al **Lejano Oeste** o "nadar" en el **fondo del mar**. **Y todo gracias a** la imaginación de sus **vecinos**.

La tradición de decorar las calles **se remonta** al siglo XVIII, cuando Gracia todavía era un pueblo a las **afueras** de la ciudad de Barcelona (**se unió** definitivamente en 1850). La preparación **dura** casi 12 meses pero el resultado final **justifica** los **centenares** de horas **empleadas**. A los pocos días de finalizar las fiestas, los vecinos **empiezan ya** a **generar** ideas para la **ornamentación** de las calles del próximo año.

**Una vez escogido** el tema para la **escenografía**, los **improvisados artistas deberán** pensar cómo van a **llevar a cabo** su idea y qué materiales necesitan **recolectar** para **diseñar** las diversas formas y texturas.

Desde hace varios años la mayoría de vecinos **reciclan** objetos y **envases** de la **vida cotidiana** para **elaborar** sus creaciones: **periódicos**, **botellas de plástico**, **vasos de yogur**, **alambres**, **cajas de cartón** o **hueveras**. **Resulta** realmente **asombroso** ver el **espectáculo** que con cosas tan simples **se consigue**.

**Una veintena** de calles, **vestidas con sus mejores galas**, **acoge** conciertos, espectáculos con **magos** y **orquestas populares** cada noche.

A lo largo de sus aceras tienen barras en las que los propios vecinos sirven copas a los visitantes, que bailan y beben hasta bien entrada la noche. De esta manera, los organizadores de las calles consiguen dinero para pagar los costes de la elaboración de los decorados.

Tanto esfuerzo vecinal se ve recompensado el primer día de fiesta mayor cuando un jurado popular entrega diversos premios a las mejores calles: a la más original, la mejor iluminada, la que más ecológica y la más bella. La curiosidad de los que se acercan hasta Gracia por conocer a las calles agraciadas hace que sean estas vías las más visitadas y, en consecuencia, las que más bebidas venden y dinero recaudan.

Además de estas fantásticas calles decoradas, en las fiestas de Gracia se celebran clases de baile, exhibiciones de castellers, desfiles de gigantes y cabezudos, chocolatadas populares, carreras, exposiciones y mucha, mucha música forman parte de la oferta festiva de estos cálido días de verano en Barcelona aunque, sin duda, lo que las hace especiales es la decoración de sus calles.

A pesar de que en agosto la ciudad suele quedarse con la mitad de sus ciudadanos puesto que es el mes preferido por los españoles para sus vacaciones de verano, Gracia atrae cada mes de agosto (en su tercera semana) a más de un millón y medio de visitantes… y es que perderse estas fiestas estando en Barcelona sería un pecado.

**oír:** to hear

**todo el mundo:** everyone

**piensa/pensar:** (they) think/to think

**cuyos:** whose

**encanto propio:** their own charm

**tiene lugar/tener lugar:** it takes place/to take place

**Martes de Carnaval:** Shrove Tuesday

**para saber:** in order to know

**hay que tener en cuenta:** one must take into account

**Cuaresma:** Lent

**mantenida/mantener:** maintained/ to maintain

**en cualquier lugar:** anywhere

**se remontan/remontarse:** they go back/to go back (in time), to date from

**siglo XVI:** 16th century

**puertos marítimos:** seaports

**entonces:** then

**gaditanos:** people from Cádiz

**copiaron/copiar:** they copy/to copy

**con el tiempo:** with time, eventually

**lo adaptaron/adaptar:** they adapted it/to adapt

**sus propias costumbres:** their own customs

**hecho:** fact

**bastante:** pretty

**gente:** people

**no se reúne/reunirse:** they do not gather/to gather

**ocurre/ocurrir:** it happens/to happen

**se llenan de/llenarse:** they get full of/ to get full of

**disfraces:** costumes

**verdaderamente:** truly

**cantando/cantar:** singing/to sing

**disfrutando/disfrutar:** enjoying/ to enjoy

**olvidar:** to forget

**marcadas:** marked

# El carnaval de Cádiz
## ESPAÑA

Al **oír** la palabra "carnaval" **todo el mundo piensa** en Brasil, pero hay una ciudad en España, llamada Cádiz, **cuyos** carnavales tienen un **encanto propio.** Como en el resto de los lugares que celebran estas fiestas, el carnaval de Cádiz **tiene lugar** durante el mes de febrero. Su fecha central es el **Martes de Carnaval** que este año es el 8 de febrero. **Para saber** la fecha aproximada de la celebración de los carnavales, **hay que tener en cuenta** que tienen lugar 40 días antes de **Cuaresma**, costumbre **mantenida en cualquier lugar** con tradición católica.

Los orígenes del Carnaval de Cádiz **se remontan** al **siglo XVI**, cuando la ciudad tenía uno de los **puertos marítimos** más importantes del mundo. Fue **entonces** cuando los **gaditanos copiaron** el carnaval de Venecia y **con el tiempo**, **lo adaptaron** a **sus propias costumbres**.

Un **hecho bastante** curioso es que durante esta fiesta, la **gente no se reúne** en un lugar específico como **ocurre** en muchas ciudades, sino que todas las calles de Cádiz **se llenan de** gente con **disfraces verdaderamente** originales, **cantando** y **disfrutando** de unos días dedicados a **olvidar** las prohibiciones y restricciones **marcadas** por la religión.

Durante la Guerra Civil y los 40 años de dictadura franquista, los carnavales **fueron prohibidos** en todo el territorio español. **Sin embargo**, Cádiz **se opuso** a esta norma y **continuó celebrándolos**.

Los principales **acontecimientos** celebrados durante los carnavales de Cádiz son la **coronación** de la Diosa del carnaval y la **lectura** del **pregón**. También **destacan** los **desfiles** que **discurren** por toda la ciudad, los **pasacalles**, las **fiestas infantiles** y los **bailes de disfraces**. Pero sin duda, lo que hace a este carnaval uno de los más famosos de España son las canciones de las **comparsas**, que destacan por su sátira y comicidad.

En el Gran Teatro de la Falla se celebra el **concurso** oficial de canciones and baile, donde **se escogerá** a la mejor composición. **Existen** varios grupos de amigos, llamados comparsas o agrupaciones carnavalescas que cantan **coplas** o canciones, **satirizando** a **personajes** o hechos importantes de la **actualidad**. Sus canciones son verdaderamente originales y es imposible no **sonreír** (¡o **reír a carcajadas**!) mientras se escuchan.

**¡Son un verdadero espectáculo**!

**fueron prohibidos/prohibir:** thcy were banned/to ban

**sin embargo:** however

**se opuso/oponer:** opposed/to oppose

**continuó/continuar:** it continued/to continue

**celebrándolos/celebrar:** celebrating them/to celebrate

**acontecimientos:** events

**coronación:** crowning, coronation

**lectura:** reading

**pregón:** street cry

**destacan/destacar:** they stand out/ to stand out

**desfiles:** parades

**discurren/discurrir:** they flow/to flow

**pasacalles:** a type of "unofficial" parade usually early in the morning, with bands playing typical songs, and they aim to wake up people to go on with the carnivals.

**fiestas infantiles:** parties for children

**bailes de disfraces:** costume balls

**comparsas:** teams of singers who write and sing their own songs

**concurso:** contest

**se escogerá/escoger:** will be chosen/to choose

**existen/existir:** exist/to exist

**coplas:** popular songs from Andalucía

**satirizando/satirizar:** satirizing/to satirize

**personajes:** celebrities, characters

**actualidad:** current affairs

**sonreír:** smile

**reír a carcajadas:** to roar with laughter

**¡Son un verdadero cspectáculo!:** They are an amazing show!

# Celebración de Navidad
## COLOMBIA

Navidad, **época** en la que los cristianos **conmemoran** el **nacimiento** de Jesús, pero al margen del **significado religioso,** la **gente** en Colombia **aprovecha** la ocasión **para reunirse con** los **seres queridos** y **manifestarles**, con **regalos y comida,** su **cariño y amor.** En Colombia, diciembre es época de **aguinaldos** y fiestas; también es un mes **propicío** para el **descanso** y las vacaciones. Los niños **esperan con ansiedad** la Navidad, la cual transforma los paisajes tradicionales con **luces multicolores** en **árboles, pesebres,** calles, establecimientos públicos y en la mayoría de **hogares.**

CELEBRACIÓN NAVIDEÑA COLOMBIANA:

Hay cuatro días que son especiales. Los más importantes son el 24 y 31 de diciembre. Le **siguen** en importancia el 8 de diciembre y **menor proporción** el 28 de diciembre.

El 8 de diciembre es **el dia de las veltas.** Ese día se celebra la anunciación del arcángel a María, aunque realmente **muy pocos** colombianos **lo saben.** Este día, y algunas veces también el 7 de diciembre, celebramos en Colombia "El dia de las velitas" o **"El alumbrado"** en el cual todas las familias colombianas

**encienden centenares** de velas en los andenes de las calles y **ventanas de sus casas**, convirtiendo las ciudades y los campos en una **hermosa tierra alumbrada** por miles y miles de pequeñas lucecitas. Los niños felices **prenden** sus **chispitas mariposas** y los **juegos pirotécnicos adornan** cada calle.

El 24 de diciembre es la Navidad. Durante los nueve días anteriores a la navidad **se reza** la novena de aguinaldos, la cual comienza a las seis de la tarde. Los **vecinos** van de **casa en casa cantando villancicos**, y **con el interés de recibir dulces y postres** al final de cada novena.

La noche es una fiesta, todos **bailan** al ritmo de salsa. **Canciones** especiales de estas fechas **suenan y resuenan una y otra vez**. A las 12 de la noche **se reparten** los aguinaldos. Después la fiesta **continúa hasta el amanecer**. La mañana del 25 es la fecha en la que los niños encuentran los regalos que les envía "el niño Dios" quien es el **encargado de traer** los regalos en Colombia.

El 28 de diciembre es el **día de los santos inocentes**. Este día es el equivalente al April Fool's Day americano. Está **permitido** hacer **bromas** a los amigos y **familiares**. Durante este día **se debe andar** con **mucho cuidado** y con los **ojos bien abiertos** para **no caer** en alguna "**inocentada**".

El 31 de diciembre es la fiest de fin de año. Muchas veces es una fiesta mucho mayor que la del 24. Las mamás y las abuelas **expresan** su amor con la **cena** que preparan para la medianoche. En muchas regiones del país, **se acostumbra** hacer un **muñeco con ropa vieja**, **relleno de guasca de plátano** y de **pólvora**. A las 12 de la noche en punto, mientras todos **se abrazan** y **se desean** un feliz año, el muñeco es **incinerado** ante la vista de todos en **señal** de que el año **ha muerto** y como bienvenida al nuevo año. También es muy común la creencia en los **agüeros** de fin de año, como por ejemplo ponerse **ropa interior amarilla**; **correr con las maletas en las manos** dándole la vuelta a la casa **para poder viajar** el año **siguiente**; **comer doce uvas** al ritmo de las doce **campanadas**, y mucho más.

---

**se reza/rezar:** it is recited/to recite
**vecinos:** neighbors
**casa en casa:** house to house
**cantando/cantar:** singing/to sing
**villancicos:** Christmas carols
**con el interés de:** with the interest of
**recibir:** to receive
**dulces y postres:** sweets and desserts
**bailan/bailar:** they dance/to dance
**canciones:** songs
**suenan y resuenan una y otra vez:** sound and resound again and again
**se reparten/repartir:** they are distributed, given out/to give out
**continúa/continuar:** it continues/ to continue
**hasta el amanecer:** until dawn
**encargardo de:** in charge of
**traer:** to bring
**día de los santos inocentes:** Innocent Saints Day
**permitido/permitir:** allowed/to allow
**bromas:** jokes
**familiares:** relatives
**se debe andar:** one must walk
**mucho cuidado:** very carefully
**ojos bien abiertos:** eyes wide open
**no caer:** do not fall
**inocentada:** practical joke
**expresan/expresar:** they express/to express
**cena:** dinner
**se acostumbra:** it is customary
**muñeco con ropa vieja:** doll made with old clothes
**relleno de guasca de plátano:** full of bark from the plantain tree
**pólvora:** gunpowder
**se abrazan:** they hug each other
**se desean:** they wish each other
**incinerado/incinerar:** incinerated/ to incinerate
**señal:** sign, signal
**ha muerto:** has died
**agüeros:** omens, superstitions
**ropa interior amarilla:** yellow underwear
**correr con las maletas en las manos:** to run with suitcases in hand
**para poder viajar:** to be able to travel
**siguiente:** following
**comer doce uvas:** eat twelve grapes
**campanadas:** bells (of midnight)

# Examina tu comprensión

## La Mamá Negra, page 64

1. *La Mamá Negra* is the celebration of two events. What are they?

2. How is the *Mamá Negra* represented in the parade?

3. *Huacos* are part of the celebration. Who are they?

4. What do the following symbolize during this celebration: the star angel, the Moorish King, the captain?

## El día de los muertos, page 66

1. The Day of the Dead is the time to reflect on what?

2. What is a popular saying as the celebration begins?

3. Party food includes food molded in the shape of bones and little skulls. What is the main ingredient of each of these?

## Festeja su independencia Chile, page 68

1. What is the name of the National Independence Day celebrated in Chile?

2. How long does this celebration last?

3. Describe the entertainment and street vendors.

4. Describe the most popular game during this time.

## ¡Menudo tomate!  page 70

1. Describe how the *La Tomatina* celebration started.

2. During the first *Tomatina* celebration the town hall ordered how many tomatoes and how long did it take the citizens to throw them?

3. To prepare for "battle" what do the people do?

# Test your comprehension

## La Virgen de la Candelaria, page 74

1. When does this event take place and what is it celebrating?

2. Puno was designated the capital of what? Why?

3. The festivities culminate in what stadium and what takes place here?

## La fiesta con más Gracia, page 78

1. Who conducts or puts together this event? What materials are used to decorate the streets?

2. Some of the "best streets" are judged. What critera is used to judge the streets? What reward (if any) do the winners receive?

## La pascua y Semana Santa, page 76

1. What takes place on Good Friday?

2. What is Saturday dedicated to?

## El carnaval de Cádiz, page 80

1. The Carnival of Cádiz is celebrated during what month?

2. What is the reason/origin of the celebration?

3. What event takes place in the *Gran Teatro de la Falla*?

Cuando hay gente unida que cree en algo firmemente,
ya religión, política o sindicato, algo sucede.

César Chávez

# Personas

# La magia de García Márquez
## COLOMBIA

**Conocí** a Gabriel García Márquez **por primera vez** cuando tenía diecisiete años. **Fue entonces** cuando leí *El coronel no tiene quien le escriba*. Esta **narración corta se convirtió** en la puerta que **se abriría** para **descubrir el mundo mágico** de quien para mí es y seguirá siendo **el mejor escritor** Latinoamericano. *Crónicas de una muerte anunciada* **ha sido** la única **novela de suspenso** que **he leído alguna vez** y, su **obra maestra**, *Cien años de soledad*, se convirtió en mi **libro más leído** y base fundamental de mi **tesis de maestría**.

Este **célebre escritor** nació en Aracataca, Colombia, un 6 de marzo de 1928. **Sus primeros ocho años** de vida fueron los más importantes de su vida, años **cuando vivió** con sus **abuelos maternos**, Nicolás Márquez y Tranquilina Iguaran. **En algún momento** de su vida **pensó** estudiar **derecho** pero, **según él**, "**me aburría a morir esa carrera**". Así **se adentró** en **el mundo de las palabras** y las páginas blancas. Comienza en el **periodismo** trabajando en "El Heraldo", mientras empieza a trabajar en su primera novela *La Hojarasca*.

**Su carrera periodística lo lleva** a conocer Europa y **más tarde** los Estados Unidos, donde **viajó** por los caminos de sus **escritores favoritos**: Kafka, Faulkner, Virginia Wolf y Hemingway. En los últimos años, García Márquez ha vivido en México **junto a su esposa** Mercedes Barcha. Su libro más reciente, *Vivir para contarla*, es su autobiografía donde **pueden encontrarse** muchos de los **personajes** de sus libros. **Desde muy joven me sentí atraída hacia** el escritor y sus palabras. **Quizás sean** nuestros **años felices de infancia**, el **compartir** esa **abuela enérgica que adivinaba el futuro**, nuestro gusto por Hemingway o el **haber conocido el sur estadounidense**. Gabriel García Márquez **no necesita magia** para escribir. Él es la magia **transformada** en palabras.

# Las hazañas de Rita Moreno
## PUERTO RICO

Muchos la **recuerdan** como la Anita de de la película *West Side Story*. Para los puertorriqueños, Rosita Dolores Alverio representa uno de **nuestros orgullos** más importantes. Esta **dama** del **cine** y la televisión nació el 11 de diciembre de 1931 en el **pequeño pueblo** de Humacao. Aquí vivían sus padres, **trabajadores** y **amantes de la tierra**.

La Depresión de los años 30 los llevó a abandonar la isla **para probar suerte** en las **frías calles** de Nueva York. **Aunque el cambio fue drástico** y existía la **barrera del lenguaje**, Rita **demostró** desde pequeña su inmenso talento.

**Mucho tiempo ha pasado** desde *West Side Story*, la historia moderna de Romeo y Julieta. Desde entonces ha trabajado en más de 70 películas **a lo largo de** su **exitosa carrera**. *King of the Corner* **ha sido** su más reciente **aparición** y muchos la **podrán** recordar como Juana en American Family, donde también **se destacan** otros hispanos **notables**.

Rita Moreno ha sido la **única** hispana que ha ganado los **premios** Oscar, Tony, Emma y Grammy. Por su hazaña, aparece en el *Libro Guinness de Récords*. En 2004, el presidente George Bush **le otorgó** la **Medalla Presidencial de la Libertad** en honor a todos sus **logros** y **labor cívica**.

Rita Moreno, siempre **orgullosa** de su origen y su **herencia**, **pasará a la posteridad** como una de las artistas más famosas y **queridas** de la historia.

---

**hazañas:** outstanding achievements
**recuerdan/recordar:** they remember/ to remember
**nuestros orgullos:** our pride
**dama:** lady
**cine:** cinema
**pequeño pueblo:** small village; town
**trabajadores:** hard workers
**amantes de la tierra:** lovers of the land
**para probar suerte:** to try one's luck
**frías calles:** cold streets
**aunque el cambio fue drástico:** although the change was drastic
**barrera del lenguaje:** language barrier
**demostró/demostrar:** she showed/ to show
**mucho tiempo ha pasado:** a long time has gone by
**a lo largo de:** throughout
**exitosa carrera:** successful career
**ha sido/ser:** it has been/to be
**aparición:** appearance
**podrán/poder:** they will be able to/can; to be able to
**se destacan/destacar:** stand out/ to stand out
**notables:** outstanding
**única:** only one
**premios:** awards
**le otorgó/otorgar:** he awarded/ to award, to grant
**Medalla Presidencial de la Libertad:** Presidential Medal of Freedom
**logros:** achievements
**labor cívica:** civil work
**orgullosa:** proud
**herencia:** heritage
**pasará a la posteridad:** she will go down in posterity; history
**queridas:** beloved

# Diego Rivera
## MÉXICO

La **primera vez** que **supe de** Diego Rivera fue por mi **acercamiento** y admiración hacia Frida Kahlo, su **amada**, pero también una gran artista. Es difícil **pensarlos separados** y la relación que **tuvieron** tan tormentosa, **dolorosa**, **amorosa** y pasional hace que esta **pareja sea** una de las más **recordadas** de su **época**. **Además del amor que se tenían el uno al otro**, les **unió** también su amor por la **pintura** y la **política**. **Se admiraron mutuamente** y **se amaron**, pero también **se odiaron**.

Diego Rivera nació en 1886 en Guanajuato (México) y fue uno de los pintores más famosos e importantes del mundo. **Mujeriego**, **imponente**, **escandaloso**, **feo** y **encantador**, Rivera fue uno de los máximos representantes, **si no el mayor**, del muralismo mexicano, **aunque** su obra también incluye trabajos como **pintor de caballete**, **dibujante** e ilustrador. Su **aporte** al mundo del arte moderno fue decisivo.

Diego Rivera fue un pintor revolucionario que siempre **buscó** llevar su arte, de **gran contenido social**, a la **gente**, a las calles, a los **techos** y **paredes** de **edificios públicos** ya que consideraba que el arte **debía** servir a la **clase trabajadora** y estar **a su alcance**.

Estudió Bellas Artes en México y luego en Europa, donde vivió varios años, **se enriqueció** con los distintos movimientos culturales y pictóricos. También visitó la Unión Soviética, **cuna** de sus ideales políticos. **De regreso** a México en 1921, **fundó** el Partido Comunista Mexicano y **se casó con** la pintora Frida Kahlo. Ambos **combinaron** su trabajo artístico con una **agitada** actividad política. En Rivera estaban tan **mezcladas** ambas expresiones que en la mayoría de sus murales **se ven reflejados** sus ideales: revolución social mexicana, resistencia a la opresión **extranjera**, la **valoración del indígena**, sus raíces, el **pasado** y el futuro de su país.

Su fama le llevó también a vivir y exponer su obra en Estados Unidos, aunque en su **país natal** es donde **se encuentra** su **legado** más importante. **Decoró** muchos edificios y ministerios públicos; dos de los más conocidos e importantes son *La Tierra Fecunda* en la Escuela Nacional de Agricultura de Chapingo y el mural con su **propia interpretación** sobre la historia de México, en el Palacio Nacional de la capital.

**Murió** el 24 de noviembre de 1957 en su casa de San Ángel de la ciudad de México.

*"Era un hombre adorable que **no sabía dar la cara** en su vida personal pero que en su vida pública era un **luchador**. Era muy **capaz de pararse** en público y **demoler**, por ejemplo, a los Rockefeller en 10 minutos."* Louise Nevelson

*"**Vuelvo a verte** con tu estatura monumental, tu **vientre** siempre adelantándosete, tus **zapatos sucios**, tu viejo sombrero alabeado, tu **pantalón arrugado**, y pienso que nadie **podría** llevar con tanta **nobleza** cosas tan **estropeadas**."* Elena Poniatowska

**se enriqueció/enriquecer:** he became enriched/to enrich
**cuna:** cradle
**de regreso:** back from
**fundó/fundar:** he founded/ to found
**se casó con:** he married
**combinaron/combinar:** they combined/to combine
**agitada/agitar:** agitated/to agitate
**mezcladas/mezclar:** mixed/ to mix
**se ven reflejados/reflejar:** they are seen reflected/to reflect
**extranjera:** foreign
**valoración del indígena:** valuation of indigenous people
**pasado:** past
**país natal:** country of origin
**se encuentra/encontrarse:** it is found/to find
**legado:** legacy
**decoró/decorar:** he decorated/ to decorate
**propia interpretación:** own interpretation
**murió/morir:** he died/to die
**no sabía:** he wasn't able (literally he didn't know)
**dar la cara:** to face the consequences of one's acts
**luchador:** fighter
**capaz de pararse:** able to stand up
**demoler:** to demolish
**vuelvo a verte/volver:** I see you again/to see
**vientre:** abdomen, stomach
**zapatos:** shoes
**sucios:** dirty
**pantalón:** pants
**arrugado:** wrinkled
**podría/poder:** nobody could/can
**nobleza:** nobility
**estropeadas:** damaged

| | |
|---|---|
| **llenó:/llenar:** it fulfilled /to fulfill | |
| **perdí/perder:** I lost/to lose | |
| **otra serie de cosas:** many other things | |
| **hubieran podido:** could have | |
| **reemplazó/reemplazar:** replaced/ to replace | |
| **desesperada:** desperate, hopeless | |
| **más vale:** it is better | |
| **le robamos/robar:** we steal/to steal | |
| **vislumbrar:** to glimpse | |
| **dolor:** pain | |
| **tristeza:** sadness | |
| **luz:** light | |
| **fuerza:** strength | |
| **quizás:** perhaps | |
| **modo:** way, manner | |
| **no la aguantarían/aguantar:** they wouldn't tolerate/to tolerate | |
| **le cambió/cambiar:** it changed her/ to change | |
| **no pudo/poder:** she wasn't able/to be able, can | |
| **hijos:** children | |
| **dolor físico:** physical pain | |
| **columna:** spinal column | |
| **pierna:** leg | |
| **cuerpo:** body | |
| **comenzó/comenzar:** she started/to start | |
| **sin prestar mucha atención:** without paying much attention | |
| **postrada/postrarse:** prostrated/to prostrate oneself, kneel down | |
| **mitigar:** to mitigate | |
| **largas horas:** long hours | |
| **a través de:** through | |
| **se expresaba/expresarse:** she expressed herself/to express | |
| **se liberaba/liberarse:** she liberated herself/to liberate | |
| **implosiva:** implosive | |
| **arrasadora/arrasar:** devastating/to devastate, to destroy | |
| **liberarse:** to go free | |
| **aseguraba/asegurar:** she assured/ to assure | |
| **cuadros:** paintings | |
| **seres queridos:** loved ones | |
| **le preguntaban/preguntar:** she was asked/to ask | |
| **autorretratos:** self portraits | |
| **se retrataba:** she painted a self-portrait | |
| **conocía/conocer:** she knew/to know | |
| **femeninos:** feminine | |
| **feroces:** ferocious | |

# Frida Kahlo
## MÉXICO

"La pintura **llenó** mi vida. **Perdí** tres hijos y **otra serie de cosas** que **hubieran podido** llenar mi horrible vida. Todo eso lo **reemplazó** la pintura". "Para estar **desesperada**, **más vale** ser productiva. Siempre es algo que **le robamos** a la pura y simple autodestrucción…"

Estas palabras son de Frida Kahlo y dejan **vislumbrar** algo de lo que fue su vida. Una vida llena de **dolor**, **tristeza**, desesperación pero también de **luz**, pasión, amor, **fuerza** y resistencia. Una vida corta pero intensa. ¿Por qué será que la mayoría de los que viven una vida tan intensa, viven pocos años? **Quizás** porque de otro **modo no la aguantarían**.

Nació en México en 1907. En la adolescencia tuvo un terrible accidente que **le cambió** la existencia para siempre. Como consecuencia, no sólo **no pudo** tener **hijos**, sino que el **dolor físico** la acompañó en todo momento: la operaron más de siete veces de la **columna**, tres de una **pierna** (que al final terminó perdiendo), y todo su **cuerpo** fue un constante sufrir. **Comenzó** a pintar "**sin prestar mucha atención**", casi por casualidad, **postrada** en una cama y para **mitigar** su soledad y sus **largas horas** de convalecencia. **A través de** su obra **se expresaba** y **se liberaba**: "La fuerza de lo que no se expresa es **implosiva**, **arrasadora**, autodestructiva. Expresar es **liberarse**", **aseguraba.**

Sus **cuadros** están llenos de símbolos. Todos representan su realidad, su vida y la de sus **seres queridos**. Cuando **le preguntaban** por qué pintaba tantos **autorretratos**, ella contestaba que **se retrataba** a sí misma porque pasaba mucho tiempo sola y porque era el motivo que mejor **conocía**. Sus cuadros son **femeninos**, sinceros, sensibles y **feroces**.

Se **casó con** Diego Rivera, famoso muralista mexicano. Su amor por él fue inmenso, **inagotable**, incondicional. **Juntos participaron** políticamente en el partido nacional-socialista y **viajaron** por Europa y Estados Unidos, donde Frida exhibió por primera vez, en Nueva York, su obra individualmente.

Fue una relación tormentosa que **superó** las infidelidades de él, los **amoríos** de ella, las obligaciones de trabajo de Diego, los problemas de salud de Frida, varios abortos, el divorcio y otra vez el matrimonio. La pasión que los **unió** los **acompaño** hasta sus últimos días.

Frida murió en 1954. Su último cuadro, una naturaleza muerta en el que **se ven** unas **sandías abiertas**, se titula *Viva la vida*. Sus últimas frases escritas en su diario íntimo, "**Espero alegre** la **salida**…y espero no **volver** más", **resumen su paso** por esta vida.

**se casó con/casarse:** she married/to marry
**inagotable:** inexhaustible, tireless
**juntos:** together
**participaron/participar:** they were involved/to be involved
**viajaron/viajar:** they traveled/to travel
**superó/superar:** she overcame/to overcome
**amoríos:** love affairs
**unió/unir:** it joined/to join
**acompañó/acompañar:** it accompanied/to accompany
**se ven/ver:** they are shown/to show
**sandías abiertas:** open watermelons
**espero/esperar:** I hope/to hope
**alegre:** happy
**salida:** exit
**volver:** to return
**resumen:** summary
**su paso:** her route

**CULTURE NOTE** People often ask if Castilian Spanish, as it is spoken in Spain, is different from the Spanish of Latin America. In addition to a different accent, there are some differences in grammar, vocabulary, and at times, pronunciation. Two of the greatest differences are the *leísmo* of Spain and the use of the pronoun *vos* instead of *tú*. Another major difference is that *vosotros* is often used as the plural of *tú* (the singular familiar "you") in Spain, while in Latin America *ustedes* is usually used. Another difference is that many Spaniards often pronounce the "z" and the "c" before "i" or "e" like the "th" in thin, while many Latin Americans pronounce it the same as the "s". Speakers in some areas (Argentina in particular) often pronounce the "ll" and "y" like the "s" in *measure*. In some areas, you will hear speakers drop "s" sounds, so *está* sounds like *etá*. In some areas, the "j" sounds like the "ch" in *loch* (difficult for many native English speakers to master), while in others it sounds like the English "h". In some areas, the "l" and the "r" at the end of a word sound alike. Over time you may be able to tell where someone is from based on their accent. Rest assured, regardless of where you study, whether your accent is Castilian or Mexican or Bolivian, with good pronunciation you will be understood most anywhere in the Spanish-speaking world.

# Celia Cruz
## CUBA

Celia Cruz **nació** el 21 de octubre de 1925 en La Habana, Cuba. Su vocación era la música pero **aparte de** su talento, Celia con moral e integridad **alcanzó** su misión de **entusiasmar al mundo**. **Puesto que** ella **no pudo** tener niños, **adoptó** a **centenares** de **ahijados** y **demostró** respeto **hacia** su audiencia con positivismo y **fe**.

En el año 1961, Celia y Pedro Knight hicieron de Manhattan su **hogar**. **Al lado** de Tito Puente, Celia alcanzó una **meta** importante: ser la primera mujer hispana en el Carnagie Hall. En 1974 la vida de Celia **comenzó** con músicos como Héctor Lavoe, Cheo Feliciano, Johnny Pacheco, Rubén Blades y Willie Colón, entre muchos otros. Celia, la **fiel dama sonriente** y devota de la Virgen de la Caridad del Cobre, fue **siempre humilde**, pero **obtuvo frutos** como ser nominada 12 **veces** al Grammy **ganándolo** por primera vez en 1989. **Cantó** con Pavarotti y Liza Minelli entre otros artistas. **Recibió doctorados** de la Universidad de Yale, la Universidad Internacional de la Florida y la Universidad de Miami. **Participó** en varias **películas y telenovelas**. Sus manos estan en el Paseo de la Fama en Hollywood, en Miami, e **incluso** muchas ciudades tienen calles que **llevan** su nombre. Celia Cruz obtuvo también la Medalla Presidencial de las Artes de las **manos** del presidente Bill Clinton. A los 77 años, el 16 de Julio del 2003 Celia Cruz abandonó esta tierra luego de sufrir un **tumor cerebral**. En su **velorio**, que **duró** días, cantó Patti LaBelle, y asistió gente de todas partes del mundo, entre ellos sus amigos íntimos y su **amado** Pedro, con quien un par de días antes Celia cumplió 41 años de unión. Su cuerpo fue enterrado en Nueva York **junto a** un **puño de tierra** que **trajo** desde Guantánamo años antes, cuando **supo** que no podría **volver** a su isla. Su música **sigue sonando** en los **rincones más remotos** del mundo y su legado **no tendrá fin** pues fue una dama que **convirtió** su vida en la **fuerza** de su canción.

---

**nació/nacer:** was born/to be born
**aparte de:** apart from
**alcanzó/alcanzar:** it reached/to reach
**entusiasmar al mundo:** to delight the world
**puesto que:** since
**no pudo:** she was not able to
**adoptó/adoptar:** she adopted/to adopt
**centenares:** hundreds
**ahijados:** godchildren
**demostró/demostrar:** she showed/to show
**hacia:** towards
**fe:** faith
**hogar:** home
**al lado:** beside
**meta:** goal, objective
**comenzó/comenzar:** began/to begin
**fiel:** faithfuly
**dama:** lady
**sonriente/sonreír:** smiling/to smile
**siempre:** always
**humilde:** humble, modest
**obtuvo/obtener:** obtained/to obtain
**frutos:** profits
**veces:** times
**ganándolo:** winning it/to win
**cantó/cantar:** she sang/to sing
**recibió/recibir:** she received/to receive
**doctorados:** doctorates
**participó:** she participated/to participate
**películas y telenovelas:** films and soap operas
**incluso:** even
**llevan/llevar:** take/to take
**manos:** hands
**tumor cerebral:** brain tumor
**velorio:** wake
**duró/durar:** it lasted/to last
**amado:** beloved
**junto a:** next to
**puño de tierra:** handful of earth
**trajo/traer:** she brought/to bring
**supo/saber:** she knew/to know
**volver:** to return
**sigue sonando:** it keeps on sounding
**rincones más remotos:** outermost corners
**no tendrá fin:** will not end
**convirtió/convertir:** changed/to change
**fuerza:** strength

# Rubén Darío
## NICARAGUA

**Pensar** en Nicaragua es **acordarse inevitablemente** de Rubén Darío y de esos poemas que a uno **le enseñaron** en el **colegio secundario** y que **hacían**, y hacen, **suspirar**.

La poesía es una de las artes más **queridas** de este país gracias a su gran poeta y escritor, uno de los mayores **exponentes** de todo Centroamérica. Desde su **infancia** fue un **niño prodigio**, **aprendió** a **leer** cuando **apenas** tenía tres años y **antes** de **cumplir los trece**, ya **había escrito** su primer poema.

**Tuvo** una vida **agitada**, **gozó** con exceso de todos los **placeres mundanos**. Fue **hombre de amores tempestuosos,** temperamental y sensual.

El **afán** de perfección fue una de sus características más **destacadas**. El ritmo, las nuevas combinaciones **métricas** y la armonía en sus composiciones **aportaron innovaciones** fundamentales en toda la literatura de **lengua** castellana. Fue el gran **inspirador** y máximo representante del Modernismo, **corriente** literaria que **se destacó** por la renovación radical en los conceptos básicos de la poesía, **otorgándole riqueza** y musicalidad.

**Combinó** su pasión por la escritura con **trabajos periodísticos** y diplomáticos que **le permitieron** viajar por algunos países.

La poesía de Rubén Darío no sólo **se lee**, sino que **se escucha** como una **melodía cautivante**, como una canción que emociona y **llega** al **alma**.

---

**pensar:** to think
**acordarse:** to remember
**inevitablemente:** inevitably
**le enseñaron/enseñar:** one was taught/ to teach
**colegio secundario:** secondary school
**hacían/hacer:** they made/to make
**suspirar:** to sigh
**queridas:** beloved
**exponentes:** exponents
**infancia:** childhood
**niño prodigio:** child prodigy
**aprendió/aprender:** he learned/to learn
**leer:** to read
**apenas:** hardly
**antes:** before
**cumplir los trece:** to reach the age of 13
**había escrito/escribir:** he had written /to write
**tuvo/tener:** he had/to have
**agitada:** agitated
**gozó/gozar:** he enjoyed/to enjoy
**placeres mundanos:** material pleasures
**hombre de amores tempestuosos:** man of tempestuous loves (love affairs)
**afán:** effort
**destacadas:** outstanding
**métricas:** metrics
**aportaron/aportar:** they contributed/ to contribute
**innovaciones:** innovations
**lengua:** language
**inspirador:** inspiring
**corriente:** tendency
**se destacó/destacarse:** he stood out/ to stand out
**otorgándole/otorgar:** bestowing upon it/to bestow
**riqueza:** wealth
**combinó/combinar:** he combined/ to combine
**trabajos periodísticos:** journalistic work
**le permitieron/permitir:** they allowed him/to allow
**se lee/leer:** it is read/to read
**se escucha/escuchar:** it is listened/ to listen
**melodía cautivante:** gripping melody
**llega/llegar:** it reaches/to reach
**alma:** soul

**con el paso de los años:** as years went by
**se transformó/transformarse:** became/ to become
**lucha:** struggle
**pobres:** poor
**mirada desafiante:** defiant look
**morir:** to die
**dispara/disparar:** shoot/to shoot
**cobarde:** coward
**estás matando/matar:** you are killing/ to kill
**inventadas/inventar:** made up/to invent
**contribuyeron/contribuir:** they contributed/to contribute
**construcción:** building
**guerrero:** warrior
**implacable:** relentless, implacable
**pocos:** few
**saben/saber:** they know/to know
**con exactitud:** precisely, exactly
**pormenores:** details
**como sucede:** as it happens
**se convierten/convertir:** they become/ to become
**justamente:** precisely
**supera/superar:** it exceeds/to exceed
**desvirtúa:** it distorts
**de carne y hueso:** real, only human
**nació/nacer:** he was born/to be born
**chiquito:** child
**sufrió/sufrir:** he suffered/to suffer
**hacer la educación:** took his education
**hogar:** home
**no le impidió/impidió:** it didn't prevent him from/to prevent from
**sobresalir:** to stand out
**entre los demás:** among the rest
**doctorarse:** to get one's doctorate
**realizó/realizar:** he made/to make
**descubriendo/descubrir:** discovering/ to discover
**miseria:** extreme poverty
**masas:** masses, people
**se formó:** he was educated
**conoció/conocer:** he met/to meet
**se vinculó:** he joined
**médico:** doctor
**sindicatos:** labor unions
**participó/participar:** he participated/ to participate
**posteriormente:** later
**partió/partir:** he left/to leave
**encuentro:** gathering
**integrante:** member
**luchaba/luchar:** he fought/ to fight

# El Che Guevara
## ARGENTINA

**Con el paso de los años,** el Che Guevara **se transformó** en icono de la revolución, la **lucha** y la defensa de los **pobres.** Su **mirada desafiante** en la fotografía que lo inmortalizó en posters, y sus últimas palabras antes de **morir**, "**Dispara, cobarde,** sólo **estás matando** a un hombre", **inventadas** o reales, **contribuyeron** a la **construcción** de esta imagen de **guerrero implacable.** En realidad, **pocos saben con exactitud** quién fue Ernesto Guevara, cuáles fueron sus ideales y los **pormenores** de su vida privada y de combate. **Como sucede** con la mayoría de las personas famosas que **se convierten** en mito, es **justamente** esa imagen mítica la que **supera,** y a veces también **desvirtúa,** al hombre real, al **de carne y hueso.**

Ernesto Guevara de la Serna **nació** en Rosario (Argentina) el 14 de junio de 1928. Desde **chiquito sufrió** de asma, por lo que tuvo que **hacer la educación** primaria en su **hogar,** pero esto **no le impidió sobresalir entre los demás.**

En 1953, tras **doctorarse** en Medicina en la Universidad de Buenos Aires, **realizó** su segundo viaje por Centroamérica y Sudamérica gracias al que, **descubriendo** la **miseria** dominante entre las **masas** y la omnipresencia del imperialismo, **se formó** políticamente con inclinación a la ideología marxista. Durante este viaje **conoció** también a varios revolucionarios cubanos, guatemaltecos y de otros países del continente (entre ellos a quien sería su futura esposa, Hilda Gadea Ontalia, economista exiliada peruana). **Se vinculó** al Partido Guatemalteco del Trabajo, trabajó como **médico** en los **sindicatos** y **participó** activamente en la política interna del país.

**Posteriormente partió** a México donde conoció a los hermanos Castro, Fidel y Raúl. Después de este **encuentro,** el Che se convirtió en un **integrante** del grupo de revolución cubana que **luchaba** contra el dictador Fulgencio Batista, presidente de Cuba en ese momento.

En 1955 **se casó** con Hilda Gadea, con quien tuvo una **hija. Sin embargo**, este **nacimiento no logró mantener** a la **pareja** unida y se divorciaron al poco tiempo. Tres años después, el Che se casaría **de nuevo** con Aleida March Torres, una joven cubana de 22 años, con la que tuvo cuatro **hijos**. A finales de 1956, en el **yate** Granma, el Che y una **superpoblación** de **tripulantes desembarcaron** en el este de Cuba para **dar comienzo** a la guerrilla revolucionaria. Desde entonces, participó activamente en varios **combates** y **batallas** hasta que, en enero de 1959, Cuba fue liberada y Batista tuvo que partir al **exilio**. En honor a los **servicios prestados** al país, Ernesto Guevara fue declarado ciudadano cubano por el **Consejo de Ministros**.

Durante varios años **cumplió funciones** oficiales dentro del **gobierno** cubano, tuvo responsabilidades de carácter militar y económico (una de sus funciones fue la de Presidente del Banco Nacional de Cuba) y viajó por Egipto, Sudán, Pakistán, India, Indonesia y Ceilán, entre otros países. En octubre de 1960, Estados Unidos **decretó** el embargo **comercial** a Cuba y al año siguiente **rompieron** relaciones diplomáticas. Desde varios puestos políticos y militares, el Che **siguió** su lucha revolucionaria **sin descanso** durante años, además de escribir **numerosos** artículos y varios libros donde **volcó** sus ideas y **pensamientos.** Su **carrera** y funciones políticas **le llevaron** a viajar **por todo el mundo**. Para poder **seguir adelante** con sus ideales progresistas, **solicitó** a la Dirección de la Revolución Cubana su **liberación** en las responsabilidades que tenía con ese país para **reiniciar** la **lucha armada** en solidaridad con los pueblos del mundo.

A finales de 1966 entró clandestinamente a Bolivia para **unirse** inmediatamente a un pequeño grupo de combatientes bolivianos, cubanos y de otras nacionalidades. Así, **fundó** el Ejército de Liberación de Bolivia, instalando una guerrilla que **pudiera irradiar** su influencia hacia Argentina, Chile, Perú, Brasil y Paraguay. El 8 de octubre de 1967, a los 39 años de edad, después de **ser apresado** y **ser seriamente herido**, el Che fue ejecutado por soldados bolivianos. En La Habana, en la Plaza de la Revolución, Fidel Castro informó a medio millón de **acongojados** cubanos, la **triste noticia** de la muerte del Comandante Ernesto Che Guevara.

**se casó/casarse:** he got married/to get married
**hija:** daughter
**sin embargo:** however
**nacimiento:** birth
**no logró/lograr:** it didn't succeed in/to succeed in
**mantener:** to keep
**pareja:** couple
**de nuevo:** again
**hijos:** children
**yate:** yacht
**superpoblación:** overpopulation
**tripulantes:** crew members
**desembarcaron/desembarcar:** they disembarked/to disembark
**dar comienzo:** to begin, to start
**combates:** combat
**batallas:** battles
**exilio:** exile
**servicios prestados:** services given
**Consejo de Ministros:** cabinet meeting
**cumplió funciones:** he worked as
**gobierno:** government
**decretó/decretar:** it decreed/to decree
**comercial:** trade
**rompieron/romper:** they broke/to break
**siguió/seguir:** he continued/to continue
**sin descanso:** without having a rest
**numerosos:** several
**volcó/volcar:** he dumped/to dump, to empty out
**pensamientos:** thoughts
**carrera:** career
**le llevaron:** they made him
**por todo el mundo:** around the world
**seguir adelante:** to keep going
**solicitó/solicitar:** he asked/to ask
**liberación:** freeing, liberation
**reiniciar:** restart
**lucha armada:** armed struggle
**unirse:** to join
**fundó/fundar:** he founded/to found
**pudiera/poder:** it could/can
**irradiar:** to radiate
**ser apresado/apresar:** to be captured/to catch
**ser seriamente herido:** to be seriously injured
**acongojado:** distressed
**triste:** sad
**noticia:** news

# Unamuno, el eterno poeta
## ESPAÑA

Este **escritor** inmortal **nació** en Bilbao, España, en 1864. **Sin embargo**, **no fue** allí donde **conocí** su historia sino en la ciudad donde vivió gran parte de su vida y **donde hoy descansa su cuerpo**, Salamanca. Desde mi habitación **podía** ver su **sepultura** y en muchas ocasiones tuve conversaciones imaginarias con él.

En 1891, llegó a esta ciudad donde también **contrajo matrimonio** con Concepción Lizarraga. En su *Diario Intimo* quedan los **recuerdos** de su amor y sus crisis personales **en torno** a la religión.

En 1900 fue nombrado **rector** de la famosa y antigua Universidad de Salamanca, aunque sus ideas políticas lo **despojaron** del **cargo** 14 años más tarde. Estas **mismas afiliaciones** con el Partido Socialista le llevaron a ser **deportado** a la isla de Fuerteventura, luego a Hendaya y finalmente a París.

Regresó a Salamanca en 1931 **para morir** allí **de manera extraña** el 31 de diciembre de ese mismo año. Su cuerpo y su genio se fueron con el **Año Viejo**.

Cuando estaba en la **escuela superior**, **sufrí** sus agonías **a través de** *San Manuel Bueno, Mártir*. Durante mi **estadía** en Salamanca, descubrí al otro hombre, a quien muchos llamaron loco. Para mí, *Niebla* representa su **obra maestra**. En ella presenta la tragedia realista del **ser humano** y todos los **demonios** y ángeles con los que **batallamos**.

**Después de todo**, todos tenemos algo de locos, ¿no?

---

**eterno:** eternal
**escritor:** writer
**nació/nacer:** he was born/to be born
**sin embargo:** nevertheless
**no fue/ser:** it was not/to be
**conocí/conocer:** I knew about/to know about
**donde hoy descansa su cuerpo:** where his body lies today
**podía/poder:** I was able to/to be able to
**sepultura:** grave
**contrajo matrimonio/contraer matrimonio:** he got married/to get married
**recuerdos:** memories
**en torno:** revolved around
**rector:** dean
**despojaron/despojar:** they stripped/to strip, to take away from
**cargo:** position
**mismas afiliaciones:** same affiliations
**deportado/deportar:** deported/to deport
**para morir:** to die
**de manera extraña:** in a strange way
**año viejo:** New Year's Eve
**escuela superior:** university, college
**sufrí/sufrir:** I suffered/to suffer
**a través de:** through
**estadía:** stay
*Niebla:* *Fog* (Unamuno's novel)
**obra maestra:** masterpiece
**ser humano:** human being
**demonios:** devils
**batallamos/batallar:** we battle/to battle
**después de todo:** after all

# Hispanos para la historia
## MÉXICO

Anthony Quinn fue un hispano famoso. **Nació** Antonio Rodolfo Oaxaca Quinn el 21 de abril de 1915 en Chihuaha, México de padre **irlandés** y madre mexicana. **Se movió** a los Estados Unidos **siendo** aun muy pequeño. **En las calles del barrio** al este de Los Ángeles, **vende periódicos y lustra zapatos** para **ayudar** a su familia **antes de convertirse** en uno de los actores más importantes de la nación americana.

**Entre sus películas mas destacadas** están: *Caminando en las nubes* (*A Walk in the Clouds*) 1995, *Ángelo vengador* (*Avenging Angelo*) 2002, *El viejo y el mar* (*The Old Man and the Sea*) 1990) y *Onassis* 1998. Hizo un total de 158 películas. También fue productor, director de cine y **ganador** del **premio** Oscar en **varias ocasiones**. Anthony Quinn **murió** el 3 de junio del 2001 **a causa de complicaciones respiratorias**.

Una de sus **citas** famosas **se refiere** a sus **comienzos de su carrera** cuando "*Todos decían que para lo único que servía era para hacer papeles de indio*".

Este hispano **demostró** que era **mucho más grande** y **se convirtió en un inmortal del cine**.

**nació/nacer:** was born/to be born
**irlandés:** Irish
**se movió/mover:** he moved/to move
**siendo:** when he still was
**en las calles del barrio:** the streets of the neigborhood
**vende periódicos y lustra zapatos:** sells newspapers and shines shoes
**ayudar:** to help
**antes de convertirse:** before becoming
**entre sus películas mas destacadas:** among his most outstanding movies
**ganador:** winner
**premio:** award
**varias ocasiones:** various occasions
**murió/morir:** he died/to die
**a causa de complicaciones respiratorias:** caused by respiratory complications
**citas:** quotations
**se refiere/refeir:** refers/to refer
**comienzos de su carrera:** beginning of his career
**Todos decían que para lo único que servía era para hacer papeles de indio:** Everybody used to say that I was only good to play the indian.
**demostró/demostrar:** showed/to show
**mucho mas grande:** a lot bigger
**se convirtió en un inmortal del cine:** he became immortal on the big screen

# Andrés Segovia
## ESPAÑA

**está considerado/estar considerado:**
  he is considered/to be considered
**eruditos:** scholars
**esfuerzos:** efforts
**del plebeyo:** of the peasants
**búsqueda:** quest; search
**se inició/iniciar:** he started/to start
**temprana edad:** early age
**tío:** uncle
**le cantaba/cantar:** sang/to sing
**fingía/fingir:** pretended/to pretend
**rasguear:** to strum
**luthier:** brand name of a guitar
**cercano:** close by, near
**entonces:** then
**le acompañó/acompañar:** it went
  with/to go with, to accompany
**desalentó/desalentar:** it discouraged/
  to discourage
**debería haber tocado/tocar:** he
  should have played/to play
**verdadero:** real
**se propuso como meta:** he was
  determined to set a new goal
**llevar:** to take, taking
**consiguió/conseguir:** he reached/to
  reach, to get
**buscaba/buscar:** he was looking for/to
  look for
**incluyó /incluir:** included/to include
**supuestamente serios:** so-called
  serious
**público:** audience
**se reiría/reirse:** it would laugh/to
  laugh
**tendría/tener:** it would have/to have
**salir:** to leave
**creían/creer:** they believed/to believe
**asombró/asombrar:** he amazed/
  to amaze, to surprise
**los asistentes:** those present
**se encontró/encontrarse:** he found/
  to find
**no podía/poder:** it wasn't able/
  to be able
**producir:** to produce
**suficiente sonido:** enough sound
**llenar:** to fill
**salón:** hall

Andrés Segovia **está considerado** como el padre del movimiento clásico moderno de la guitarra por la mayoría de los **eruditos** modernos. Muchos piensan que sin sus **esfuerzos**, la guitarra clásica todavía se consideraría como un instrumento humilde **del plebeyo**.

La **búsqueda** de Segovia para elevar la guitarra a una posición prominente en el mundo de la música **se inició** a la **temprana edad** de cuatro años. Su **tío le cantaba** canciones en su regazo mientras él **fingía rasguear** una guitarra imaginaria. Afortunadamente había un **luthier cercano** y **entonces** la guitarra **le acompañó** siempre. Aunque su familia lo **desalentó** (según ellos, **debería haber tocado** un instrumento **verdadero**), él continuó persiguiendo su sueño. Segovia **se propuso como meta llevar** los estudios de guitarra a todas las universidades del mundo. Y así fue. Segovia **consiguió** lo que **buscaba**.

Este guitarrista universal dio su primer concierto en España a los 16 años, aunque su debut profesional no llegó hasta los 20. Su programa original **incluyó** transcripciones de Tárrega, así como sus propias transcripciones de Bach y de otros maestros. Muchos músicos **supuestamente serios** creyeron que el **público se reiría** tanto de Segovia, que **tendría** que **salir** del escenario porque **creían** que no se podía tocar música clásica con una guitarra. Sin embargo, Segovia **asombró** a **los asistentes** con su arte. El único problema con el que **se encontró** fue que la guitarra **no podía producir suficiente sonido** como para **llenar** el **salón**.

Con el paso de los años, Segovia perfeccionó su técnica experimentando con maderas y diseños nuevos, para aumentar la amplificación natural de la guitarra. Más adelante, con la llegada de las cuerdas de nylon, las guitarras empezaron a producir tonos más constantes, a la vez que proyectaban el sonido más lejos.

La búsqueda de Segovia le llevó a Norteamérica en 1928 para ofrecer su primer concierto en Nueva York. Una vez más, su público quedó abrumado con la técnica de su guitarra y la maestría de sus manos, consiguiendo así que sus disidentes empezaran a apreciar la guitarra clásica. Su éxito en la ciudad de los rascacielos le condujo a otras ofertas para más presentaciones en América y Europa e, incluso, un viaje a Oriente en 1929. Segovia y la guitarra clásica habían llegado.

Mientras viajaba por el mundo, el músico español y su guitarra se hicieron más y más populares. A partir de entonces, compositores de todo el mundo empezaron a crear piezas originales específicas para guitarra.

Asimismo, Segovia adaptó obras maestras a la guitarra. De hecho, su trascripción del Chaconne de Bach es una de las piezas más famosas y difíciles de dominar. Al escuchar la realizada por el maestro español, parece como si la intención de Bach hubiera sido componerla originalmente para guitarra en vez de para violín.

Además de crear un amplio repertorio y de mejorar la calidad sonora de la guitarra, Segovia consiguió pasar su legado de conocimientos a una nueva generación. El compositor español tuvo muchos alumnos a lo largo de su carrera. Entre los más famosos se encuentran Christopher Parkening, John Williams, Elliot Fisk y Oscar Ghiglia. Estos discípulos, entre muchos otros, continúan hoy la tradición de Segovia, a la vez que extienden la presencia, el repertorio y los límites musicales de la guitarra clásica.

**con el paso de los años:** as years went by
**perfeccionó/perfeccionar:** he improved/to improve; to perfect
**maderas:** woods, timbers
**diseños:** designs
**aumentar:** to increase
**más adelante:** later
**llegada:** arrival
**cuerdas de nylon:** nylon strings
**tonos más constantes:** more consistent tones
**a la vez:** at the same time
**más lejos:** further
**llevó/ llevar:** it took /to take
**quedó:** was
**abrumó/abrumar:** overwhelmed/ to overwhelm
**maestría:** expertise, skill
**consiguiendo:** obtaining; reaching
**éxito:** success
**rascacielos:** skyscrapers
**condujo/conducir:** it led him/to lead
**habían llegado/llegar:** they had arrived/to arrive
**viajaba/viajar:** he traveled/to travel
**se hicieron/ hacerse:** they became/ to become
**a partir de entonces:** from then on
**empezaron/empezar:** they started/ to start
**crear:** to create
**piezas originales:** original pieces
**asimismo:** also; as well
**adaptó/adaptar:** he adapted/to adapt
**obras maestras:** masterpieces
**dominar:** to master
**parece/parecer:** it seems/to seem
**hubiera sido componerla:** it would have been to compose it
**amplio/ampliar:** expanded/to expand
**repertorio:** repertoire
**calidad sonora:** sound quality
**pasar:** to go to
**legado:** legacy
**conocimientos:** knowledge
**alumnos:** students
**extienden/extender:** they spread/ to spread

es curioso: it is funny, it is curious
uno no valora/valorar: one does not
  appreciate/to appreciate
cerca: close
se encuentra/encontrarse: it is/to be
demasiado lejos: too far away
a pesar de: in spite of
haber nacido/nacer: having been
  born/to be born
crecido/crecer: grown/to grow
recién cumplidos los 18 años: right
  after my 18th birthday
estadía: stay
me prestó/prestar: lent me/to lend
obra: work
fuego: fire
a través: throughout
personajes: characters
míticos: mythical
tomo: volume
incluye/incluir: it includes/to include
mitos y leyendas: myths and legends
llegada: arrival
comprende/comprender: it includes/
  to comprise, to include
finales: end
siglo: century
cubre/cubrir: it covers/to cover
en detalle: in detail
acontecimientos: events
le valió/valer: won him/to win
Premio del Libro Americano:
  American Book Award
redescubrimiento: rediscovery
escritor: writer
periodista: journalist
saltó a la fama mundial: he became
  famous all around the world
obra periodística: journalistic work
venas: veins
trabajo de investigación: investigative
  work
dejaron/dejar: they left/to leave
legado: legacy
más poderosas: most powerful
utiliza/utilizar: it uses/to use
se ha quedado/quedarse: it has
  stayed/to stay
conmigo: with me
es aquella que: it is the one that
colonizadores: colonists, settlers
abrieron/abrir: they opened/to open
se drena/drenar: is drained/to drain

# Eduardo Galeano
## URUGUAY

**Es curioso** como a veces **uno no valora** lo que tiene **cerca** hasta el momento en que **se encuentra** ya **demasiado lejos**. **A pesar de haber nacido** y **crecido** en Uruguay, mi primer contacto con la obra del escritor uruguayo Eduardo Galeano fue **recién cumplidos los 18 años**, durante una **estadía** en Alemania, y gracias a un amigo venezolano que **me prestó** uno de sus libros.

La introducción a Galeano fue nada más y nada menos que con su famosa **obra** *Memorias del **fuego***. En esta trilogía el autor describe la historia de América **a través** de pequeñas historias y **personajes**, muchos reales y otros **míticos**. En el primer **tomo incluye mitos y leyendas** indígenas, memorias previas a la **llegada** de los europeos. El segundo tomo **comprende** la historia de las Américas durante el período que va desde la llegada de los españoles hasta **finales** del **siglo** XIX.

Por último, en el tercer tomo, **cubre en detalle** los **acontecimientos** del siglo XX. Esta obra **le valió** el **Premio del Libro Americano** en 1989, y para mí, representó el **redescubrimiento** de América Latina.

Este **escritor, periodista** y poeta uruguayo **saltó a la fama mundial** con su **obra periodística** *Las **venas** abiertas de América Latina*. En ese gran **trabajo de investigación**, el autor describe lo que años de colonización **dejaron** como **legado** al continente americano. Una de las imágenes **más poderosas** que **utiliza** y que **se ha quedado conmigo** a través de los años **es aquella que** compara a países latinoamericanos con una mano abierta, donde por sus venas las vías de comunicación que los **colonizadores abrieron se drena** al continente de sus riquezas.

**Fuerte** crítico social y activista, Galeano, que **ha sido traducido** a casi 20 idiomas, es un viejo **defensor** de los **grupos menos privilegiados** de la sociedad. Entre sus trabajos **más conocidos se encuentran** *Días y noches de amor y de **guerra**, Nosotros decimos no, El libro de los **abrazos*** y Las ***palabras andantes.***

Sus intereses son muy **amplios**, **como lo demuestra su libro** *El fútbol a sol y **sombra***, donde habla sobre su **deporte** favorito, o el libro ***Patas arriba**: la escuela del mundo **al revés***, donde **cuestiona** varios aspectos de la vida moderna. Su libro más reciente **se titula** *Bocas del tiempo* y **abarca** temas tan diversos como el agua, la música y la guerra.

Es imposible estar al día con la obra de un autor tan **prolífico**. Con esa forma tan rica y poética que lo caracteriza, Galeano escribe constantemente. Con innumerables **ensayos** y artículos periodísticos, **nos brinda** su opinión y **mirada crítica acerca** de los diferentes acontecimientos mundiales. A través de sus **preguntas nos lleva a reflexionar**, a pensar; a veces **nos hace reír**, otras, **nos saca una lágrima.**

**Exiliado** durante la dictadura militar de los años 70 y 80, Galeano **se encuentra instalado actualmente** en su **ciudad natal**, Montevideo. Su casa, **ubicada** en el **barrio** de Malvín, es **fácilmente** identificable por las **pinturas** en rojo que decoran la **fachada** y que son obra del **propio escritor**. Viviendo a tan pocas **cuadras** del Río de la Plata, a Galeano **se le puede ver a menudo caminando a lo largo** de la **rambla**, disfrutando del aire y del **mar**. O **se le puede encontrar** en uno de los **tantos** cafés que **pueblan** las **esquinas** de la ciudad y que, **como él bien dice**, **invitan** a la **charla** y la confesión.

**fuerte:** strong
**ha sido traducido/tranducir:** (his work) has been translated/to translate
**defensor:** defender
**grupos menos privilegiados:** least privileged groups
**más conocidos:** famous, more known
**se encuentran/encontrarse:** they are/to be
**guerra:** war
**abrazos:** hugs
**palabras andantes:** walking words
**amplios:** broad
**como lo demuestra su libro:** as it is shown in his book
**sombra:** shade
**deporte:** sport
**patas arriba:** in a mess
**al revés:** upside down
**cuestiona/cuestionar:** he questions/to question
**se titula/titularse:** it is entitled/to be entitled
**abarca/abarcar:** it covers/to cover
**prolífico:** prolific, productive
**ensayos:** essay
**nos brinda/brindar:** it provides us/to provide, to offer
**mirada crítica:** critical look
**acerca:** about
**preguntas:** questions
**nos lleva a reflexionar:** he makes us reflect
**nos hace reír:** he makes us laugh
**nos saca una lágrima:** he makes us cry
**exiliado:** exiled
**se encuentra instalado:** he lives
**actualmente:** these days
**ciudad natal:** home town
**ubicada:** located
**barrio:** neighborhood
**fácilmente:** easily
**pinturas:** paintings
**fachada:** facade
**propio escritor:** the writer himself
**cuadras:** blocks
**se le puede ver:** (Galeano) can be seen
**a menudo:** often
**caminando/caminar:** walking/to walk
**a lo largo:** along
**rambla:** boulevard
**mar:** sea
**se le puede encontrar:** he can be found
**tantos:** many
**pueblan/poblar:** they populate/to populate
**esquinas:** corners
**como él bien dice:** as he well says
**invitan/invitar:** they invite/to invite
**charla:** chat

# Examina tu comprensión

## García Márquez, page 88

**1.** What career did Márquez pursue before he started to write?

**2.** What genre are his books?

**3.** What other career did Márquez work in?

**4.** Who are the favorite writers admired by Márquez?

## Diego Rivera, page 90

**1.** Who was the woman in Rivera's life who assisted with his political paintings?

**2.** Rivera had a distinctive style of painting in what venue?

**3.** His mural on the national palace was his interpretation of what?

**4.** What were the ideals reflected in Diego's murals?

## Frida, page 92

**1.** When Kahlo was young she had an accident that changed her life. What were the consequences of her accident?

**2.** What was her first painting?

**4.** Who did Kahlo marry and how did that change her passion for painting?

## Celia Cruz, page 94

**1.** Cruz had a vocation in music but a mission for what?

**2.** Cruz holds the honor of being the first Hispanic woman to do what?

**3.** Cruz died at age 77 of what illness?

## Rubén Diarío, page 95

**1.** Darío was a child prodigy who is well known as what?

# Test your comprehension

## Che Guevera, page 96

**1.** As a child Guevara was home schooled. Why?

**2.** During his medical studies what did he discover? What did this prompt him to do?

**3.** How did Che Guevara die and where?

## Andrés Segovia, page 100

**1.** At what age did Segovia's love for music/guitar begin? When was his first concert?

**2.** Segovia encountered a unique problem with his guitar/music. What was this problem and how did he fix it?

**3.** Segovia adapted other masterpieces to guitar. What is considered the most famous and difficult?

## Unamuno, page 98

**1.** Unanamo held what position at the University of Salamanca? What led to this position ending?

**2.** What did Unanamo's *Diario Intimo* contain?

## Eduardo Galeano, page 102

**1.** In the trilogy *Memorias del Fuego*, what is discussed/described in each section?

**2.** Where does Galeano live and what might you see him doing there?

Dime cómo te diviertes y te diré quién eres.

José Ortega y Gasset

# Deportes

| | |
|---|---|
| **imitar:** to imitiate | |
| **los pájaros:** the birds | |
| **enclavado:** located | |
| **corazón:** heart | |
| **se encuentra/encontrar:** it is located/ to be located | |
| **más lindos:** most beautiful | |
| **altura:** height | |
| **sobre el nivel del mar:** above sea level | |
| **zona serrana:** mountain region | |
| **se destaca/destacar:** it stands out/ to stand out | |
| **no sólo...sino también:** not only... but also | |
| **paisajes de cuento:** fairy tale landscapes | |
| **abanico:** range | |
| **actividades recreativas:** recreational activities | |
| **sin duda:** without a doubt | |
| **estrella:** star | |
| **vuelo libre:** free flight | |
| **aladeltas:** hang gliders | |
| **parapentes:** paragliders | |
| **planeadores:** gliders | |
| **intentar:** to try | |
| **aves:** birds | |
| **y lo mejor:** and the best part | |
| **no hay que hacer ningún curso especial:** there is no need to take a special course | |
| **primer vuelo:** first flight | |
| **animarse:** to fancy to go or do it | |
| **contactar:** to contact | |
| **pilotos biplaza:** two seat pilot | |
| **se encuentran/encontrarse:** there is/to be | |
| **mirador:** viewpoint | |
| **sagrado:** sacred | |
| **rampa de despegue:** takeoff ramp | |
| **allí:** there | |
| **proporciona/proporcionar:** it provides/to provide | |
| **casco:** helmet | |
| **detalla/detallar:** details/to give the details of, to list | |
| **travesía:** flight | |
| **una vez:** once | |
| **sentidos:** senses | |
| **se exacerban/exacerbar:** they are exacerbated/to exacerbate | |
| **mente:** mind | |
| **se pone en blanco:** it goes blank | |
| **disfrute:** enjoyment | |
| **lo invade/invadir:** it invades/to invade | |
| **flotar:** to float | |
| **pluma:** feather | |
| **no sería/ser:** it would not be/to be | |
| **cruzarse:** to pass somebody | |
| **mitad del vuelo:** middle of the flight | |
| **aterrizaje:** landing | |
| **justo al lado:** right beside | |
| **si hace calor:** if it is hot | |
| **refrescarse:** to cool down | |
| **cálidas aguas:** warm waters | |

# El arte de imitar a los pájaros
## ARGENTINA

A sólo 90 kilómetros de Córdoba capital, **enclavado** en el **corazón** del Valle de Punilla, **se encuentra** uno de los pueblos **más lindos** de esta región: La Cumbre. A 1.100 metros de **altura sobre el nivel del mar**, esta **zona serrana se destaca no sólo** por sus incomparables **paisajes de cuento sino también** por su enorme **abanico** de posibilidades para realizar **actividades recreativas** y de turismo aventura. **Sin duda**, la **estrella** en este tema es el **vuelo libre**. Desde **aladeltas** a **parapentes**, pasando por **planeadores**, todo es válido a la hora de **intentar** imitar a las **aves**. **Y lo mejor: no hay que hacer ningún curso especial** para el **primer vuelo**, sólo **animarse**.

Para volar en parapente, lo primero es **contactar** con alguno de los **pilotos biplaza** o ir directamente a Cuchi Corral, donde **se encuentran** el antiguo **mirador sagrado** y la **rampa de despegue**. **Allí**, el instructor **proporciona casco** y **detalla** las cuestiones mínimas a tener en cuenta durante la **travesía**. **Una vez** en el aire, los **sentidos se exacerban**, la **mente se pone en blanco** y el **disfrute lo invade** todo. Volar es **flotar**, flotar en el aire. Como una **pluma**, como un pájaro. O como un cóndor, al que por otra parte **no sería** raro **cruzarse** en **mitad del vuelo**.

El **aterrizaje** es suave, **justo al lado** del Río Pintos. Y **si hace calor**, y uno puede **refrescarse** en sus **cálidas aguas**, la gloria es completa.

# Acampando en San Felipe
## MEXICO

**No hay nada como acampar** al **aire libre** bajo las **estrellas, fuera** de la ciudad y **gozando** de la **naturaleza**. Uno de los mejores lugares para acampar en México es en las **playas** de San Felipe, **situadas** al norte del estado de Baja California, cerca de Mexicali (México). Con sus playas **calientes**, San Felipe **atrae** a mucha gente que quiere **escapar** de la vida de las **ciudades**. Este lugar es uno de los favoritos para **jugar** en la **arena** y el **mar**.

San Felipe es árido y caliente, y el **terreno** que **lo rodea** es extremadamente desértico, **aunque** este **ambiente solitario** es lo que muchas personas encuentran **relajante**. Aquí **reinan** la **paz** y la **tranquilidad**. El **reloj parece caminar** más **despacio** y uno **se siente** como transportado a otro tiempo, a otro lugar, **alejado** de cualquier preocupación.

Situado al lado del **Golfo** de Baja California, San Felipe **proporciona** una experiencia **encantadora** a aquellos que **disfrutan** del calor. Las aguas del golfo son **tibias** a todas horas del día. Uno puede **nadar** por la noche y **sentir** el agua caliente, o **estirarse** en la arena y **mirar** al **cielo lleno de** estrellas. San Felipe es uno de los mejores lugares para observar las **maravillas** celestiales. No hay muchas **luces** fuera de la ciudad, y el cielo es tan **claro** y lleno de estrellas **brillantes** que en las noches en que no hay **luna**, las mismas estrellas **dan** suficiente luz como para **alumbrar** las playas. Es tan increíble que es difícil de **creer incluso estando** allí.

**acampando/acampar:** camping/ to camp
**no hay nada como:** there is nothing better than
**acampar:** to camp
**aire libre:** outdoors
**estrellas:** stars
**fuera:** out
**gozando/gozar:** enjoying/to enjoy
**naturaleza:** nature
**playas:** beaches
**situadas:** located
**calientes:** hot
**atrae/atraer:** it attracts/to attract
**escapar:** to get away
**ciudades:** cities
**jugar:** to play
**arena:** sand
**mar:** sea
**terreno:** land
**lo rodea/rodear:** it surrounds it/ to surround
**aunque:** even though
**ambiente:** atmosphere
**solitario:** solitary
**relajante:** relaxing
**reinan/reinar:** they reign/to reign
**paz:** peace
**tranquilidad:** calmness, tranquility
**reloj:** clock
**parece/parecer:** it seems/to seem
**caminar:** to walk
**despacio:** slow
**se siente/sentirse:** one feels/to feel
**alejado:** far away
**golfo:** gulf
**proporciona/proporcionar:** it provides/to provide
**encantadora:** charming
**disfrutan/disfrutar:** they enjoy/ to enjoy
**tibias:** tepid
**nadar:** to swim
**sentir:** to feel
**estirarse:** to stretch
**mirar:** to look
**cielo:** sky
**lleno de:** plenty of
**maravillas:** wonders
**luces:** lights
**claro:** light
**brillantes:** gleaming
**luna:** moon
**dan/dar:** they give/to give
**alumbrar:** to light, to illuminate
**creer:** to believe
**incluso:** even
**estando/estar:** being/to be

**miles:** thousands
**visitan/visitar:** they visit/to visit
**buscando/buscar:** searching/to search
**en verdad:** really
**condiciones ideales:** ideal conditions
**aguas cálidas:** warm waters
**unas 700 millas:** some 700 miles
**gente amable:** nice people
**precios razonables:** reasonable prices
**la estación del año:** season of the year
**algunas de ellas:** some of them
**especialmente acondicionadas:** specially prepared, equipped
**estancia tranquila:** calm stay
**sin vida nocturna:** without nightlife
**por lo general:** generally
**más apropiado:** more appropriate
**desde ... hasta:** from ... to
**por otra parte:** on the other hand
**si queremos/querer:** if we want/ to want
**dirigirnos/dirigir:** to direct us to/ to direct
**tanto....como:** both...and
**en cambio:** on the other hand
**estará en pleno auge:** it will be at its very peak
**teniendo en cuenta:** taking into account
**planear:** to plan
**siempre hay que pensar:** it is always necessary to think
**elegir:** to choose
**excursiones diarias:** daily tours
**coche de alquiler:** rental car
**entre ciudades:** among cities
**pasaremos más tiempo/pasar:** we'll spend more time/to spend
**carretera:** road
**debido principalmente a:** mainly due to
**seguridad:** security
**cualquier lugar del país:** any place in the country
**índices de criminalidad:** crime rates
**confiados:** confident
**muy poco frecuentes:** very infrequent
**salpicadero:** dashboard
**reloj:** watch
**antes de ir:** before going

# Surfing en Costa Rica
## COSTA RICA

**Miles** de personas **visitan** Costa Rica **buscando** las mejores zonas para practicar el surf. Y Costa Rica reúne **en verdad** las **condiciones ideales** para la práctica de este deporte: **aguas cálidas, unas 700 millas** de costa, **gente amable** y unos **precios razonables**. Las zonas para practicar el surf en Costa Rica están definidas por su localización y **la estación del año**. Podemos distinguir cuatro zonas: La Costa Pacífica Norte, con playas como Tamarindo o Playa Negra, **algunas de ellas especialmente acondicionadas** para los surfeadores que prefieren una **estancia tranquila, sin vida nocturna**. Esta zona es **por lo general** el destino **más apropiado desde** diciembre **hasta** abril.

**Por otra parte, si queremos** practicar el surf entre los meses de mayo y noviembre, será preferible **dirigirnos tanto** a la Costa Pacífica Sur (Playas de Matapalo o Pavones) **como** a la Costa Pacífica Central (Playa Hermosa, Dominical). **En cambio**, la Costa del Caribe **estará en pleno auge** entre noviembre y marzo. **Teniendo en cuenta** estas características, podemos **planear** nuestras vacaciones, aunque **siempre hay que pensar** que estas diferencias son generales. Una buena idea para disfrutar de nuestro viaje a Costa Rica y practicar el surfing es **elegir** una ciudad, y desde ésta hacer **excursiones diarias** a otras ciudades en **coche de alquiler**. La distancia **entre ciudades** varía entre una hora y diez minutos. Así, **pasaremos más tiempo** en el agua y menos en la **carretera**.

Costa Rica es uno de los países con más turismo, **debido principalmente a** su **seguridad** en prácticamente **cualquier lugar del país**. Sus **índices de criminalidad** son bastantes bajos. Pero no seamos **confiados**, aunque en los hoteles los robos son **muy poco frecuentes**. ¡No es una buena idea guardar en el **salpicadero** del auto nuestro **reloj**, pasaporte u otros objetos valiosos **antes de ir** al agua!

# Escalando el Nevado Sajama
## BOLIVIA

**¿Quién no pensó alguna vez** en tocar el **cielo** con las **manos**? **Escalar** el Nevado Sajama y llegar a la **cima** es una forma de **sentir algo parecido**. Nevado Sajama es el **pico** más alto del Bolivia. Son 6542 metros de **roca maciza** que se elevan en la provincia de Oruro.

Aunque esta aventura **no es fácil** ni es para cualquiera, el que **se proponga** realizarla y se prepare con varios días de **entrenamiento** y un **buen guía de montaña**. La preparación consiste básicamente en **ejercicios físicos** de aclimatación a la **altura** y una **alimentación adecuada**. Los **entendidos recomiendan pasar** varios días en la base del cerro, y hacer **ascensos** y **descensos** a montañas cercanas **combinándolos** con **días de descanso** y un plan **alimentario energético**. En estas altitudes el clima es riguroso y muchas veces hostil por lo que es muy importante **contar con indumentaria** especial y por supuesto el equipo básico: **arnés de cintura**, **mosquetones de seguridad** y **calzado de gran adherencia**.

La escalada es un deporte considerado de **alto riesgo**, en el que no sólo se utiliza la **fortaleza física** de **brazos** y **piernas** sino también **destreza técnica** y claridad mental para tomar las decisiones **adecuadas** a cada paso. Es una experiencia fascinante y **única** en la que **se templa** el espíritu, **se construye** una fuerza de **voluntad de acero** y el compañerismo juega un **papel** fundamental.

será/ser: it will be/to be
chiquitos: boys, male children
varones: males
cumpleaños: birthdays
regalan/regalar: they give
pelota de fútbol: soccer ball
camiseta: t-shirt
equipo: team
intuye/intuir: he suspects/to suspect
temprana edad: early age
ciertas: certain
habilidades: skills
hará planes: they make plans
proyectará/proyectar: they project/
   to project
soñará/soñar: he will dream/to dream
verlo: to see him
preferido: favorite
siempre: always
hay tiempo: there is time
picadito: game without a serious
   rivalry, usually between friends
ida al campo: trip to the country side
juntarse: to get together
acompañado: accompanied
asado: roast
no hay mejor: there is not a better
siguiente: following
se comentarán/comentar: they
   mention; comment/to comment
hazañas: deeds, exploits
desaciertos: mistakes, errors
jugador: player
desmesurada: excessive
como si: as if
valores: values
decisivos: decisive
piel de gallina: goose bumps (literally:
   chicken skin)
aficionados: fans, enthusiasts
genera/generar: it generates/
   to generate
amargura: bitterness
llanto: crying
gritos: shouts
seguidores: fans

# El fútbol, pasión de multitudes
## ARGENTINA

¿Por qué **será** que de **chiquitos**, a los **varones** argentinos, en alguno de sus **cumpleaños** les **regalan** una **pelota de fútbol** o la **camiseta** de algún **equipo**? Si algún padre **intuye** que su hijo desde **temprana edad** tiene **ciertas habilidades** con ese deporte, **hará planes**, **proyectará** ilusiones y **soñará** con **verlo** jugar en su equipo **preferido**.

Los domingos **siempre hay tiempo** para un **picadito** con los amigos, para una **ida al campo** en grupo o, simplemente, para **juntarse** a ver por televisión al equipo de sus sueños. Si todo esto viene luego **acompañado** de un **asado**, **no hay mejor** domingo. Al día **siguiente se comentarán** las **hazañas** o **desaciertos** de cada **jugador** con una pasión **desmesurada**, **como si** en cada relato se jugaran **valores** e ideales importantísimos y **decisivos**. El fútbol en Argentina es pura pasión y emoción, un deporte que pone la **piel de gallina** a sus **aficionados** y que **genera** tensión, alegría, **amargura**, **llanto** y **gritos** entre sus **seguidores**.

Gran parte del fenómeno en que el fútbol **se ha convertido** en Argentina **se lo debemos** a su máximo ídolo, Diego Armando Maradona. "El Pelusa", como **se le conoce mundialmente**, **ha dejado** un **legado sin igual** así como miles de niños que quieren **imitarlo**. Verlo en el campo era ver jugar al mejor. Maradona **mostraba** una habilidad superior con el balón, una **gracia digna de dioses**, una magia de otra dimensión. **Se desplazaba** como quien lo hace suspendido a unos centímetros **del suelo**. El campo era su **hogar**, la pelota una extensión de su **cuerpo**, sus compañeros de equipo un apoyo y sus rivales, obstáculos necesarios, pero **fáciles de sortear**, hasta llegar al gol. El número 10 que llevaba a su **espalda** coincidía, **sin duda**, con la **calidad** de sus habilidades como futbolista.

**se ha convertido/convertir:** it has become/to become
**se lo debemos/deber:** we owe it/to owe
**se le conoce/conocer:** he is known/to know
**mundialmente:** worldwide
**ha dejado/dejar:** he has left/to leave
**legado sin igual:** unrivaled legacy
**imitarlo/imitar:** imitate him/to imitate
**mostraba/mostrar:** he showed/to show
**gracia digna de dioses:** grace worthy of gods
**se desplazaba/desplazar:** he moved/to move
**del suelo:** from the ground
**hogar:** home
**cuerpo:** body
**fáciles de sortear:** easy to avoid, easy to get around
**espalda:** back
**sin duda:** without a doubt
**calidad:** quality

**Comunidad Autónoma:** Autonomous Region

**País Vasco:** Basque country

**hace varios siglos:** several centuries ago

**en la actualidad:** nowadays

**no sólo ... sino también:** not only ...but also

**concretamente:** in particular

**apuestas:** betting

**permitidas:** allowed

**es más:** furthermore

**ha llegado/llegar:** it arrived/ to arrive

**fiesta alegre:** joyful party

**se practicaba/practicar:** it was played/ to play

**en realidad:** in fact

**hacía referencia:** it referenced

**frontón:** arena for Jai Alai

**en sí:** in/by itself

**pelota:** ball

**posteriormente:** afterwards

**empezó a utilizarce:** it started to be used

**quizás:** perhaps

**bases y reglas:** rules and basis

**a pesar de:** in spite of

**no todo el mundo:** not everybody

**con detalle:** in depth

**no ha sufrido variaciones:** it didn´t change

**acción:** action

**velocidad:** speed

**cancha:** court

**paredes:** walls

**aunque:** though

**se mencionó/mencionar:** it was mentioned/to mention

**anteriormente:** before

**hecha de granito:** made of granite

**suficientemente sólido:** strong enough

**soportar:** to support; to hold up

**golpes:** hits

**por último:** finally

**pantalla de seguridad:** security screen

**alambre:** wire

# El jai alai
## ESPAÑA

Este deporte, nacido en la **Comunidad Autónoma** del **País Vasco hace varios siglos,** es **en la actualidad** muy popular **no sólo** en esta región española, **sino también** Latinoamérica y Estados Unidos, **concretamente** en los estados de Florida o Connecticut, donde las **apuestas** están **permitidas**. **Es más**, incluso **ha llegado** a países como China y Egipto.

El término "Jai Alai"es una palabra de origen vasco que significa **"fiesta alegre"**, pues este juego **se practicaba** normalmente durante las fiestas anuales. **En realidad**, Jai Alai **hacía referencia**, originariamente, al **frontón**. El juego **en sí** se llama "**pelota**" o "Pelota vasca". **Posteriormente** el nombre "Jai Alai" **empezó a utilizarse** también para hacer referencia al juego. **Quizás** resulte interesante describir las **bases y reglas** de este juego, pues, **a pesar de** su popularidad, **no todo el mundo** lo conoce **con detalle**. Desde el nacimiento de este juego, hace más de 500 años, **no ha sufrido** muchas variaciones, y sus principales características siguen siendo la **acción** y la **velocidad**.

Jai Alai, o pelota vasca, se juega en una **cancha** con tres **paredes**, también llamada frontón (**aunque** su nombre original es Jai Alai, como **se mencionó anteriormente**). La pared principal de la cancha está **hecha de granito** ya que es un material **suficientemente sólido** para **soportar** los **golpes** de la pelota y las otras dos paredes están hechas de cemento. **Por último**, hay una **pantalla de seguridad** hecha de **alambre**, situada en la parte de la cancha sin pared, para proteger a los espectadores.

Los pelotaris, o **jugadores**, tienen que **lanzar** la pelota contra la pared principal **usando** una **cesta de mimbre atada al brazo** del jugador.

El **propósito** de este juego es lanzar la pelota contra la pared **de forma que** el jugador contrario **no pueda golpearla a su regreso**. La pelota, que está hecha de **caucho** y que puede **alcanzar** una velocidad de 230 kilómetros por hora, puede golpear la pared lateral o la posterior, pero nunca la zona de los espectadores. Un **dato muy significativo** es que estas pelotas tienen una vida de **tan sólo** 20 minutos. Con esto, podemos **hacernos una idea** de la fuerza y la velocidad con que se lanzan las pelotas contra el frontón.

Las reglas de juego son **bastante parecidas** a las del tenis. El jugador debe lanzar la pelota **por encima** de la línea de servicio y debe **rebotar** entre las líneas 4 y 7 del frontón. **Si no lo consigue**, el equipo contrario ganará un punto. **La mayoría de** las variantes de Jai Alai se juega a siete puntos, que **se doblan después de la primera vuelta**. Es un **juego de rotación** con ocho jugadores/equipos. Estos equipos también pueden ser dobles, **es decir, formados** por dos jugadores, uno en la parte **delantera**, y otro en la parte **trasera**. El juego es eliminatorio: el equipo ganador jugará **con el siguiente**, y así sucesivamente **hasta que haya un sólo ganador**.

Esta es una descripción básica, pues **existen** muchas variantes del juego en todo el mundo, **desde** la forma inicial de juego, en el norte de España, **hasta** las reglas **fijadas** en países donde este juego **llegó gracias a** por los emigrantes vascos.

---

**jugadores:** players
**lanzar:** to throw
**usando:** using
**cesta de mimbre:** wicker basket
**atada al brazo:** attached to the arm
**propósito:** purpose
**de forma que:** so that
**no pueda golpearla:** he cannot hit it
**a su regreso:** when it comes back
**caucho:** rubber
**alcanzar:** to reach
**dato muy significativo:** very significant data
**tan sólo:** only
**hacernos una idea:** we can get an idea
**bastante parecidas:** much alike
**por encima:** over
**rebotar:** to bounce
**si no lo consigue:** if he cannot make it
**la mayoría de:** most of
**se doblan/doblar:** they are doubled/to double
**después de la primera vuelta:** after the first round
**juego de rotación:** rotation play
**es decir:** that is to say
**formados:** formed
**delantera:** front
**trasera:** back
**con el siguiente:** with the next one
**hasta que haya un sólo ganador:** there is a single winner
**existen/existir:** they exist/to exist
**desde … hasta:** from … to
**fijadas:** fixed
**llegó/llegar:** it arrived/to arrive
**gracias a:** thanks to

# Sierra Nevada, el paraíso blanco
## ESPAÑA

Sierra Nevada es la principal **estación de esquí** del sur de Europa y **se encuentra situada** a **tan sólo** 30 kilómetros de la ciudad de Granada, en Andalucía. **Gracias a** su altitud (entre 2.000 y 3.300 metros), se puede **disfrutar** de la **nieve** durante todo el **invierno** y hasta bien entrada la **primavera**, **a veces** incluso hasta el mes de mayo. Hay **posibilidad** de practicar **no sólo** el esquí **sino también** el *snowboard*, el esquí **parapente**, el **patinaje sobre hielo** y **un sinfín de** actividades más. **De hecho**, estas instalaciones **cuentan con** 53 **pistas**, un *snowpark*, 338 **cañones de nieve** y varios restaurantes.

Sierra Nevada **posee instalaciones** de **alta calidad**, con unas **cabinas remontadoras con cabida** para 14 personas. Las **pistas** son **anchas** y con una buena **señalización**, y hay para **todo el mundo**, **tanto** si los visitantes son principiantes (pistas **largas** y con poca **pendiente**) **como** si son expertos **esquiadores** (pistas rojas y negras), **sin olvidar** los **niveles** intermedios: las pistas azules, también largas y **cómodas**. En la década de los 90, estas pistas **acogieron** la final de la Copa de Europa de Esquí Alpino y los Campeonatos del Mundo.

**Sin embargo**, en Sierra Nevada no sólo se practican deportes de nieve. Para aquellos que quieran algo diferente y que quieran disfrutar de la **naturaleza**, existen actividades variadas como **montar a caballo** o hacer rutas en **bicicleta de montaña**. El **emplazamiento** es ideal, pues **nos encontramos** en el Parque Natural de Sierra Nevada, declarado Reserva de la Biosfera por la UNESCO en 1986. El parque tiene una superficie aproximada de 83.000 hectáreas y **se extiende** por las provincias de Granada y Almería. Posee una **amplia** variedad de **paisajes** y **climas** con una de las diversidades botánicas más importantes de Europa.

# Conociendo Guatemala a caballo
## GUATEMALA

Una forma diferente de conocer este **hermoso país** es, **sin duda**, **haciendo** una excursión a caballo. Es realmente la forma ideal de combinar el turismo activo con **experiencias únicas**. **No importa si** usted **nunca** ha **montado a caballo** o es un experto.

Los **recorridos** de estas excursiones son muy variados y **se puede** disfrutar de la **belleza** de los **paisajes** y recorrer zonas **no frecuentadas** por el **turismo masivo**. Las posibilidades son innumerables, entre las cuales se puede **citar** las **visitas** a granjas, pasar por **pueblos indígenas aislados**, por ruinas coloniales y por **bosques tropicales** y volcanes, o también disfrutar de las espectaculares vistas desde **diversos miradores**, explorar **cuevas** y **dormir bajo las estrellas**.

Actualmente existen diversas ofertas en el **mercado**. Algunas de ellas proporcionan **no sólo** excursiones a caballo, **sino también** diversos itinerarios utilizando **vehículos "todo terreno"**, sin olvidar la oportunidad de **navegar** los **ríos guatemaltecos** en **barca** y visitar interesantes sitios mayas, como Topoxté o Ixtinto. **Recuerde** que siempre será preferible si en la excursión les acompañan **guías bilingües** y en caso de tratarse de una excursión a caballo, es importante que éstos estén bien **alimentados** y **entrenados**.

Una excursión a caballo es la forma perfecta de conocer y **amar** la biodiversidad de las tierras y la cultura de Guatemala.

Finalmente, unos **consejos prácticos**: es conveniente llevar **botas de equitación**, **pantalones largos**, protector solar, **gafas de sol**, **prismáticos**, **ropa para lluvia** y **sobre todo**, lo más importante, **deseo de disfrutar** de un **viaje relajado**, en unos **parajes inolvidables**.

---

**hermoso país:** beautiful country
**sin duda:** without doubt
**haciendo/hacer:** making/to make
**experiencias únicas:** unique experience
**no importa si:** it doesn't matter if
**nunca:** never
**montado a caballo:** rode a horse
**recorridos:** routes
**se puede/poder:** you can/can
**belleza:** beauty
**paisajes:** landscapes
**no frecuentadas/to frequent:** not frequented/to frequent
**turismo masivo:** massive tourism
**citar:** to arrange
**visitas:** visits
**granjas:** farms
**pueblos indígenas aislados:** isolated indigenous towns
**bosques tropicales:** tropical forests
**diversos miradores:** diverse viewpoints
**cuevas:** caves
**dormir bajo las estrellas:** to sleep under the stars
**mercado:** market
**no sólo...sino también:** not only... but also
**vehículos todo terreno:** all-terrain vehicles
**navegar:** to navigate
**ríos guatemaltecos:** Guatemalan rivers
**barca:** boat
**recuerde/recordar:** remember/ to remember
**guías bilingües:** bilingual guides
**alimentados/alimentar:** fed/to feed
**entrenados/entrenar:** trained/to train
**amar:** to love
**consejos prácticos:** practical advice
**botas de equitación:** horseback riding boots
**pantalones largos:** long pants
**gafas de sol:** sunglasses
**prismáticos:** binoculars
**ropa para lluvia:** rain clothing
**sobre todo:** above all
**deseo de disfrutar:** a desire to enjoy
**viaje relajado:** relaxed travel, trip
**parajes inolvidables:** unforgettable places

# El senderismo en el Perú
PERU

**Seguir senderos** zigzagueantes, pasar por **angostos puentes abismales hechos de soguillas**, **cruzar** ríos **caudalosos**, **atravesar** desiertos, ascender montañas, **bajar colinas** o **abrirse paso** por una tropical **selva** son solamente algunas de las emociones que **nos ofrece** el senderimo en la increíble geografía peruana.

El Perú, **mítico país** de los incas, **no sólo** es conocido por su **milenaria** cultura y sus fabulosas construcciones prehispánicas **sino** que, gracias a la incomparable belleza de sus paisajes, es también un **auténtico edén** para los **caminantes**. Este país sudamericano es excelente para los amantes del senderismo ya que cuenta con elementos **de sobra** para la práctica de este deporte: una **costa bañada de tranquilas aguas**, una sierra cruzada por montañas, varios ríos y una selva amazónica.

Las **sendas** del Perú ofrecen **interminables** alternativas y muchas combinaciones **geniales** para caminantes de **todos los niveles** de experiencia. **Existen** caminos con diferentes grados de dificultad para este deporte. Uno puede **recorrer** senderos **apacibles** o atravesar desiertos, **llanuras, cañones, cerros, bosques, cataratas** y selvas. **Todo depende del** grado de aventura, **riesgo** y emoción que **desee** experimentar. Otra gran alternativa es **seguir** el famoso Camino Inca.

---

**senderismo:** trekking
**seguir:** to follow; to go through
**senderos:** paths
**angostos:** narrow
**puentes:** bridges
**abismales:** enormous
**hechos de soguillas:** made of small ropes
**cruzar:** to cross (a river)
**caudalosos:** abundant, plentiful
**atravesar:** to cross (the desert)
**bajar:** to go down
**colinas:** hills
**abrirse paso:** to open one's path
**selva:** jungle
**nos ofrece/ofrecer:** it offers us/ to offer
**mítico país:** mythical country
**no sólo… sino:** not only...but
**milenaria:** thousand-year-old
**auténtico edén:** authentic paradise
**caminantes:** walkers
**de sobra:** more than enough
**costa bañada de tranquilas aguas:** coast bathed by calm waters
**sendas:** paths
**interminables:** endless
**geniales:** brilliant
**todos los niveles:** all levels
**existen/existir:** they exist/to exist
**recorrer:** to travel
**apacibles:** mild, calm
**llanuras:** plains
**cañones:** canyons
**cerros:** hills
**bosques:** forests
**cataratas:** waterfalls
**todo depende del:** it all depends on
**riesgo:** risk
**desee/desear:** one wishes/to wish
**seguir:** to follow

Los incas **no conocieron** el **caballo** y **tampoco** la **rueda** por **lo que hicieron a pie** todo viaje o recorrido. Este pueblo fue caminante por excelencia. Como toda gran civilización, los andinos contaban con una **compleja red de caminos** que llegaron a **alcanzar** 16.000 kilómetros.

Los incaicos **construyeron trochas** y senderos de **piedra** que **cruzaban** montañas, **sitios desolados** y frías **punas**. Estas **vías peatonales** variaban en **calidad y tamaño**. Algunas sendas podían ser de seis u ocho metros de **ancho** y otras de sólo un metro de **anchura**. Generalmente estas rutas se hacían en **línea recta**, aunque sí contaban con **escalinatas**, veredas **inclinadas** y **túneles abiertos** en roca viva.

El **tramo** más conocido de esta **arteria** de comunicaciones fue el llamado Camino Inca que **se encuentra** en el Cuzco. **Fue descubierto** por Hiram Bingham entre 1913 y 1915. Este famoso **trayecto nace** en el kilómetro 88 de la **línea férrea** que va de la ciudad del Cuzco a Machu Picchu, desde donde uno baja del tren y parte a pie. La versión clásica de esta caminata puede **durar** cuatro días, pero existen otras alternativas que duran uno o dos días de viaje.

Actualmente **decenas** de **miles** de turistas llegan cada año a Cuzco para recorrer este paso. La **riqueza** de la flora y fauna, los exquisitos paisajes a 4.000 metros de altura, los senderos rodeados de vegetación selvática y los **escondidos restos** arqueológicos incaicos que se encuentran por el itinerario son sólo parte de esta experiencia para el caminante. Sin duda, el **premio** más fabuloso es **concluir** esta aventura llegando a las ruinas de Machu Picchu, la **joya** arqueológica de América.

---

**no conocieron/conocer:** they didn't know/to know
**caballo:** horse
**tampoco:** neither
**rueda:** wheel
**lo que hicieron/hacer:** they made it/to make
**a pie:** on foot
**compleja:** complicated
**red de caminos:** road network
**alcanzar:** to reach
**construyeron/construir:** they built/to build
**trochas:** narrow trails
**piedra:** rock
**cruzaban/cruzar:** they crossed/ to cross
**sitios desolados:** desolate places
**punas:** bleak, desolate plateau
**vías peatonales:** pedestrian routes
**calidad y tamaño:** quality and size
**ancho:** wide
**anchura:** width
**línea recta:** straight line
**escalinatas:** steps
**inclinadas:** inclined, slanted
**túneles abiertos:** open tunnels
**tramo:** section, stretch
**arteria:** main road, artery
**se encuentra/encontrarse:** it is located/to be located
**fue descubierto/descubrir:** it was discovered/to discover
**trayecto:** route
**nace/nacer:** it starts, it begins/ to start, to begin
**línea férrea:** rail line, railway
**durar:** to last
**decenas:** ten, group of ten
**miles:** thousands
**riqueza:** wealth
**escondidos/esconder:** hidden/ to hide
**restos:** remains
**premio:** award, prize
**concluir:** to conclude
**joya:** jewel

# Examina tu comprensión

## Imitar a los pájaros, page 108

**1.** What type of special training is needed to do paragliding in Argentina?

**2.** In the direction of Cuchi Corral there is a takeoff ramp that is popular. What is unique about this site?

**3.** Floating in the air over this area, a wonderful soft landing ends the flight in what location?

## Acampando en San Felipe, page 109

**1.** San Felipe is one of the most popular places in Mexico to camp. Where is it located?

**2.** Although San Felipe has warm beautiful beaches, what type of land surrounds this area?

**3.** At nightime San Felipe is one of the best places to observe what?

## Surfing en Costa Rica, page 110

**1.** What conditions make surfing in Costa Rica ideal?

**2.** What months/locations are the best for surfing?

**3.** A bit of practical advice is given at the end of this article. What is it?

## El fútbol, page 112

**1.** What is a favorite birthday present for little boys in Argentina?

**2.** What is a popular Sunday outing in Argentina?

**3.** What types of emotion does *fútbol* generate?

# Test your comprehension

## El jai alai, page 114

**1.** What is the origin/meaning of the term *Jai Alai*? What other name can be given to the game?

**2.** What are the main characteristics of the game?

**3.** Describe the *Jai Alai cancha*.

**4.** The rules of *Jai Alai* are similiar to what other sport?

## Sierra Nevada, page 116

**1.** What time is the best for skiing in the Sierra Nevadas?

**2.** How are the trails marked to indicate levels?

**3.** What other activities can be enjoyed on the mountain?

## El senderismo en el Perú, page 118

**1.** What makes Peru an excellent place for trekking?

**2.** The type of trek you choose depends on what things?

**3.** What makes the Incan town an excellent place for walking?

**4.** The famous "Camino Inca" can take how many days?

La música es el arte más directo,
entra por el oído y va al corazón.

Magdalena Martínez

# Música

| | |
|---|---|
| **estilos:** styles | |

**estilos:** styles
**tan populares:** so popular
**han saltado fronteras:** they have
  crossed (literally jumped) borders
**importar:** to matter
**fácilmente:** easily
**reconocible:** recognizable
**debido a:** due to
**en cuanto a:** regarding
**creencia:** belief
**se trata de/tratarse:** it is about/to be
  about
**parecido:** similar
**nos recuerda/recordar:** it reminds us
  of /to remind
**rayador de queso:** cheese grater
**cara:** face
**adoran/adorar:** they adore/to adore,
  to love
**cualquier lugar:** anywhere
**en cuanto a:** regarding
**temas:** topics
**versan/versar:** they are about/to be
  about
**originariamente:** originally
**género:** genre
**fuera dado a conocer/dar a conocer:**
  it was released/to release
**medios de comunicación:** media,
  means of communication
**base:** basis
**actual:** current
**focos:** centers
**por la tarde:** in the evening
**más tarde:** later
**comenzaron/comenzar:** they began/
  to begin
**acelerar:** to accelerate
**nuevo paso de baile:** new dance step
**pasó a ser/pasar a ser:** it became/
  to become

# Bailando al son de merengue
## REPÚBLICA DOMINICANA

Estos dos **estilos** de música dominicanos **tan populares han saltado fronteras** y ahora nos invitan a bailar sin **importar** dónde estemos.

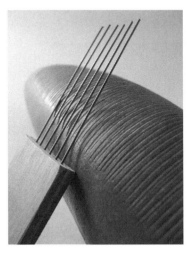

El merengue es **fácilmente reconocible debido a** su ritmo rápido de 2/2 y 2/4. Hay varias opiniones **en cuanto a** sus orígenes, pero la **creencia** más común es que **se trata de** una combinación de elementos africanos y europeos. Los instrumentos utilizados para el merengue son el melodeón (instrumento **parecido** al acordeón), la güira (cuya apariencia **nos recuerda** a un **rayador de queso**), y la tambora (un tambor de doble **cara**). Los dominicanos **adoran** el merengue y es normal verles bailando y cantando este ritmo en **cualquier lugar**.

**En cuanto a** la bachata, este estilo tiene un ritmo más melancólico de 4/4 y los **temas** que trata **versan** sobre la vida rural y las relaciones entre hombres y mujeres. **Originariamente**, y antes de que este **género fuera dado a conocer** por la industria discográfica y los **medios de comunicación,** los tríos y cuarteros de guitarra (**base** de la **actual** bachata), servían como informales **focos** de reunión en casas y patios, normalmente los domingos **por la tarde**. Durante los años 60, este estilo estaba clasificado como una subcategoría de la música de guitarra, pero algunas décadas **más tarde**, sus músicos **comenzaron** a **acelerar** el ritmo y se creó un **nuevo paso de baile**. Fue así como la bachata **pasó a ser** considerada música de baile.

# Los instrumentos musicales
## VENEZUELA

Venezuela tiene una tradición muy **rica** en lo que **se refiere** a música, danza y fiestas populares, ya que en todas estas expresiones **se mezclan** la tradición indígena, afro-venezolana y **criolla**. Esa **suma** de varias culturas hace que el **resultado** sea un **legado verdaderamente próspero**. Si hablamos de música, Venezuela **se destaca** por el gran **desarrollo** que cada comunidad hizo de los instrumentos musicales artesanales y tradicionales utilizados para acompañar bailes y cantos en celebraciones, fiestas y ceremonias religiosas. **Se pueden encontrar** más de 100 tipos, subdivididos en **instrumentos de viento** o **aerófonos**, de **cuerda** o **cordófonos**, los **construidos** con una membrana o membranófonos y los idiófonos.

Algunos ejemplos de aerófonos son: la **flauta** en diferentes formas y materiales; una trompeta construida con una **concha de caracol marino llamada** guarura con un orificio en la parte superior que **le sirve** de **boquilla**; el ovevi mataeto, hecho con un **cráneo de venado** con **cuernos**, **recubierto** con **cera** negra y un solo orificio en la base para emitir el **soplo**; y el isimoi o pito grande, una especie de clarinete hecho con un **tubo grueso** de **hoja de palmera**. **Dentro de** los cordófonos existen, entre otros, el arpa aragüeña con 35 cuerdas; el bandolín o mandolina que es un **laúd** con ocho cuerdas; y el cuatro venezolano, una guitarra pequeña de cuatro cuerdas que se usa en **casi todas** las festividades religiosas y **profanas**. El furruco es un membranófono hecho con una **lata** y una membrana de cuero **atada** y **tensada** con cuerdas, que **se frota** con un **palo** hasta transmitir una vibración o **sonido**. La mina y la curbata son tambores hechos con un **tronco de aguacate** y una membrana de cuero de **venado**, que **se ejecutan** siempre juntos y acompañan el canto y el baile que **se realizan** durante la celebración de la fiesta de San Juan Bautista en la región de Barlovento. Los idiófonos son instrumentos musicales cuyo sonido se produce por la vibración del **propio** material del que **se componen** al ser **golpeados**, **rascados** o **frotados**. En este caso, los distintos tipos de maracas son usadas en fiestas y principalmente en **rituales chamánicos**. **Dan ganas de tocar algo, ¿no?**

**rica:** rich
**se refiere/referirse:** it refers/to refer
**se mezclan/mezclar:** they mix/to mix
**criolla:** Creole
**suma:** addition
**resultado:** result
**legado:** legacy
**verdaderamente:** truly, really
**próspero:** prosperous, successful
**se destaca/destacar:** it stands out/ to stand out
**desarrollo:** development
**se pueden/poder:** they can/can
**encontrar:** to find
**instrumentos de viento, aerófonos:** wind instruments
**cuerda:** string
**cordófonos:** stringed instruments
**construidos/construir:** built/to build
**flauta:** flute
**concha de caracol marino:** conch sea shell
**llamada/llamar:** called/to call
**le sirve/servir:** it serves as/to serve
**boquilla:** mouthpiece
**cráneo de venado:** deer skull
**cuernos:** horns
**recubierto/recubrir:** covered/to cover
**cera:** wax
**soplo:** blow
**tubo grueso:** thick tube
**hoja de palmera:** palm leaf
**dentro de:** inside
**laúd:** lute
**casi todas:** almost all
**profanas:** secular
**lata:** can
**atada/atar:** tied/to tie
**tensada/tensar:** tightened/to tighten
**se frota/frotar:** it is rubbed/to rub
**palo:** stick
**sonido:** sound
**tronco de aguacate:** avocado tree trunk
**venado:** deer
**se ejecutan/ejecutar:** they are played/ to play, to perform
**se realizan/realizarse:** they take place/ to take place
**propio:** own
**se componen/componerse:** they are made of/to be made of
**golpeados/golpear:** beaten/to beat
**rascados/rascar:** scratched/to scratch
**frotados/frotar:** rubbed/to rub
**rituales chamánicos:** shamanic rituals
**Dan ganas de tocar algo, ¿no?:** It makes you want to play something, doesn't it?

# El arte flamenco
## ESPAÑA

La palabra "flamenco" **se suele** identificar con una guitarra, el pueblo **gitano**, las **palmas** y el **zapateao**. **Ciertamente**, todos estos son **símbolos típicos** del flamenco, aunque **se podría decir** que son sólo la **apariencia**. El flamenco es mucho más, es un arte que **se manifiesta en** el baile, en el **cante** y la guitarra. **Sin embargo**, en mi opinión, hay algo no tangible que **lo hace** muy especial: el **sentimiento**.

Sobre los orígenes del flamenco existe una gran controversia pues, **en realidad**, los textos más antiguos **en los que se hace referencia** a este arte son del siglo XVIII. Aunque está **claro que** su **lugar de nacimiento** fue Andalucía, existen varias teorías sobre sus creadores. Una de ellas identifica a la **raza gitana**, que llegó a la Península Ibérica **procedente de** la India en el siglo XIV, aproximadamente. Otros **estudiosos consideran** que el flamenco es una **mezcla de** todas las culturas existentes en el sur **de lo que hoy llamamos** España, la bizantina, la **judía** y la **musulmana**. Otras teorías hablan del origen musulmán, **debido a** la dominación árabe del sur **durante casi** ocho siglos. **En definitiva**, **la mayor parte de** las personas que han estudiado este tema opinan que el pueblo gitano fue el **principal precursor**, pero que su arte se vio muy influenciado por la cultura que **les rodeaba** en esa región de la Península.

En la historia del flamenco existen tres **puntos principales**, **relacionados** con las **ciudades** de Cádiz, Triana y Jerez de la Frontera, donde **nacieron** las principales escuelas. Aquí comienza este arte, **tal y como** se conoce hoy, pues hasta ese momento, el flamenco era algo popular, sin **reglas** fijas, **nacido** del sentimiento y para expresar emociones.

**Al principio**, el flamenco era **sólo** cante, **es decir**, no existía **ni** el acompañamiento de guitarra **ni** el baile. Sólo **se seguía** el ritmo con las palmas. **Posteriormente,** durante lo que se conoce como "la **edad dorada** del flamenco" entre la **última mitad** del siglo XIX y principios del XX, el flamenco **adoptó** su **forma actual** al **incluir** instrumentos y baile. **Empezaron** a **proliferar** los cafés cantantes, momento en el que nacieron todas las variantes de este hermoso arte. Estos cafés evolucionaron **a mediados** del siglo XX **hasta convertirse** en los actuales **tablaos**. Así, **poco a poco**, el flamenco se fue extendiendo internacionalmente hasta el punto de **ser mostrado** en festivales y teatros.

En el flamenco actual, el **papel** de la guitarra y del **guitarrista** puede ser **no sólo** de acompañamiento, **sino también** de solista. Es el caso del gran Paco de Lucía, o de Manolo Sanlúcar, **verdaderos** revolucionarios de la guitarra flamenca.

Así, algo tan popular en sus **comienzos** es **hoy en día** un arte único y universal.

---

**puntos principales:** main points
**relacionados/relacionar:** related/ to relate
**ciudades:** cities
**nacieron/nacer:** they were born/ to be born
**tal y como:** just as
**reglas:** rules
**fijas:** fixed
**nacido:** born
**al principio:** at first
**sólo:** only
**es decir:** that is to say
**ni... ni:** neither ... nor
**se seguía/seguir:** one would follow/ to follow
**posteriormente:** later, subsequently
**edad dorado:** golden age
**última mitad:** last half
**adoptó/adoptar:** it adopted/to adopt
**forma actual:** present, current form
**incluir:** to include
**empezaron/empezar:** they started/ to start
**proliferar:** to proliferate, spread
**a mediados:** in the middle
**hasta:** until
**convertirse:** to become
**tablaos:** flamenco bars
**poco a poco:** little by little
**ser mostrado/mostrar:** to be shown/ to show
**papel:** role
**guitarrista:** guitarist
**no sólo... sino también:** not only... but also
**verdaderos:** real, authentic
**comienzos:** beginnings
**hoy en día:** nowadays

# El reguetón está "rankeao"
## PUERTO RICO

El reguetón es un **nuevo estilo** de **música latina bailable** que nació en Puerto Rico hace aproximadamente 10 años. Es una **mezcla de** rap, hip hop y reggae **jamaiquino**, con la influencia de ritmos típicamente puertorriqueños como **la bomba y la plena**. **Posee el ritmo básico** del reggae y **algunas de** las tendencias vocales del hip hop. **Además**, incluye los sonidos de **tambores** derivados de la bomba y plena. **Esto lo hace** ser un ritmo bien **pegajoso** y de gran popularidad entre la juventud hispana.

El reguetón **se dirige** principalmente a los **jóvenes**. Sus **líricas exponen** la realidad de las **calles**, hacen críticas sociales y, **por supuesto**, **hablan del** amor y la pasión. **Algunas veces** es también **conocido** como *perreo*, **término alusivo** a **la manera** de bailarlo que **emplea movimientos de caderas** que **algunos consideran** eróticos.

El *perreo* **se baila pegando el cuerpo con otro**, **ejerciendo** diferentes movimientos y **rozando** de **frente, lado o espalda** a la otra persona. Se puede hacer el famoso paso de "**hasta abajo**" que consiste en mover la pelvis suavemente **hasta llegar al suelo**.

El reguetón también **promueve** un **estilo de vestimenta** y una nueva forma de expresión verbal. La moda del reguetón incluye **mahones de piernas anchas**, **camisetas tropicales** en tamaños grandes, **calzado deportivo** tipo canvas y en algunos casos **tatuajes** y *body piercing*.

El reguetón también se caracteriza por tener una **jerga muy callejera**, **llena de** anglicismos y con un vocabulario propio que incluye **palabras** como:

- pichaera – ignorar
- guerlas o gatas – **muchachas**
- guillao – **orgulloso** y **presumido**
- flow – **estilo**
- yales – **mujeres**
- gata fina – una chica **conservadora**
- corillo – grupo de personas
- rankearse – **subir de categoría**
- **perrear**

El **gusto** por este peculiar ritmo **ha crecido enormemente** y está **alcanzando** ya un importante reconocimiento internacional. **Se ha hecho popular** en otras islas del Caribe y **naciones vecinas**, entre ellas la República Dominicana, Panamá, Nicaragua, Méjico, Colombia y algunas regiones de Cuba. **Ya ha comenzado a escucharse** en los Estados Unidos, particularmente en Florida, Nueva York y Miami **debido a** la gran concentración de puertorriqueños e hispanos **que habitan** en estas regiones.

En la actualidad, Tego Calderón, Daddy Yankee, Ivy Queen, Nikky Jam y Don Omar son algunos de los más importantes **exponentes** del reguetón en Puerto Rico y Latinoamérica. Sus **conciertos se llenan a capacidad** y sus discos **se venden** como **pan caliente**. **Definitivamente**, este **género** de rápido **crecimiento promete seguir cautivando** a muchos. **Es por esto** que hacemos **un llamado** a todas las *guerlas* y chicos **que quieran** *rankearse* para que **se unan** al *corillo* y **aprendan** a *perrear* al ritmo del reguetón.

**jerga muy callejera:** street slang
**llena de:** full of
**palabras:** words
**muchachas:** girls
**orgulloso:** proud
**presumido:** vain
**estilo:** style
**mujeres:** women
**conservadora:** conservative
**subir de categoría:** to reach a higher class
**perrear:** a term given by Puerto Ricans to the way reggaeton is danced
**gusto:** taste
**ha crecido/crecer:** it has grown/ to grow
**enormemente:** enormously
**alcanzando/alcanzar:** reaching/ to reach
**se ha hecho popular:** it has become popular
**naciones vecinas:** neighboring nations
**ya ha comenzado a escucharse:** it started to be listened to
**debido a:** due to
**que habitan/habitar:** that live/ to live
**exponentes:** advocates
**conciertos:** concerts
**se llenan a capacidad:** they fill to capacity
**se venden/vender:** they are sold/ to sell
**pan caliente:** hot bread
**definitivamente:** definitely
**género:** type of music
**crecimiento:** growth
**promete/prometer:** it promises/ to promise
**seguir:** to follow
**cautivando:** captivating/to captivate
**es por esto:** it is because of this
**un llamado:** a call
**que quieran/querer:** that want to/ to want to
**se unan/unir:** they join/to join
**aprendan/aprender:** they learn/ to learn

**pista:** dance floor
**querido:** beloved
**te vuela a ver:** I see you again
**no habrá/haber:** there won't be/to be
**penas:** sorrows
**ni olvido:** nor oblivion (void, emptiness)
**cantaba/cantar:** he sang/to sing
**lo llamaban/llamar:** he used to be called/to call
**cariñosamente:** affectionately
**cantante:** singer
**además de:** besides
**marca indiscutible:** indisputable mark
**porteño:** inhabitant of Buenos Aires
**los comienzos:** the beginnings
**ribera:** riverside
**principios:** beginnings
**escenario:** place, scenario
**época:** time, period, age
**crecimiento demográfico:** population growth
**países:** countries
**hombres:** men
**marineros:** sailors
**artesanos:** craftsmen
**peones:** unskilled laborers
**abandonado/abandonar:** abandoned/to abandon
**en busca de/buscar:** in search of/to search
**otro:** another
**mitigar:** to alleviate
**soledad:** loneliness
**frecuentaban/frecuentar:** they frequented/to frequent
**burdeles:** bordellos
**lupanares:** brothels
**agrupaciones:** associations
**improvisaban/improvisar:** they improvised/to improvise
**flauta:** flute

# El tango: pasión en la pista
## ARGENTINA

"Mi Buenos Aires **querido**, cuando yo **te vuelva a ver**, **no habrá** más **penas ni olvido**" cantaba Carlos Gardel. "El Zorzal" o "El Mudo", como **lo llamaban cariñosamente**, fue el **cantante** argentino más importante y una de las figuras más representativas del tango.

**Además de** baile, música, canción y poesía, el tango es sobre todo un fenómeno cultural y la **marca indiscutible** del ser **porteño**.

### LOS COMIENZOS

Este género musical nació en la **ribera** del Riachuelo a **principios** de 1880 en un **escenario** particular. En esa **época**, Buenos Aires era una ciudad en expansión con un gran **crecimiento demográfico** producto de la inmigración de muchos **países** de Europa como Italia, España, Francia, Alemania o Polonia. Estos inmigrantes eran principalmente **hombres: marineros, artesanos, peones** y otros trabajadores que habían **abandonado** a sus familias **en busca de** nuevas y mejores posibilidades de vida en **otro** continente. Para **mitigar** su **soledad frecuentaban burdeles** y **lupanares**, donde diferentes **agrupaciones** de músicos **improvisaban** melodías con **flauta**, violín y guitarra.

Así **se empezó** a bailar el tango, al principio sólo entre hombres, y luego **junto a** las mujeres **del lugar**. Los primeros tangos **carecían de letra**, pero **posteriormente** algunos músicos **añadieron** canciones a los **acordes** que **describían** el ambiente en el que se encontraban, unas escenas a menudo un tanto obscenas o que **demostraban** poca educación. Por esto, y **debido a** su origen en los **ambientes prostibularios,** el tango **fue considerado** durante mucho tiempo una música prohibida.

LOS AÑOS DE GLORIA

Con el tiempo, los **lugares de baile fueron cambiando**. El tango llegó a los barrios y comenzó a bailarse en **salones públicos**, patios de casas particulares y **grandes galpones**. La década de 1940 **quedó grabada** en la historia del tango como su **época de oro**. El cantante **adquirió** más **protagonismo** en la orquesta, transformándose en un instrumento más de la misma. Y las letras **asumieron** un **nuevo perfil**: en sus versos le cantaban al amor y a la mujer en un tono diferente, más poético que en sus **inicios** y **exaltando** la ciudad, el barrio y los **protagonistas del baile.**

UN PRESENTE DE **ÉXITO**

Hoy, el tango **ha traspasado fronteras** y barreras culturales y su música y su baile **se disfrutan alrededor** del mundo. En casi todos los países existen academias o salones donde **avezados** bailarines demuestran sus habilidades y donde la música, seductora y melancólica, **les transporta** a otras épocas.

# Las sevillanas
## ESPAÑA

Las sevillanas son **actualmente unos de los bailes más típicos** de España, y **son conocidas** internacionalmente. **¡Incluso** hay **"bailaores"** y "bailaoras" en **Japón**! Y es que las sevillanas son más que música y danza; su **ritmo** y **sensualidad hacen que nuestros pies y brazos se muevan al ritmo**; sus **letras producen alegría**, **melancolía**, **tantas emociones**.

**Veamos brevemente** la historia de las sevillanas. **A partir de** la **fundación** de la **Feria de Abril** de Sevilla, la **seguidilla** sevillana (posiblemente con orígenes en la antigua Castilla) **fue llamada** Sevillana. **Más tarde**, con la **aparición** de las **grabaciones de discos**, en los años 60, las sevillanas fueron conocidas en toda España, con **nuevos grupos** como "Los del Río" o "Los Marismeños".

Durante los años 80 y 90, las sevillanas **cruzaron las fronteras** españolas. Una de las más famosas es "**El Adiós**", de "Los amigos de Gines". Actualmente, **nacen nuevas sevillanas cada año**; **mejor dicho**, nuevas letras, pues la música y el ritmo, la base de las sevillanas, **no cambian mucho**. Una **regla general** para el visitante a la Feria de Abril en Sevilla es, primero, ver **cómo bailan los demás**, y luego, **perder la vergüenza** y **pasarlo lo mejor posible**. Este es el **alma** de la Feria.

**Usted se divierte viendo y oyendo** a los demás, y viceversa. No es necesario **aprender** este baile en una academia, y **seguramente**, unas tapas y más de dos **manzanillas harán que**... ¡**se pierda la vergüenza**!

Es como una fiesta en familia, pero en un **entorno lleno de ritmo**, **palmas** y el color de los **trajes de faralaes**. Las sevillanas tienen un formato bien definido: **se componen de** 4 partes (La **Primera** o entrada, La **Segunda**, La **Tercera** y La **Cuarta**). **Cada una** de estas partes tiene 3 **versos** (o coplas). **A continuación** está la letra de una de las sevillanas más conocidas: El Adiós.

El Adiós
(La primera o entrada)
**Algo se muere** en el alma **cuando** un **amigo se va**

(La segunda)
Cuando un amigo se va
algo se muere en el alma
cuando un amigo se va
algo se muere en el alma
cuando un amigo se va

(La tercera)
cuando un amigo se va
y **va dejando** una **huella**
**que no se puede borrar**
y va dejando una huella
que no se puede borrar

(La cuarta)
**No te vayas** todavía,
no te vayas por favor
no te vayas todavía
que **hasta la guitarra mía llora**
cuando **dice** adiós.

**En este caso**, la letra es **triste**, **pues habla de** la **despedida** de un amigo.

En conclusión, la experiencia de **oír** una sevillana, y de **ver cómo se baila**, es **única**. Incluso para **aquellos que no hemos nacido rodeados** por esta forma de **vivir** la **vida**.

**entorno lleno de ritmo:** environment full of rhythm
**palmas:** clapping
**trajes de faralaes:** typical dress with flounces and colors
**se componen de/componer:** they are composed of/to compose
**primera:** first
**segunda:** second
**tercera:** third
**cuarta:** fourth
**cada una:** each one
**versos:** verses
**a continuación:** next
**algo:** something
**se muere/morir:** it dies/to die
**cuando:** when
**amigo:** friend
**se va/ir:** he/she goes away/to go
**va dejando/dejar:** he/she is leaving/to leave
**huella:** trace
**que no se puede borrar:** that cannot be erased
**no te vayas:** don't go
**hasta la guitarra mía:** even my guitar
**llora/llorar:** it cries/ to cry
**dice/decir:** it says or tells/to tell
**en este caso:** in this case
**triste:** sad
**pues habla de:** as it talks about
**despedida:** farewell
**oír:** to listen
**ver cómo se baila:** to see how it is danced
**única:** unique
**aquellos que no hemos nacido:** those of us who weren't born
**rodeados/rodear:** surrounded/to surround
**vivir:** to live
**vida:** life

# El mariachi
## MÉXICO

La música mariachi es una de las tradiciones más memorables de México. El nombre "mariachi" **viene** originalmente de los indios coca y significa "música". La música de mariachi es música folclórica de México y se considera una de las formas musicales más románticas del mundo. Un **conjunto** completo de mariachi tiene tres o más violines, dos **trompetas**, una guitarra, una **vihuela** y un guitarrón. **De vez en cuando** también se usan el **arpa** y la **guitarra de golpe**. El guitarrón es un **tipo** de instrumento **en forma de** guitarra pero con un **cuello corto** y una **barriga** grande en la **parte de atrás**. Este instrumento **toca** la parte de **bajo** y, **junto con** la vihuela, otra variante de la guitarra, **imparte** el ritmo distintivo del sonido mariachi **mientras** los violines, las trompetas y la guitarra tocan la melodía y la parte segunda o harmonía. Normalmente, todos los músicos cantan pero a veces hay un solista.

La **vestimenta** del mariachi es de tipo **charro**, similar al **traje** que usan los **vaqueros** mexicanos pero mucho más elegante. Este traje típico normalmente está formado por **botas**, un **sombrero** grande, un **moño** o **corbata**, un **chaleco** o **chaqueta corta**, pantalones bien **ajustados** con una **correa ancha** y botonaduras o **botones brillantes** en los **lados** de los pantalones. Las bandas mariachi usualmente tocan en las **bodas**, **fiestas de cumpleaños**, **días festivos**, **serenatas** y **servicios religiosos**.

Algunas canciones populares de mariachi son: *Las Mañanitas, Cielito Lindo, México Lindo, Guadalajara, El Rey* y muchas más que **forman parte** del repertorio de cualquier grupo mariachi. Unos cantantes famosos de mariachi son Pedro Infante, Vicente Fernandez, Javier Solis y Jorge Negrete.

La música mariachi **ha sido** usada en muchas **películas** mexicanas y **aún se puede escuchar en vivo** en muchos restaurantes mexicanos.

---

**viene/venir:** it comes/to come
**conjunto:** band
**trompetas:** trumpets
**vihuela:** name of a small classical guitar used in mariachi bands
**de vez en cuando:** once in a while
**arpa:** harp
**guitarra de golpe:** Mexican variation of the Spanish guitar
**tipo:** kind
**en forma de:** with the shape of
**cuello corto:** short neck
**barriga:** belly
**parte de atrás:** back side
**toca/tocar:** it plays/to play
**bajo:** bass
**junto con:** coupled with
**imparte/impartir:** it gives/to give
**mientras:** while
**vestimenta:** clothes
**charro:** horseman
**traje:** costume
**vaqueros:** cowboys
**botas:** boots
**sombrero:** hat
**moño:** lace bow
**corbata:** tie
**chaleco:** vest
**chaqueta corta:** bolero jacket
**ajustados:** tight
**correa:** strap
**ancha:** wide
**botones:** buttons
**brillantes:** shiny
**lados:** sides
**bodas:** weddings
**fiestas de cumpleaños:** birthday parties
**días festivos:** holidays
**serenatas:** parties on the streets that take place at night
**servicios religiosos:** religious services
**forman parte/formar parte:** they are part of/to be part of
**ha sido/ser:** it has been/to be
**películas:** movies, films
**aún:** still
**se puede/poder:** one can/can
**escuchar:** to listen
**en vivo:** live

# Los gamberros universitarios
## ESPAÑA

Son la representación más **gamberra** de las universidades españolas, pero **a sus espaldas llevan** una tradición **centenaria**. Los **tunos**, **ataviados** con sus **capas** y sus **pantalones bombachos** negros, **llenan** con su **alegre** música la noche de las ciudades universitarias. Los tunos del siglo XXI son **herederos** de una antigua tradición que **se remonta** al siglo XIII. En el año 1212, bajo el **reinado** de Alfonso VIII, **se fundó** en Palencia el primer *Studium Generale*, **precedente** de las futuras universidades. A estos Estudios Generales, y a los que se crearon por todo el país, **acudían** también jóvenes de pocos **recursos económicos**, a los que se conocía como "sopistas".

Los sopistas eran estudiantes **pobres** que con su música, su **simpatía** y su **picardía recorrían** conventos, calles y plazas **a cambio de** un plato de sopa (de ahí proviene su nombre) y de unas **monedas** que **les ayudaran** a pagar sus estudios. Además de sus instrumentos siempre llevaban **consigo** una **cuchara** y un **tenedor de madera**, lo que **les permitía** comer en cualquier lugar donde tenían ocasión. Estos **cubiertos** de madera **siguen siendo** hoy en la **actualidad** el símbolo de todas las tunas universitarias.

Las tunas, **tal cual las conocemos** hoy en día, **aparecieron** en el siglo XVI ya que gracias a la creación de residencias universitarias para estudiantes pobres, los sopistas **dejaron de mendigar**. Las características de las tunas son muy particulares. Están integradas **únicamente** por hombres y su **vestimenta** es muy peculiar, toda negra y prácticamente idéntica a la de los estudiantes de las primeras universidades españolas. Cada miembro del grupo, que **suele estar formado** por unas ocho o diez personas, lleva un instrumento, a excepción del cantante principal. **Predominan** las guitarras, los **laúdes** y las **bandurrias**, aunque el instrumento más característico de las tunas es la **pandereta**. **La razón de ser** de estos grupos siempre **ha sido** la mujer; a ella **van dedicadas** todas sus canciones, todas sus **actuaciones**. Sin embargo, **conquistando** o sin conquistar **féminas**, el objetivo de las tunas es disfrutar de la compañía de los amigos y hacer de la noche una fiesta.

**gamberros universitarios:** university hooligans
**gamberra:** mischievous
**a sus espaldas:** on their back
**llevan/llevar:** they carry/to carry
**centenaria:** hundred-year-old
**tunos:** members of a *tuna* (a *tuna* is a music group of university students)
**ataviados:** dressed
**capas:** capes, cloaks
**pantalones bombachos:** baggy pants
**llenan/llenar:** they fill/to fill
**alegre:** lively
**herederos:** heirs
**se remonta/remontarse:** it goes back/to go back
**reinado:** kingdom
**se fundó/fundar:** it was founded/to found
**precedente:** previous
**acudían/acudir:** they went/to go
**recursos económicos:** financial means
**pobres:** poor
**simpatía:** charm
**picardía:** craftiness
**recorrían:** they used to go around
**a cambio de:** in exchange for
**monedas:** coins
**les ayudaran/ayudar:** would help them/to help
**consigo:** with them
**cuchara:** spoon
**tenedor de madera:** wooden fork
**les permitía/permitir:** it allowed them/to allow
**cubiertos:** cutlery
**siguen siendo/ser:** they still are/to be
**actualidad:** nowadays
**tal cual:** the way
**las conocemos:** we know them
**aparecieron/aparecer:** they appeared/to appear
**dejaron de/dejar de:** they stopped/to stop
**mendigar:** to beg
**únicamente:** solely
**vestimenta:** clothing
**suele estar formado:** it usually consists of
**predominan:** they predominate
**laúdes:** lutes
**bandurrias:** a kind of wind instrument
**pandereta:** tambourine
**la razón de ser:** the objective
**ha sido/ser:** it has been/to be
**van dedicadas:** they are dedicated
**actuaciones:** performances
**conquistando/conquistar:** winning/to win (hearts)
**féminas:** female, women

**hoy en día:** nowadays
**constituye/constituir:** it constitutes/to constitute
**posee/poseer:** it has/to have
**distingue/distinguir:** it distinguishes/to distinguish
**países vecinos:** neighboring countries
**basado/basar:** based/to base
**se toca/tocar:** it is played/to play
**chico:** literally, it means "small" but in this case is also the name of one of the drums
**repique:** peal (of bells), it is the name of one of the drums
**crean/crear:** they create/to create
**mantiene/mantener:** it maintains/to maintain
**toque creativo:** creative touch
**puede repetirse/repitir:** it can be repeated/to repeat
**conjuntos:** band
**decenas:** tens
**comienzos:** beginnings
**hogar:** home
**barrios:** neighborhoods
**al atardecer:** at dusk
**fines de semana:** weekends
**verano:** summer
**extraño:** strange, foreign
**se reúnen/reunirse:** they gather/ to gather
**convocatorias:** calls (to a meeting)
**se ha afincado/afincarse:** it has established itself/to establish itself
**han surgido/surgir:** they have emerged/to emerge
**aficionados:** fans
**dar rienda suelta:** to give free rein to
**ganas:** desire
**punto de encuentro:** meeting point
**esquina prefijada:** prearranged corner
**antemano:** beforehand
**se congregan/congregar:** they congregate/ to congregate
**propio:** own
**se juntan/juntarse:** they get together/to get together
**seguidores:** followers, fans
**calentar:** to warm up
**lonjas:** strip of leather (that covers the top of the drum)
**alrededor:** around
**fogata:** bonfire
**recorrer:** to visit, to go around
**repitiendo/repetir:** repeating/ to repeat

# El candombe
### URUGUAY

**Hoy en día**, el candombe **constituye** una de las expresiones musicales más particulares que **posee** el Uruguay y que lo **distingue** de los **países vecinos**. De origen africano, el candombe está **basado** en la percusión. **Se toca** con tres tambores, **chico**, **repique** y piano, que al ser tocados juntos **crean** el ritmo del candombe. El chico **mantiene** la métrica y el piano mantiene la base del ritmo, mientras que el repique le da el **toque creativo**. Este núcleo de tres tambores **puede repetirse** varias veces hasta formar **conjuntos** de varias **decenas**. Su combinación crea ritmos que invitan a bailar y que desde sus **comienzos** en su nuevo **hogar** americano estuvieron asociados con el carnaval.

En varios **barrios** de Montevideo, **al atardecer** y, sobre todo durante los **fines de semana** de **verano**, no es **extraño** escuchar grupos de personas que **se reúnen** a tocar candombe con sus tamboriles. Inicialmente, los barrios donde se realizaban estas **convocatorias** eran Barrio Sur y Palermo, donde la comunidad negra **se ha afincado** tradicionalmente. Más recientemente **han surgido** otros puntos en Montevideo donde **aficionados** al candombe se reúnen cada semana para **dar rienda suelta** a sus **ganas** de tamborilear. Generalmente, el **punto de encuentro** es en alguna **esquina prefijada** de la ciudad, a una hora y día determinados de **antemano**. Allí **se congregan** las personas, muchas de ellas cargando con su **propio** tamboril, aunque a menudo también **se juntan** vecinos curiosos y **seguidores** de esta expresión musical.

Después de **calentar** las **lonjas alrededor** de una **fogata**, comienzan a tocar y **recorrer** las calles, **repitiendo** así una costumbre que llegó a las costas del Río de la Plata gracias a los esclavos africanos.

Desde **principios** del siglo XIX, cuando los esclavos fueron introducidos al país por el puerto de Montevideo, la cultura africana **mantuvo** una **fuerte presencia** entre el **aluvión** de culturas de todo el mundo que **convergían** en la capital. **Sin embargo**, es difícil determinar con claridad los comienzos del candombe en el Uruguay. **Sin duda,** presente en las fiestas de los negros esclavos, el *candomblé* era parte danza y parte música, resultando un camino muy efectivo para que mantuvieran sus raíces africanas. Además de mantenerse vivo **dentro de** la comunidad negra, en la década de los años 40 el candombe comenzó a hacerse un lugar entre los ciudadanos uruguayos de otros grupos étnicos.

A este cambio **contribuyeron** artistas de otras **ramas** y **se manifestó**, por ejemplo, en los **cuadros** de uno de los pintores uruguayos más famosos, Pedro Figari. Este pintor **revalorizó** el carnaval tanto como a sus participantes y su música al **plasmarlos** en sus pinturas. Otro artista que **jugó un papel clave** en la expansión del candombe fue el músico Alfredo Zitarrosa, que en varios de sus temas hace referencia al candombe. En uno de ellos dice: "Para **ahuyentar** al Mandinga, macumba, macumbembé, hay que **tirar una flecha**, y bailar el *candomblé*." Así, esta expresión musical fue **poco a poco ganando** aceptación entre un **público más amplio**. Más tarde **aparecerían** otros músicos **destacados**, tales como José Carvajal, **más conocido como** "El Sabalero", que **compuso** temas de candombe **extremadamente** populares en la década de los años 60. Más recientemente, muchos otros músicos y cantautores uruguayos, como Jaime Ross, Rubén Rada o Fernando Cabrera, **se han incursionado** en el candombe. En los **últimos** 20 años, este ritmo musical ha **disfrutado** de un **auge creciente**, **gracias en parte a** la revalorización del carnaval uruguayo como **patrimonio** cultural nacional. **No sería de extrañar** que **de ahora en más**, el candombe **expanda** su **contagioso ritmo más allá de las fronteras** uruguayas.

**principios:** beginnings
**mantuvo/mantener:** it maintained/to maintain
**fuerte presencia:** strong presence
**aluvión:** downpour
**convergían/converger:** they converged/to converge
**sin embargo:** however
**sin duda:** without a doubt
**dentro de:** inside
**contribuyeron/contribuir:** they contributed/to contribute
**ramas:** lines of work, branches
**se manifestó/manifestarse:** it was shown/to be shown
**cuadros:** paintings
**revalorizó/revalorizar:** he revalued/to revalue
**plasmarlos/plasmar:** he captured them/to capture
**jugó un papel clave:** he played a key role
**ahuyentar:** to scare away
**tirar una flecha:** to shoot an arrow
**poco a poco:** little by little
**ganando/ganar:** winning/to win
**público más amplio:** a broader public
**aparecerían/aparecer:** they would appear/to appear
**destacados:** outstanding
**más conocido como:** better known as
**compuso/componer:** he composed/to compose
**extremadamente:** extremely
**se han incursionado/incursionar:** they have tackled (a subject)/to tackle
**últimos:** last
**disfrutado/disfrutar:** enjoyed/to enjoy
**auge creciente:** increasing peak
**gracias en parte a:** thanks in part to
**patrimonio:** heritage
**no sería de extrañar:** it would be hardly surprising
**de ahora en más:** from now on
**expanda/expandir:** it expands/to expand
**contagioso ritmo:** infectious rhythm
**más allá de las fronteras:** beyond the borders

instrumentos exóticos: exotic
  instruments
solemnidad evocativa: evocative
  solemnity
público selecto: select public
ritmo precolombino: precolumbian
  rhythm
vida del increíble hombre andino:
  life of an incredible Andean man
diversas etapas: diverse stages
se desarrollaron/desarrollar: it was
  developed/to develop
acompañadas de/acompañar:
  accompanied by, with/to accompany
varios tipos de ritmos: various types
  of rhythms
alegres: happy
tristes: sad
solemnes: solemn
guerreros: warlike
no se podían cambiar: could not be
  changed
dura: hard
faena: work
se aliviaba/aliviar: was relieved/
  to relieve
piezas: pieces
fecha: date
se convertía/convertía: it was turned
  into; it was changed/to change
dejaran/dejar: they left/to leave
caracterizaba: characterized
nueve flautas: nine flutes
amarradas: tied together
en fila: in line
hechas de carrizo: made of reed
confeccionada de arcilla: made of
  clay
plata: silver
carrizo: reed
huesos humanos: human bones
piel de puma: puma skin
marcar: to mark
también: also
caracol marino: marine snail
agudo: sharp; high-pitched

# La música andina
## PERU

Por sus **instrumentos exóticos** y su **solemnidad evocativa**, la llamada música de los andes tiene un **público selecto** en el planeta. Este **ritmo precolombino** de los quechuas y aymaras formó parte esencial en la **vida del increíble hombre andino**.

Las **diversas etapas** de la vida de los indígenas de los Andes **se desarrollaron acompañadas de varios tipos de ritmos**: alegres, tristes, solemnes, festivos o **guerreros**. Cada lugar u ocasión tenía sus propios cantos y bailes que **no se podían cambiar**. Una **dura faena se aliviaba** con la ejecución de **piezas** musicales, y la celebración de una **fecha** festiva **se convertía** en motivo para que los indígenas **dejaran** por un momento esa melancolía que les **caracterizaba**.

LOS INSTRUMENTOS MUSICALES

El elemento más característico de esta melodía fue la zampoña, que era una especie de **nueve flautas amarradas en fila hechas de carrizo**. La quena era una flauta **confeccionada de arcilla**, **plata**, **carrizo** o de **huesos humanos**. En la percusión, el tambor, fabricado con **piel de puma** o piel humana, fue un elemento básico para **marcar** el ritmo. **También** existía el "pututo" o **caracol marino** que emitía un sonido **agudo** como de ultratumba, un sonido realmente mágico.

El arte musical andino precolombino no conoció los instrumentos de **cuerda** y su ritmo **estuvo basado** en la **escala pentatónica.**

Con la **llegada** de los españoles **se incorporó** a esta **orquesta** el **arpa**, y **nació** en estas **tierras** una **especie de** guitarra pequeña llamada "charango", hecha con de la **concha del armadillo.**

## LA **ACTUAL** MÚSICA ANDINA

Hoy la música de los Andes ya **no se conserva** "pura". Este concepto está **casi extinto**. Con el paso del tiempo **se añadieron** instrumentos europeos, **creándose** así una interesante fusión.

**Hay abundantes** grupos que aún **cultivan** este género con gran talento en Perú, Bolivia, Chile, Ecuador, Colombia y Argentina. Durante los años 60 y 70 muchos de estos grupos fueron **enviados** al exilio europeo por sus ideas socialistas o antimilitaristas. Ya en Europa, estos **sonidos** indígenas **atrajeron** la atención internacional. *El Cóndor Pasa,* creada en 1913 por el peruano Daniel Alomía Robles, es el **tema maestro** de la música andina. Paul Simon descubrió esta canción en París y **de ahí la hizo** conocida a todo el mundo en 1970.

La **complicada y hermosa ejecución** de *El Cóndor Pasa* es sólo un ejemplo del **reconocimiento** a este **género** musical indígena después de siglos de **haber sido marginado** por el **mundo occidental.**

venado: deer
toro: bull
por lo menos: at least
algunos: some
forman parte: they are part of
bellas: beautiful
estéticas: aesthetic
fuente: source
conexión: connection
forma de expresar: form of expression
alegría: joy
goce: enjoyment
inmemoriales: immemorial
festejar: to celebrate
invocar: to invoke
dioses: gods
cortejar: to court, to woo
como casi todos: like almost all
rico: rich
si bien: although
se representan/representar: they are performed/to perform
Fin de Año: New Year's Eve
Año Nuevo: New Year's Day
leyenda: legend
cuenta/contar: tells/to tell
a mediados de: the middle of
matrimonio: married couple
salió/salir: (the marriage) went out/to go out
cazar: to hunt
amenazado/amenazar: threatened/to threaten
pidió auxilio: asked for help
suplicó/suplicar: begged, implored/to beg, to implore
patrono del municipio: patron saint of the town
salvara del peligro: to save from danger
cazadores: hunters
mataron/matar: they killed/to kill
se celebra/celebrar: is celebrated/to celebrate
acecha/acechar: lies in wait for/to lie in wait for
pareja: couple
son: sound, tune, melody
arco: arch
flecha: arrow
alrededor: around

# Las danzas tradicionales
## EL SALVADOR

El tigre, el **venado** y el **toro** no son sólo animales, **por lo menos** no en El Salvador. Aquí también son los nombres de **algunos** de los bailes tradicionales más populares que **forman parte** de la cultura, las raíces y las costumbres salvadoreñas.

El baile es una de las formas de expresión y comunicación más **bellas** y **estéticas**. Es **fuente** y emisión de energía, **conexión** con el mundo exterior e interior y una **forma de expresar** muchas emociones, principalmente **alegría** y **goce**. Desde tiempos **inmemoriales**, el hombre bailó, bailó para celebrar y **festejar**, para **invocar dioses** o para **cortejar**.

El Salvador, **como casi todos** los países de Centroamérica, es **rico** en danzas tradicionales, y **si bien** toda ocasión es buena para el baile, la mayoría de ellas **se representan** durante las fiestas de **Fin de Año**, **Año Nuevo** y fiestas patronales.

DANZA DEL TIGRE Y EL VENADO

Esta danza representa una **leyenda** del pueblo de San Juan Nonualco, en el departamento de La Paz. La historia **cuenta** que, **a mediados de** 1800, un **matrimonio** mayor **salió** a **cazar** un venado y al verse **amenazado** por la presencia de un tigre, **pidió auxilio** y **suplicó** al Señor de la Caridad, **patrono del municipio**, que los **salvara del peligro**.

Los **cazadores mataron** al tigre y en honor a este santo **se celebra** una danza en la que varios personajes representan aquel momento: el tigre **acecha** al venado y a la **pareja** bailando al **son** del tambor, mientras el matrimonio armado con **arco** y **flecha** baila también **alrededor** del tigre.

El público observa cómo el tigre ataca a los viejos y aplaude cuando éstos **lo degüellan** y **reparten** las porciones del animal **entonando** frases humorísticas **dirigidas** a las personas del pueblo: "**Lo de adelante** para el **comandante**", "lo de atrás para el **juez de paz**", "la cabeza para Teresa" o "los **riñones** para los **mirones**".

## LOS TOROS DE LA ASCENSIÓN

Esta tradición, también procedente de San Juan Nonualco, celebra el **hecho ocurrido** a un **personaje** llamado Isidro Labrador, que **se dedicaba** a la agricultura para **alimentar** a su familia. Un **Jueves de Ascensión** (día en el que **se conmemora** la **subida** de Cristo al **cielo**) Isidro **se disponía** a **labrar** la tierra y cuando **arreaba** a los **bueyes**, uno de ellos le dijo: "Isidro, hoy no trabajaremos, mañana sí". Él insistió pero **obtuvo** la misma **respuesta** y al darse cuenta de lo que se conmemoraba ese día, **se arrodilló** pidiendo perdón a Dios.

Basado en este suceso **se mantiene** la celebración del Jueves de Ascensión como el día dedicado a los toros. En todos los **barrios**, los habitantes **fabrican** un toro (**armazón** con **varas** de **bambú forradas** con **cuero** o **piel de toro** y en los extremos, **cuernos** y **cola**) que pasean por las calles, acompañados de música y **quema** de **pólvora**. En las **capillas** o ermitas se adornan altares y **se reza** el **rosario**. Luego de las **oraciones** y el baile, **se inician** competencias con los toros.

Éstos y otros tantos bailes y tradiciones mantenidos a lo largo de años reafirman el **compromiso** de **promover** las raíces del país.

---

**lo degüellan/degollar:** they beheaded him/to behead
**reparten/repartir:** they give out/ to give out
**entonando/entonar:** singing, saying/to sing, to say
**dirigidas/dirigir:** addressed/ to address
**lo de adelante:** in the front part
**comandante:** commander
**juez de paz:** justice of the peace
**riñones:** kidneys
**mirones:** curious people,
**hecho ocurrido:** made occur
**personaje:** character
**se dedicaba/dedicarse:** he was dedicated/to be dedicated
**alimentar:** to feed
**Jueves de Ascensión:** Ascension Day
**se conmemora/conmemorar:** it is commemorated/to commemorate
**subida:** ascension
**cielo:** heaven
**se disponía/disponerse:** he got ready/to get ready, to prepare
**labrar:** to farm
**arreaba/arrear:** he was urging on/ to urge on, to drive
**bueyes:** oxen
**obtuvo/obtener:** he got/to get
**respuesta:** answer
**se arrodilló/arrodillarse:** he knelt down/to kneel down
**se mantiene/mantener:** is kept/ to keep
**barrios:** neighborhoods
**fabrican/fabricar:** they make/ to make
**armazón:** shell
**varas:** rods, sticks
**bambú:** bamboo
**forradas/forrar:** covered/to cover
**cuero:** leather
**piel de toro:** bull skin
**cuernos:** horns
**cola:** tail
**quema:** burn
**pólvora:** gunpowder
**capillas:** chapels
**se reza/rezar:** it is said/to say
**rosario:** rosary
**oraciones:** prayers
**se inician/iniciar:** they start/ to start
**compromiso:** commitment
**promover:** to promote

# Examina tu comprensión

## Bailando al son de merengue, page 124

**1.** The origin of the merengue is a combination of what two cultural influences?

**2.** What are the primary instruments used in the merengue?

**3.** During what years was this style of music classified as a sub-category of guitar music?

## Los instrumentos musicales, page 125

**1.** Some of the wind instruments such as the flute and trumpet are made from what animal-based materials?

**2.** The thick tube of the clarinet is made from what type of leaf?

**3.** The *Mina* and the *Curbata* are tamborines made of what type of tree?

## El arte flamenco, page 126

**1.** Flamenco is demonstrated in what three ways?

**2.** Although the origin of flamenco is uncertain, where is the birthplace?

**3.** Flamenco started as song and then evovled to include what?

**4.** What is the role of the guitar and the *guitarrista*?

## El reguetón está "rankeao", page 128

**1.** *Reguetón* is a mixture of what influences, rhythms and sounds?

**2.** *Reguetón* lyrics express what?

**3.** List the "slang" associated with *Reguetón* and what these words mean.

# Test your comprehension

## El tango, page 130

**1.** In 1880 immigrants from what countries came to Buenos Aires?

**2.** What were the primary occupations of the immigrants?

**3.** What was the original environment where the tango was danced?

**4.** In what decade did the tango become more accepted by all societal classes?

## El mariachi, page 134

**1.** What is the origin of the word *mariachi* and what does it mean?

**2.** What instruments make up a *mariachi* band?

**3.** Describe the *guitarrón*.

## El candombe, page 136

**1.** Where and when might you hear *candombe*?

**2.** What is the origin of *candombe* and what importance does it serve?

**3.** *Candombe* has been expressed in what other art forms?

## La música andina, page 138

**1.** The sounds of Andean music are varied, evoking five types of rhythms. What are they?

**2.** One instrument characteristic of the Andean melody is the *Zampoña*. How is it constructed?

**3.** What American performer made Andean music well-known in the 1970s?

Las buenas costumbres, y no la fuerza,
son las columnas de las leyes; y el ejercicio
de la justicia es el ejercicio de la libertad.

Simón Bolívar

# Historia

# El Cinco de mayo
## MÉXICO

El cinco de mayo **conmemora** una **fecha muy importante** para los mexicanos. Las festividades de este día se celebran **por todo México**, **pero especialmente** en la **ciudad de** Puebla. En los **últimos veinte años**, las celebraciones del cinco de mayo **han adquirido** mucha popularidad en los Estados Unidos, **principalmente** en los estados de California, Arizona, Texas y Nuevo México. **De hecho**, hay muchas personas que **piensan** que en este día se celebra la Independencia de México, que es el 16 de septiembre. **En realidad**, esta fecha conmemora el **triunfo de** los mexicanos sobre el **ejército francés** en la **Batalla de Puebla** de 1862.

En 1821, **después** de **una larga lucha** por **obtener la independencia de** España, se estableció el **primer** gobierno mexicano independiente. **Durante esta época**, el gobierno mexicano **incurrió en grandes deudas** con **otros países**, principalmente Francia **e Inglaterra**. La **inestabilidad política** y la situación económica **por la cual estaba pasando** México **en ese momento impidieron** que pudiera **cumplir de inmediato** con sus **obligaciones financieras**. El **actual** presidente, Benito Juárez, **solicitó** una **moratoria** para su deuda, **que fue aceptado por** Inglaterra y España.

**Sin embargo**, el gobierno francés **se mantuvo renuente** y **envió sus tropas** a la ciudad de México con la intención de **establecer allí su propio** gobierno monárquico. **Para llegar** a su destino, tenían que pasar **por el estado de** Puebla **donde las tropas mexicanas**, **bajo el mando del** General Zaragoza, **preparaban** su defensa.

**Aunque** el ejército mexicano **no aparentaba ser** lo suficientemente **fuerte** o **capacitado para destruir** las tropas francesas, el **ímpetu de su lucha** compensó sus limitaciones y **lograron vencer** al **poderoso** ejército europeo **a pesar de** que la **victoria** en esta batalla **no logró al final ganar la guerra**. Para los mexicanos la misma **simboliza** el valor, la determinación y el patriotismo del pueblo mexicano.

Las celebraciones de este día incluyen **desfiles militares** que **rinden homenaje a** todos los héroes **que perecieron por** la **libertad de** México. El desfile generalmente culmina en el Zócalo, la plaza central de cada pueblo, **donde jóvenes** y mayores **disfrutan** de las festividades. La fiesta incluye **juegos divertidos**, **corridas de toros**, deliciosos platos típicos de la cocina mexicana, y **bandas de mariachis** que **alegran la velada** con su música y su **encanto**.

**Al final de la** noche, se oye la **pólvora de los fuegos artificiales** y un sinfín de **voces que exclaman con alegría** ¡Viva México! Este sentido **grito** refleja **el orgullo** que sienten los mexicanos por su **herencia** y el **espíritu festivo** de un pueblo que **celebra su libertad**.

**sin embargo:** nevertheless
**se mantuvo renuente:** remained reluctant
**envió sus tropas:** sent his troops
**establecer allí su propio:** to establish his own
**para llegar:** in order to arrive
**por el estado de:** through the state of
**donde las tropas mexicanas:** where the Mexican troops
**bajo el mando del:** under the command of
**preparaban/prepara:** they prepared/ to prepare
**aunque:** although
**no aparentaba ser:** did not appear to be
**fuerte:** strong
**capacitado para destruir:** able to destroy
**ímpetu de su lucha:** impetus; momentum of their fight
**lograron vencer:** managed to defeat
**poderoso:** powerful
**a pesar de:** in spite of
**victoria:** victory
**no logró al final ganar la guerra:** did not in the end win the war
**simboliza:** symbolizes
**desfiles militares:** military parades
**rinden homenaje a:** pay tribute to
**que perecieron por:** who perished for
**libertad de:** freedom of
**donde jóvenes:** where young
**disfrutan/disfrutar:** they enjoy/ to enjoy
**juegos divertidos:** playing games
**corridas de toros:** bull fights
**bandas de mariachis:** mariachi bands
**alegran la velada:** cheer up the evening
**encanto:** charm
**al final de la:** at the end of the
**pólvora de los fuegos artificiales:** powder of the fireworks
**voces que exclaman con alegría:** voices that exclaim with joy
**grito:** shout
**el orgullo:** the pride
**herencia:** legacy; inheritance
**espíritu festivo:** festive spirit
**celebra su libertad:** celebrates its freedom

**logró/lograr:** he managed/to get, to manage
**asimilar:** to assimilate
**conocimientos:** knowledge
**aportes:** contributions
**conquistaron/conquistar:** they conquered/to conquer
**crecimiento:** growth
**fue detenido/detener:** it was stopped/ to stop
**respirar:** to breathe
**mayoría:** majority
**abarcó/abacar:** it embraced/to cover, to embrace
**imperio:** empire
**sobre todo:** throughout all
**leyenda:** legend
**que cuenta:** that tells
**lago:** lake
**amados:** beloved
**barreta:** bar
**hundieron/hundir:** they sank/to sink
**cerro:** hill
**fundaron/fundar:** they founded/ to found
**sagrada:** sacred
**ombligo:** center (literally navel)
**ciudad mágica:** magical city
**enseñó/enseñar:** he taught/to teach
**ganadería:** cattle
**cerámica:** pottery
**tejido:** weaving
**cocina:** cooking, cuisine
**alcanzó/alcanzar:** reached/to reach
**extraordinaria:** extraordinary, exceptional
**casi:** almost
**llevando con ello/llevar:** taking with it/to take
**adoración:** worship
**idioma:** language

# Los hijos del sol
## PERU

Los incas fueron una magnífica civilización del siglo X que **logró asimilar** grandes **conocimientos** y **aportes** de las culturas que **conquistaron**. Aunque su **crecimiento fue detenido** por la invasión española en el siglo XVI, aún se puede **respirar** la gran influencia incaica en la **mayoría** de los países que **abarcó** este **imperio**, **sobre todo** en Perú.

Existe una **leyenda que cuenta** que el dios Inti sacó del **Lago** Titicaca, en Puno, a dos de sus **amados** hijos: Manco Cápac y Mama Ocllo. Ellos llevaban una **barreta** de oro que **hundieron** en el **cerro** Huanacaure. Aquí **fundaron** la maravillosa ciudad del Cuzco, la capital **sagrada** de los incas, a la que consideraban el **ombligo** del mundo. Esta **ciudad mágica** era el centro del imperio.

Manco Cápac, como primer inca, **enseñó** a los hombres la agricultura, la **ganadería** y la **cerámica**; y Mama Ocllo, a las mujeres, el arte del **tejido** y la **cocina**. Con el Inca Pachacútec, el imperio **alcanzó** una **extraordinaria** expansión por **casi** toda América del Sur **llevando con ello** la **adoración** al Inti, o Dios Sol y también el uso del **idioma** quechua.

Aunque **controlaron** todo el **actual Perú** y diversos territorios de Bolivia, Colombia, Ecuador, Argentina y Chile, los incas **respetaron** la cultura de los pueblos que conquistaban.

A pesar de que el Estado Inca mantenía **profundas** diferencias sociales y **utilizaba** el trabajo de la población **para su beneficio,** el pueblo **tenía asegurado** los **alimentos**, el **vestido** y la **vivienda**. Así, en una población de 12 millones no había **desocupación** ni **hambre**.

No existía **propiedad privada**, las tierras **pertenecían** al **emperador** y **eran administradas colectivamente** por **ayllus**, **quienes asignaban** a cada familia un **pedazo de tierra** para **cultivarla** para su propio **consumo** así como para dar **tributos** al rey. En las artes, las ciencias y la tecnología se alcanzó un alto nivel de desarrollo para la época, **destacando** principalmente en la **ingeniería** y la arquitectura. Los incas **construyeron** notables **palacios**, templos, canales, **puentes**, **fortalezas** y **caminos**.

Con la **muerte súbita** del **penúltimo** inca en 1526 el imperio fue dividido entre sus dos hijos Huáscar y Atahualpa, que **se enfrentaron** en una **guerra civil**.

En 1532, Atahualpa **derrotó** a Huáscar; pero ya el gran imperio se encontraba **debilitado** y **dividido sin estar preparado** para el **arribo** de los conquistadores españoles, que encontraron a su llegada una alta cultura.

controlaron/controlar: they controlled/to control
actual Perú: modern-day Perú
respetaron/respetar: respected/ to respect
profundas: deep
utilizaba/utilizar: it used/to use
para su beneficio: for it's own benefit
tenía asegurado: they had guaranteed
alimentos: food
vestido: clothes
vivienda: housing
desocupación: unemployment
hambre: hunger
propiedad privada: private property
pertenecían/pertenecer: they belonged/to belong
emperador: emperor
eran administradas/administrar: they were managed/to manage
colectivamente: collectively
ayllus: kinship-based clan
quienes asignaban/asignar: who assigned/to assign, to allocate
pedazo de tierra: a piece of land
cultivarla: to cultivate it
consumo: consumption
tributos: tribute payments
destacando/destacar: emphasizing/ to emphasize
ingeniería: engineering
construyeron/construir: they built/ to build
palacios: palaces
puentes: bridges
fortalezas: fortresses
caminos: roads
muerte súbita: sudden death
penúltimo: next to the last
se enfrentaron/enfrentar: they faced each other /to confront, to face up to
guerra civil: civil war
derrotó/derrotar: he defeated/to defeat
debilitado: debilitated, weakened
dividido/dividir: divided/to divide
sin estar preparado: unprepared
arribo: arrival

# La historia del toreo
## ESPAÑA

¿Cuál es la historia del **toreo** en España? **Se cree que** la primera corrida de toros **tuvo lugar** en Verea, en la provincia de Logroño, en el año 1133, en la **coronación del rey** Alfonso VIII. **Después de la Reconquista de España** (en la que **se liberó** a la Península del **poder musulmán**) la fiesta del toreo **se hizo** popular en toda la geografía ibérica. Durante **varios reinados** las corridas fueron **habituales**, hasta que **el Papa** Pío V **las prohibió, pues pensaba** que las corridas eran celebraciones primitivas. Pero **el pueblo ignoró** esta prohibición y **continuó** con su "fiesta". Más tarde, el Papa Gregorio VIII **derogó el decreto, asumiendo** que era una fiesta del pueblo.

Varios siglos más tarde, con la Guerra Civil Española (de 1936 a 1939), el toreo **casi desaparece, ya que los toros se utilizaban para alimentar** a las tropas. Pero cuando **el conflicto terminó**, las corridas de toros fueron restablecidas. Algunos de los toreros más representativos de esta **época** son "Manolete" y Luis Miguel "Dominguín". **Hoy en día**, el toreo **se practica** también en otros países: Portugal, Ecuador, México, etc. Incluso en Japón o Estados Unidos (en California y otros estados del oeste).

Pero ¿cómo es una corrida de toros? La corrida de toros comienza con el "**desfile**" de los toreros y toda su **cuadrilla, vestidos con trajes del siglo XVII**, que saludan al presidente. **Para anunciar** la entrada del primer toro **al ruedo**, el presidente de la plaza **agita un pañuelo blanco. Cada vez** que el torero **sale** y cuando, finalmente, **se ha matado al toro, suena una trompeta**. En la corrida **participan** tres toreros (junto con sus cuadrillas) y seis toros. Cada torero torea dos toros, los cuales **pesan entre** 500 y 800 kilos. Estos toros **nunca se han enfrentado a un hombre. Si fuera así**, el toro **enbestiría** al hombre, no a la capa del torero.

---

**Podemos diferenciar** seis **etapas** durante la corrida de toros:

Primera etapa : Durante esta fase preliminar, los **capeadores** torean al toro, para **saber** si tiene las cualidades necesarias (su fuerza, inteligencia, agilidad, etc.). Si el toro no es aceptado, el presidente de la plaza agitará un **pañuelo verde**.

Segunda etapa: Los picadores, **montados en caballos protegidos, hacen que el toro les ataque**. Cuando esto **ocurre**, **le hunden las lanzas en el cuello** para **debilitar** sus músculos. **De esta forma** el toro **bajará la cabeza** y el torero **le dará el golpe de gracia** con más facilidad.

Tercera etapa: **Colocación** de las **banderillas** en el cuello del toro. El banderillero **lleva** una banderilla **en cada mano**, **corre hacia el toro** y **le coloca** las banderillas. **Su propósito** es **regular la embestida del toro**.

Ultima etapa: Llamada "suerte" o "tercio". **Comienza** cuando el torero **agita su gorro saludando** al presidente y **pidiendo permiso** para matar al toro. El torero usualmente **dedica** el toro a alguien del público. **Para atrae**r al toro, el torero **utiliza** distintos pases, usando **su capa y espada**.

La muerte del toro: Cuando el torero **cree que** el toro está **más débil**, **intentará darle el "toque de gracia"**, insertando la espada entre la vértebra cervical, directa al **corazón** del toro. Si el "**maestro**" **ha hecho una buena "faena"**, el público agitará pañuelos blancos. Esta es la **señal** para que el presidente **premie** al torero con una **oreja** o el **rabo** del toro. **Por otro lado**, si el torero **no consigue matar** al toro por su bravura, éste **será perdonado** y **se le permitirá vivir en paz**.

---

**podemos diferenciar:** we can differentiate
**etapas:** phases
**capeadores:** people who belong to the bullfighter's team
**saber:** to know
**pañuelo verde:** green handkerchief
**montados en caballos protegidos:** mounted on protected horses
**hacen que el toro les ataque:** they provoke the bull to attack them
**ocurre/ocurrir:** happens/to happen
**le hunden las lanzas en el cuello:** they plunge their lances into the bull's neck
**debilitar:** to weaken
**de esta forma:** this way
**bajará la cabeza:** will lower its head
**le dará el golpe de gracia:** will perform the coup de grace
**colocación:** placement
**banderillas:** barbed sticks
**lleva:** he carries
**en cada mano:** in each hand
**corre hacia el toro:** runs towards the bull
**le coloca/colocar:** places/to place
**su propósito:** his aim
**regular la embestida del toro:** to regulate the charge of the bull
**comienza/comenzar:** it begins/to begin
**agita su gorro:** shakes his hat
**saludando/saludar:** saluting/to salute
**pidiendo permiso:** asking for permission
**dedica/dedicar:** he dedicates/to dedicate
**para atraer:** to attract
**utiliza/utilizar:** he uses/to use
**su capa y espada:** his cape and sword
**cree que/creer:** he thinks/to think
**más débil:** weaker
**intentará darle el toque de gracia:** he will try to administer the "death stroke"
**corazón:** heart
**maestro:** master, a good bullfighter
**ha hecho una buena "faena":** he has given a good "faena" (performance)
**señal:** signal
**premie:** to award
**oreja:** ear
**rabo:** tail
**por otro lado:** on the other hand
**no consigue matar:** he is unable to kill
**será perdonado/perdonar:** will be spared/to spare
**se le permitirá vivir en paz:** the bull will be allowed to live in peace

conmemoran/conmemorar: they commemorate/to commemorate

sin embargo: nevertheless

marca/marcar: it marks/to mark

en realidad: in fact, actually

inicio: beginning

cuenta/contar: it tells/to tell

se iba a celebrar: was going to be celebrated

partidario: supporter

tienda: store

llamado/llamar: called/to call

prestara/prestar: lend him/to lend

florero: vase

adornar: to decorate

homenajeado: the one who they paid tribute to

monarquía: monarchy

reaccionó/reaccionar: he reacted/ to react

de muy mala manera: in a very bad manner

criollos: creoles (of European descent born in a Spanish-American colony)

escuchar: to listen

se puso furioso/ponerse furioso: he became furious/to become furious

le dio una golpiza/dar una golpiza: he hit him/to hit

pelea: fight

aún: still

ilustre rol: illustrious, important role

placa: plaque

se lee/leer: it reads/to read

siguiente: following

se verificó/verificarse: it took place/ to take place

reyerta: brawl, fight

entre: between

que dio principio/dar principio: it originated/to originate, to give birth (methaporically)

a pesar del: in spite of

ímpetu: energy

líderes políticos: political leaders

obtuvo/obtener: he obtained/to obtain

# La independencia de Colombia
## COLOMBIA

El 20 de julio los colombianos **conmemoran** el Día de la Independencia de Colombia. **Sin embargo**, esta fecha **marca en realidad** el **inicio** del proceso de independencia. **Cuenta** la historia que en este día **se iba a celebrar** un banquete en honor a Francisco Villavicencio, **partidario** de la independencia.

Antonio Morales fue a la **tienda** de un español **llamado** González Llorente para que le **prestara** un **florero** con el que **adornar** la mesa del **homenajeado**. Llorente, un fanático de la **monarquía**, **reaccionó de muy mala manera** e insultó a los **criollos**. Al **escuchar** sus insultos, Morales **se puso furioso** y **le dio una golpiza** a Llorente. La **pelea** se extendió por toda la plaza y se comentó por toda la capital. Esta tienda, que **aún** existe en la Plaza de Bolívar en Bogotá, es reconocida por su **ilustre rol** en el proceso de independencia y tiene una **placa** donde **se lee** la **siguiente** inscripción: "En este lugar **se verificó** la **reyerta entre** Morales y Llorente **que dio principio** a la Revolución del 20 de julio".

**A pesar del ímpetu** que ocasionó el famoso "incidente del florero de Llorente" y la influencia de **líderes políticos** como Antonio Nariño, no fue sino hasta el 7 de agosto de 1819, nueve años más tarde, que Colombia **obtuvo** su independencia con la batalla de Boyacá.

Los patriotas **carecían** de armas o uniformes pero con su determinación y fervor **lograron vencer** al **ejército español**. Bajo el **liderazgo** de Simón Bolívar **se creó** un nuevo estado llamado la Gran Colombia en el cual **se unieron** Venezuela, Panamá, Ecuador y Colombia. Sin embargo, a pesar de que Bolívar **asumió** la presidencia de la Gran Colombia, las **facciones políticas** comenzaron a **destruir** la unión de los países que muchos querían ver convertidos en estados **soberanos**. En el 1830, Venezuela y Ecuador **se convirtieron** en naciones independientes y en 1903 Panamá obtuvo finalmente su independencia.

En la actualidad, y a pesar de los conflictos políticos por los que pasa Colombia, el **pueblo siente gran orgullo** de su **patria**. Las celebraciones para el Día de la Independencia **abundan** en las ciudades del país. **Incluso se efectúan** paradas y **manifestaciones** por la **paz. Tanto** para los colombianos que viven en su país, **como** para los que residen en el **extranjero**, el 20 de julio es un día muy especial para **recordar** la creación de la república democrática que **les dio su libertad**.

**carecían/carecer:** they lacked/to lack
**lograron/lograr:** they managed/to manage
**vencer:** to defeat
**ejército español:** Spanish army
**liderazgo:** leadership
**se creó/crear:** was created /to create
**se unieron/unir:** united/to unite
**asumió/asumir:** he assumed/to assume
**facciones políticas:** political factions
**destruir:** to destroy
**soberanos:** sovereign
**se convirtieron/convertirse:** they became/to become
**pueblo:** people
**siente gran orgullo/sentir orgullo:** he is greatly proud/to be proud
**patria:** homeland
**abundan/abundar:** they abound/to abound, to be bountiful
**incluso:** even
**se efectúan/efectuar:** they carry out/ to carry out
**manifestaciones:** demonstrations, rallies
**paz:** peace
**tanto...como:** both...and
**extranjero:** foreigner
**recordar:** to remember
**les dio su libertad:** gave them their freedom

## Vocabulario de la guerra

| | | |
|---|---|---|
| **las fuerzas aéreas:** air force | **bombardear:** to bomb | **derechos humanos:** human rights |
| **las fuerzas aliadas:** allied forces | **el alto el fuego:** cease-fire | **herir:** to wound |
| **el ataque:** attack | **el combate:** combat | **herido:** wounded |
| **atacar:** to attack | **el conflicto:** conflict | **militar:** military |
| **las fuerzas armadas:** armed forces | **la muerte:** death | **la marina:** navy |
| **el ejército:** army | **destruir:** to destroy | **la paz:** peace |
| **la batalla:** battle | **el gobierno:** government | **el/la piloto:** pilot |
| **la batería:** battery | **la granada:** grenade | **resguardar:** to protect against |
| **estar en control:** to be in control | **el helicóptero:** helicopter | **soldado:** soldier |
| **sangriento:** bloody | **las hostilidades:** hostilities | **sacudir:** to strike, to hit |
| **la bomba:** bomb | **humanitario:** humanitarian | **las tropas:** troops |

| | |
|---|---|
| **antigüedad:** antiquity | |
| **pueblos:** people | |
| **consideraron:** they considered/ | |
| to consider | |
| **bandera:** flag | |
| **profundo sentido:** deep sense | |
| **pedazo de tela:** piece of fabric | |
| **palo:** pole | |
| **estandarte:** banner | |
| **representaba/representar:** | |
| it represented/to represent | |
| **pertenencia:** belonging | |
| **diseño:** design | |
| **conocemos/conocer:** we know/ | |
| to know | |
| **sufrió/sufrir:** she suffered/to suffer | |
| **franjas:** stripes | |
| **arriba:** top, upper part | |
| **Patria Vieja:** Old Homeland | |
| **fue izada/izar:** it was hoisted/to hoist | |
| **poderes:** powers | |
| **majestad:** majesty | |
| **ley:** law | |
| **fuerza:** strength | |
| **usarse:** to use | |
| **se adoptó/adoptar:** it was adopted/ | |
| to adopt | |
| **reemplazaba/reemplazar:** it replaced/ | |
| to replace | |
| **sangre vertida:** spilled blood | |
| **campo de batalla:** battlefield | |
| **nieve:** snow | |
| **cordillera:** mountain range | |
| **limpio:** clean, clear | |
| **cielo:** sky | |
| **sin embargo:** however, nevertheless | |
| **pronto:** soon | |
| **desapareció/desaparecer:** | |
| disappeared/to disappear | |
| **actual:** current | |
| **comienzos:** beginnings | |
| **juramento:** oath | |
| **hoy en día:** nowadays | |
| **izada/izar:** raised/to raise, to hoist | |
| **figuran/figurar:** they appear/to appear | |
| **dispuestos/disponer:** arranged/ | |
| to arrange | |
| **cuadrado:** square | |
| **estrella:** star | |
| **velan/velar:** they keep watch over/ | |
| to keep watch over | |
| **en la actualidad:** at the present time | |
| **corresponde:** in accordance with | |
| **murieron/morir:** they died/to die | |

# Un símbolo de la nación
## CHILE

Desde la **antigüedad,** los **pueblos consideraron** a la **bandera** como un objeto de **profundo sentido** simbólico y espiritual. La bandera era mucho más que un **pedazo de tela** con un **palo**; era el **estandarte** que **representaba** a la nación, un símbolo de **pertenencia** y de patriotismo. Hasta llegar al **diseño** que hoy **conocemos**, la bandera chilena **sufrió** tres transformaciones. La primera bandera se componía de tres **franjas** horizontales: azul la de **arriba**, blanca la del centro y amarilla la de abajo. Esta es conocida en la historia como la Bandera de la **Patria Vieja** y **fue izada** por primera vez en 1812. Para algunos representaba los tres **poderes** del estado: **majestad**, **ley** y **fuerza**.

En 1814 dejó de **usarse** y Chile estuvo un tiempo sin bandera propia hasta que en 1817 **se adoptó** una nueva insignia llamada Bandera de la Transición. Ésta tenía tres franjas: azul, blanca y roja (la roja **reemplazaba** a la amarilla de la bandera de 1812). Estos colores simbolizaban la **sangre vertida** por los hombres chilenos en el **campo de batalla**; el blanco, la **nieve** de la **cordillera** de los Andes; y el azul, el **limpio cielo** del país. **Sin embargo**, al igual que la de la Patria Vieja, esta bandera no tuvo legalización oficial y **pronto desapareció**.

La bandera **actual** se usó públicamente y por primera vez a **comienzos** de 1818 en la proclamación de la independencia y primer **juramento** de la bandera. **Hoy en día** es **izada** en todas las fiestas patrias. En esta bandera también **figuran** los colores azul, blanco y rojo, aunque **dispuestos** de manera distinta a la anterior: la parte superior con dos colores, azul y blanco, y la parte inferior con un solo color, rojo. El azul forma un **cuadrado**, cuyas dimensiones son un tercio del largo de la franja roja, y en el centro tiene una **estrella** que representa los poderes del Estado que **velan** por la integridad de la patria. **En la actualidad**, el día de la bandera se celebra el 9 de julio y **corresponde** a la conmemoración del Combate de La Concepción de 1882, en el que **murieron** más de 70 chilenos.

# La bandera de México
## MÉXICO

Las **banderas** son más que un simple **pedazo** de **tela** con colores; son el símbolo del país al que representan. Las banderas son la imagen de la unión de la nación, de sus ideales, de su historia y también de su cultura. **Por este motivo**, el **diseño**, los colores y el **escudo** con que están confeccionadas **son escogidos** para representar **algo específico** e importante de la **patria**.

La bandera mexicana está dividida en tres partes: una verde, una blanca y una roja. Cada color tiene un **significado** especial. La **franja** verde es la de la independencia y la **esperanza**. El centro blanco representa la **pureza** de los ideales de la nación. La parte roja de la bandera representa la **sangre** que los héroes nacionales **han derramado** por la patria. En el centro del área blanca de la bandera mexicana se encuentra el escudo nacional de México, un **águila** sobre un **nopal combatiendo** contra una **serpiente**. Este **emblema** representa la **fuerza** y la historia de México.

La **leyenda cuenta** que un día unos indios aztecas **llegaron** a un gran **valle** donde había una **laguna** con un **islote** pequeño **en el medio**. Allí observaron un águila sobre un nopal **florecido devorando** una **víbora**. Los indígenas tomaron esta imagen como una **señal** de los dioses y, por eso, **construyeron allí** Tenochtitlán, lo que **hoy en día** es la capital del país, México D. F. La bandera mexicana fue creada en 1821 después de la independencia de México. El 24 de febrero es un día nacional de fiesta por lo que se celebran muchos **desfiles** y otros eventos en honor a la bandera.

**banderas:** flags
**pedazo:** piece
**tela:** cloth
**por este motivo:** for this reason
**diseño:** design
**escudo:** coat of arms
**son escogidos/escoger:** they are chosen/to choose
**algo específico:** something specific
**patria:** homeland
**significado:** meaning
**franja:** stripe
**esperanza:** hope
**pureza:** purity
**sangre:** blood
**han derramado/derramar:** they have spilled/to spill
**águila:** eagle
**nopal:** prickly pear cactus
**combatiendo/combatir:** fighting/ to fight
**serpiente:** snake
**emblema:** emblem
**fuerza:** strength
**leyenda:** legend
**cuenta/contar:** tells/to tell
**llegaron/llegar:** they arrived/to arrive
**valle:** valley
**laguna:** small lake
**islote:** islet, small island
**en el medio:** in the middle
**florecido:** flowering
**devorando/devorar:** devouring/ to devour
**víbora:** viper
**señal:** sign
**construyeron/construir:** they built/ to build
**allí:** there
**hoy en día:** nowadays
**desfiles:** parades

# San Juan
## PUERTO RICO

*"En mi* **viejo** *San Juan…"* **Así comienza** una **canción famosa** que **se ha convertido** en **himno nacional** ya que **narra** la **angustia** y **esperanza** de quienes **nos encontramos lejos** de la isla.

San Juan, la capital de Puerto Rico, está **llena de** historia, **grabada** en sus **edificios antiguos** y sus **adoquines**. La ciudad original **fue fundada** en 1508 por Juan Ponce de León. **En aquel entonces se le conocía como** "Caparra". Un **año después**, Caparra fue **reubicada** al **oeste** del lugar original. La "ciudad **amurallada**", el viejo San Juan, **nace oficialmente** en 1521, **convirtiéndóse** en la ciudad mas antigua **bajo** la bandera estadounidense y la **segunda** de las Américas.

El área hoy conocida como San Juan se divide en tres partes: el Viejo San Juan, la playa y el **área hotelera**, aparte de otras comunidades como Río Piedras, Hato Rey y Santurce. Con su población de **cerca de medio millón de habitantes**, la ciudad es el **centro de procesamiento** más grande de la isla y su **puerto** el de mas movimiento del Caribe. El puerto de San Juan es el segundo más grande de la región después de Nueva York. Pero, ¿cuál es la magia que esconde esta ciudad? A primera vista el **visitante siente** la influencia inmediata de los **ancestros españoles** aún **caminando** por sus **calles de adoquines**, **teñidos de azul** por el **pasar del tiempo**. Sus edificios coloniales hablan de **siglos lejanos**.

Estas estructuras son las que **rodean** las plazas donde jóvenes y adultos aún **se reúnen** a hablar, **escuchar** su música favorita o jugar un **partido de dominó**.

Entre las plazas preferidas de los puertorriqueños están la Plaza de San José, con su **estatua de bronce** en honor a Juan Ponce de León, La Plaza del Quinto Centenario, **celebrando** los 500 años del **descubrimiento** del **Nuevo Mundo** y la Plaza de Armas, con cuatro estatuas que representan las cuatro estaciones del año. **Yo prefiero** la Plazoleta de la Rogativa por el significado que **encierra**.

Se dice que en 1797 la **flota** británica llegó a la Bahía de San Juan para **atacar** y tomar posesión de la isla. Al verse **amenazados**, el gobernador **ordenó** una **rogativa** para **pedir la ayuda** de los santos. Las mujeres **organizaron** una procesión **repentina**. Caminaron por las calles de la ciudad **cargando antorchas** y **tocando campanas**. Ante la conmoción, los británicos **se retiraron pensando** que habían llegado **refuerzos**. Desde entonces **quedó demostrada** la **voluntad** y **valentía** de un pueblo cuando **se trata** de defender **lo suyo**.

San Juan también **cuenta con** infinidad de **parques** y **fortalezas**. Entre las mas conocidas se encuentra El Morro, con sus seis **niveles** a 140 pies sobre el **nivel del mar**. Esta **asombrosa** estructura es en realidad un **laberinto de túneles**, **calabozos**, **barracas** y rampas, **rodeadas** por las famosas **garitas** que se han convertido en símbolo nacional. A esto **se unen** las catedrales, los teatros y los museos donde se exhibe la vida, historia, cultura y evolución de un pueblo, **mezcla de sangre** taina, española y africana.

Esto es San Juan de Puerto Rico, una ciudad antigua, rodeada de belleza natural. Este es el lugar a donde millones de puertorriqueños **esperan volver** algún día **cantando** la melodía de... *En mi viejo San Juan.*

**rodean/rodear:** they surround/ to surround
**se reúnen/reunir:** they gather/to gather
**escuchar:** to listen
**partido de dominó:** game of dominoes
**estatua de bronce:** bronze statue
**celebrando/celebrar:** celebrating/ to celebrate
**descubrimiento:** discovery
**Nuevo Mundo:** new world
**yo prefiero/preferir:** I prefer/to prefer
**encierra/encerrar:** it involves/to involve
**flota:** fleet
**atacar:** to attack
**amenazados/amenazar:** threatened/ to threaten
**ordenó/ordenar:** ordered/to order
**rogativa:** rogations
**pedir la ayuda:** to ask for the help
**organizaron/organizar:** organized/ to organize
**repentina:** sudden
**cargando/cargar:** carrying/to carry
**antorchas:** torches
**tocando campanas:** ringing bells
**se retiraron:** they left
**pensando/pensar:** thinking/to think
**refuerzos:** reinforcemetns
**quedó demostrada:** it was proven
**voluntad:** will
**valentía:** bravery
**se trata/tratarse:** it is about/to be about
**lo suyo:** its own
**cuenta con:** it includes
**parques:** parks
**fortalezas:** fortresses
**niveles:** levels
**nivel del mar:** sea level
**asombrosa:** astonishing
**laberinto de túneles:** labyrinth of tunnels
**calabozos:** dungeons
**barracas:** shacks, huts
**garitas:** sentry boxes
**se unen/unirse:** they are added/to add
**mezcla de sangre:** mixture of blood
**esperan/esperar:** they hope/to hope
**volver:** to return
**cantando/cantar:** singing/to sing

# Las ruinas de Tiwanaku
## BOLIVIA

**Parece mentira** que luego de **tantos siglos**, tantos **sucesos** y tanta historia, parte de las ruinas de Tiwanaku **siga en pie**. **Si bien** el hombre **tuvo que ver** en su reconstrucción y posterior protección, **pasaron años**, décadas y hasta siglos para que estas cenizas **resurgieran** de sus **cenizas**.

**Se trata** de una antiquísima civilización cuyos **restos** aún **permanecen** en **forma megalítica** con inscripciones de símbolos que **todavía** hoy **siguen sin descifrar**. Según estudios arqueológicos **se calcula** que el origen de esta cultura **se remonta** al año 1600 AC.

Esta ciudad **desaparecida**, cuyas **milenarias** ruinas han sido **restauradas** en parte, está a sólo 72 kilómetros de la ciudad de La Paz, muy cerca del Lago Titicaca. Poco **se sabe** de ella y de su civilización, aunque historiadores y arqueólogos coinciden en que fue un gran centro urbano **sustentado** por un sofisticado sistema de agricultura en **terrazas** para producir **alimentos**, que **permitía satisfacer** las necesidades de consumo de toda esta ciudadela a semejante altura. También **destaca** por ser una metrópolis del **conocimiento** y de las ciencias ya que su pueblo, la cultura aymara, construyó monumentales **edificios** y templos con **grandísimos bloques de piedra orientados** de forma astronómica, perfeccionaron la técnica de la **momificación** y realizaron **hazañas sorprendentes** en el **campo de la medicina**.

Actualmente las ruinas de Tiwanaku están declaradas Patrimonio Histórico de la Humanidad por la UNESCO y están consideradas un **templo vivo** y un centro ceremonial por los descendientes del pueblo aymara, quienes todos los años **se dan cita** en el lugar para **rendir culto** o simplemente para **agradecer** y **acompañar** a sus ancestros. Y **no debe** ser casual que *Tiwanaku*, en **idioma** aymara, **quiera decir** "Ciudad de Dioses".

# Una pieza de historia
## HONDURAS

**Se dice** que hay evidencia de que existieron **tribus** maya en el oeste de Honduras. Pero fue Cristóbal Colón en 1502 quien primero **visitó** Trujillo y llamó al país Honduras debido a la **profundidad** del agua en la costa caribeña. La **herencia indígena** de Honduras está simbolizada por el nombre Lempira (**caballero** de las montañas) uno de los héroes nacionales **debido a** la batalla que organizó en los 1530 **contra** los españoles. Debido a la manera cruel en que **mataron** a Lempira, los hondureños **lo honraron** dándole ese nombre a su **moneda nacional.** Los españoles **llegaron** en 1525 y **denominaron** a Comayagua la capital en 1537. Fue 350 años más tarde, en 1880, cuando Tegucigalpa **se convirtió** en la capital. Debido al **oro** y la **plata encontrados** en Trujillo, holandeses y británicos **saquearon** la zona, y **no fue sino hasta** 1787 que los españoles **volvieron** a reclamar su espacio concentrándose en la zona central mientras los británicos **se enfocaron** en las costas.

En 1821 **se otorgó** la independencia a Honduras; luego de ser parte de México brevemente, **se unió** a la Federación Centro Americana. El conflicto entre liberales y conservadores llevó a Honduras a declararse nación independiente en 1838. **Desde ese entonces** ha habido **lucha de poderes**, cientos de **golpes de estado**, rebeliones e irregularidades electorales. Uno de los casos más relevantes fue de los americanos que **trataron** de **manera fallida** de obtener el control de Honduras en 1850. En 1913 los **bananos** eran el 66 por ciento de los productos de exportación del país, siendo el 75 por ciento de compañías americanas. En 1969 Honduras y El Salvador tuvieron una **guerra** (la Guerra del Fútbol) que **duró** 100 horas pero que **afectó** las relaciones entre estos **países vecinos.** En los años 80 Honduras fue **asilo** para los **Contra** cuando los sandinistas **derrocaron** al dictador nicaragüense. Tiempo después, el gobierno examinó el rol de la **base militar estadounidense**, **se negó** a **firmar** un **acuerdo**, **despidió** a los Contra de Honduras y Violeta Chamorro ganó las elecciones de Nicaragua en 1990.

**se dice/decir:** it is said/to say
**tribus:** tribes
**visitó/visitar:** he visited/to visit
**profundidad:** depth
**herencia indígena:** indigenous heritage
**caballero:** knight, horseman
**debido a:** due to
**contra:** against
**mataron/matar:** they killed/to kill
**lo honraron/honrar:** they honored him/to honor him
**moneda nacional:** national currency
**llegaron/llegar:** they arrived/to arrive
**denominaron/denominar:** they named/to name
**se convirtió/convertirse:** it was turned into/to turn into
**oro:** gold
**plata:** silver
**encontrados:** found
**saquearon/saquear:** they plundered/to plunder
**no fue sino hasta:** it was not until
**volvieron/volver:** they returned/to return
**se enfocaron/enfocar:** they focused/to focus
**se otorgó/otorgar:** it was granted/to grant
**se unió/unirse:** it joined/to join
**desde ese entonces:** since then
**lucha de poderes:** fight of powers, power struggle
**golpes de estado:** coups d'état
**trataron/tratar:** they tried/to try
**manera fallida:** unsuccessful way
**bananos:** bananas
**guerra:** war
**duró/durar:** it lasted/to last
**afectó/afectar:** it affected/to affect
**países vecinos:** neighboring countries
**asilo:** asylum
**Contra:** Somoza's National Guard
**derrocaron/derrocar:** they overthrew/to overthrow
**base militar estadounidense:** United States military base
**se negó/negarse:** he refused/to refuse
**firmar:** to sign
**acuerdo:** agreement
**despidió/despedir:** he fired/to fire

**ha oído/oír:** everybody has heard/
to hear
**judíos:** Jews
**habitaron/habitar:** they lived/to live
**todavía:** still
**suelo:** land
**sin embargo:** however
**pocos:** few
**nos acercamos/acercarse:** we get
closer/to get closer
**comienza/comenzar:** it starts/to start
**a principios:** at the beginning
**en ese entonces:** then, at that time
**fueron invadidos/invadir:** they were
invaded/to invade
**conquistados/conquistar:** conquered/
to conquer
**territorio:** land
**llevaban/llevar:** they took/to take
**esclavos:** slaves
**naufragaron/naufragar:** they were
wrecked/to be shipwrecked
**isla:** island
**pelearon/pelear:** they fought/to fight
**los unos contra los otros:** one
against the other
**con el paso del tiempo:** as time
went by
**aprendieron/aprender:** they learned/
to learn
**convivir:** to live together
**matrimonios:** marriages
**mixtos:** mixed
**así:** this way
**integrantes:** members
**fueron/ser:** they were/to be
**llamados/llamar:** called/to call
**desciende/descender:** it descends
from/to descend from
**más adelante:** further on
**se apoderaron/apoderarse:** they took
possession/to take possession
**pasó a ser/pasar a ser:** it became/
to become
**ayudados/ayudar:** helped/to help
**trataron de/tratar de:** they tried to/to
try to
**mantener:** to keep
**aunque:** even though
**sin éxito:** without success

# Los garifunas
## BELICE

Todo el mundo **ha oído** hablar alguna vez de los mayas, los aztecas, los **judíos,** los afroamericanos o de tantas otras culturas que **habitaron** algún día, y **todavía** lo hacen, **suelo** americano. **Sin embargo**, **pocos** conocen la cultura garifuna. En estas líneas **nos acercamos** a ella.

La historia de los garifunas **comienza a principios** del año 1600 en la isla de San Vicente, en el Caribe oriental, habitada **en ese entonces** por los indios arawaks. Estos **fueron invadidos** y **conquistados** por otra tribu procedente de **territorio**  norteamericano, los kalipunas, que asesinaron a los hombres arawaks y tomaron a sus mujeres como esposas. En 1635, dos buques españoles que **llevaban esclavos** nigerianos **naufragaron** cerca de la **isla**. Al principio, españoles, nigerianos y kalipunas **pelearon los unos contra los otros**, pero **con el paso del tiempo aprendieron** a **convivir** y se realizaron **matrimonios mixtos**, formándose **así** la comunidad garifuna. Sus **integrantes fueron** también **llamados** "caribes negros" (la palabra garifuna **desciende** probablemente del kalipuna).

**Más adelante,** los ingleses **se apoderaron** de San Vicente por lo que **pasó a ser** una colonia británica. Los "caribes negros", **ayudados** por los franceses, **trataron de mantener** el control independiente de la isla, **aunque sin éxito.**

En 1796, **ambos** "caribes" y franceses **se rindieron**. Los británicos deportaron a los caribes y **los dejaron** en la Isla de Roatán, **frente a** la costa de Honduras.

Los españoles, **arrebatando** la Isla de Roatán, **liberaron** a los garifunas de manos inglesas y **los llevaron** a trabajar a Trujillo, en el centro de España, como **agricultores** y en el **ejército**. Los primeros garifunas que llegaron a la costa de Belice fueron llevados por los españoles, a principios de 1800. **Al tiempo**, Belice fue ayudada por los británicos, quienes la llamaron la "Honduras británica". Los caribes que **continuaban** sirviendo en el ejército español se fueron moviendo **poco a poco hacia** el área de la "Honduras Británica" hasta que, después de la independencia centroamericana, un gran número de garifunas **huyó** hacia la costa de Belice. El 19 de noviembre se conmemora el Día del Acuerdo Garifuna, la mayor fiesta de esta comunidad.

A lo largo de todo el siglo XX, y **de forma gradual**, esta cultura **se esparció**, primero, por toda la costa de Belice y, **posteriormente**, por todo el mundo. Esto **dio como resultado** el **asentamiento** de pequeñas comunidades garifunas en otros lugares como Los Angeles, Nueva Orleans o Nueva York.

Su historia de **lucha** y trabajo ha hecho que la comunidad garifuna se caracterice, sobre todo, por su **fuerza** y su **voluntad** para **conseguir** lo que **se propone** y por defender lo propio. **Será por eso** que hoy la mayoría de ellos mantiene su música, su baile, su lengua, su religión y sus costumbres. **A pesar de** que esta cultura **se expandió** hacia otras ciudades y países, la mayor parte del pueblo garifuno reside todavía en Belice, un país donde **se entremezclan** culturas, lenguas y grupos étnicos que **conviven** en **armonía**, tolerancia y solidaridad.

---

**ambos:** both
**se rindieron/rendirse:** they surrendered/to surrender
**los dejaron/dejar:** they left them/ to leave
**frente a:** in front of
**arrebatando/arrebatar:** snatching/ to snatch
**liberaron/liberar:** releasing/to free, to release
**los llevaron/llevar:** they took them/ to take
**agricultores:** farmers
**ejército:** army
**al tiempo:** at the same time
**continuaban/continuar:** they kept/ to keep
**poco a poco:** little by little
**hacia:** towards
**huyó/huir:** they got away/to get away
**de forma gradual:** gradually
**se esparció/esparcir:** it was scattered/ to scatter
**posteriormente:** later
**dio como resultado/dar como resultado:** it gave as a result/to give as a result
**asentamiento:** settlement
**lucha:** struggle
**fuerza:** strength
**voluntad:** willingness
**conseguir:** to reach
**se propone/proponerse:** (the community) intends /to intend
**será por eso:** maybe that is why
**a pesar de:** in spite of
**se expandió/expandirse:** it spread/ to spread
**se entremezclan/entremezclarse:** they mix/to mix, to mingle
**conviven/convivir:** they live/to live
**armonía:** harmony

# Examina tu comprensión

## El cinco de mayo, page 146

**1.** Cinco de mayo is celebrated in all of Mexico, especially in what city?

**2.** Many people think Cinco de mayo is Mexican Independence Day. The actual Independence Day is when?

**3.** Cinco de mayo commemorates what event?

**4.** What does that event symbolize for the Mexicans?

## Los hijos del sol, page 148

**1.** In what century were the Incas invaded and by whom?

**2.** The legend of Cusco describes the city as what?

**3.** In 1526 the empire was divided, resulting in what event?

## La independencia de Colombia, page 152

**1.** Describe the conflict that occured between Morales and Llorente that initiated the process of independence.

**2.** How many years after this event did independence actually come to Columbia?

**3.** Under whose leadership was liberty obtained?

## Un símbolo de la nación, page 154

**1.** The flag of Chile is more than fabric. What does it represent to the people?

**2.** The three horizontal stripes represent what?

**3.** The Chilean flag is red, white and blue. What do each of these colors represent?

# Test your comprehension

## La bandera de Mexico, page 155

1. The Mexican flag is green, white and red.  List the significance of each color.

2. What is the emblem on the Mexican flag and what does it represent?

3. Describe the legend that is told in the article in your own words.

## San Juan, page 156

1. Who founded San Juan and what was the original name of the city?

2. What is the "favorite" plaza of the city and what will you find there?

3. In 1797 the city was under attack. What did the women of the city do?

4. What is El Morro?  What will you find here?

## Las ruinas de Tiwanaku, page 158

1. Why did historians and archeologists think that this area may have been a great urban center?

2. What scientific wonders were discovered here?

3. The Aymara people consider the area a temple for what purpose?

## Los garifunas, page 160

1. How was the Garifuna community formed?

2. Who "liberated" the Garifunas from the hands of the English? Where were they taken and for what purpose?

3. Despite the struggles of the Garifunas, the strength of their commitment to community helped them maintain what five elements of their culture?

La tierra que no es labrada llevará abrojos y espinas aunque sea fértil; así es el entendimiento del hombre.

Santa Teresa de Jesús

# Geografía

# El Parque Nacional Darién
## PANAMÁ

Panamá es **reconocido mundialmente** por **poseer** su capital **rodeada** de **bosques tropicales caracterizados** por la **riqueza** de su biodiversidad. Es que en este país de América Central es posible **acceder** a parques nacionales a **tan sólo** 10 minutos del área urbana. La variedad de plantas y animales que **habitan** allí es difícil de **encontrar** en otras latitudes del mundo, y su abundancia y diversidad **ha imposibilitado** una **clasificación científica definitiva**.

El **mejor ejemplo** del exuberante y **complejo** ecosistema panameño **se encuentra** en la provincia de Darién, **ubicada** en el **extremo oriental** del país. El Parque Nacional Darién **fue creado** en 1980 y **constituye no sólo** el mayor parque del país, **sino** de toda Centroamérica. En 1981 la UNESCO declaró a este paraíso tropical Patrimonio Mundial de la Humanidad por el **valor** de su **ambiente diversificado** y por la riqueza cultural de las tribus aborígenes que allí habitan.

El área protegida del Parque Nacional Darién **atraviesa casi toda** la Provincia y **abarca** desde las costas del Pacífico hasta casi la costa del Mar Caribe. **A lo largo de** esta **superficie** de aproximadamente 579.000 hectáreas, un **manto forestal** de **bosques húmedos** tropicales **definen** el paisaje. **Precisamente**, es en este parque donde nacen los ríos Tuira, Balsas, Sambú y Jaque que luego **recorren** todo el territorio.

La **cordillera** y las **serranías** de la zona son de origen volcánico por lo que resulta interesante observar **piedras** y sedimentos de lava que dan cuenta de la intensa actividad de estos **gigantes de fuego** a lo largo del tiempo.

Como se ha mencionado, también la riqueza cultural caracteriza al Parque Nacional Darién. En la región habitan tres grupos indígenas precolombinos: los Kunas, que **mantienen** poblaciones tradicionales al **pie** de la montaña **sagrada** Cerro Tarcuna; los Emberá, que **moran** en la **ribera** del Chocó; y los Wounaan, muy **cercanos** lingüísticamente y culturalmente a los Emberá. No obstante, también **cabe destacar** la presencia de poblaciones **afrodarienitas**. Estos grupos de **ascendencia** africana **han convivido** durante siglos con los indígenas de la región **creando** un mosaico etnocultural sin precedentes en Centroamérica.

**A pesar de** la riqueza y reconocimiento mundial del parque, los expertos de la zona **sostienen** que los **esfuerzos** para preservarlo **no han sido suficientes**. Entre los factores que lo **amenazan** se pueden **mencionar** el **avance de la agricultura**, el **manejo** poco responsable de las concesiones forestales, la **cacería** y la **pesca**, los residuos tóxicos, la introducción de especies **no originarias** y los **conflictos armados** del **país vecino**, Colombia.

Para la conservación de la diversidad de la región, los científicos **indican** que es **imprescindible** la regulación y control de la actividad agropecuaria y forestal y la **realización** y **profundización** de estudios de **impacto ambiental** y cultural **antes de proceder** a incorporar infraestructuras que podrían **alterar** el ecosistema.

**Sin lugar a duda**, la **estratégica ubicación** de este **pulmón** vegetal del Caribe lo convierte en un lugar de encuentro entre la riqueza natural y cultural de América Central y América del Sur. **¿Sabremos preservarla?**

---

**mantienen/mantener:** they maintain/ to maintain
**pie:** foot
**sagrada:** sacred
**moran/morar:** they live/to live
**ribera:** banks, riverside
**cercanos:** close
**cabe destacar:** it is worth pointing out
**afrodarienitas:** population of African descent from the Darien area, in Panama
**ascendencia:** ancestry
**han convivido/convivir:** they have lived together/to live together
**creando/crear:** creating/to create
**a pesar de:** in spite of
**sostienen/sostener:** they maintain/ to maintain
**esfuerzos:** efforts
**no han sido suficientes:** they have not been enough
**amenazan/amenazar:** they threaten/ to threaten
**mencionar:** to mention
**avance de la agricultura:** advances of agriculture
**manejo:** management
**cacería:** hunting
**pesca:** fishing
**no originarias:** not originally from there
**conflictos armados:** armed conflicts
**país vecino:** neighboring country
**indican/indicar:** they indicate/ to indicate
**imprescindible:** essential
**realización:** carrying out
**profundización:** deepening
**impacto ambiental:** environmental impact
**antes de proceder:** before proceeding
**alterar:** to alter, change
**sin lugar a duda:** without a doubt
**estratégica ubicación:** strategic location
**pulmón:** lung
**¿Sabremos preservarla?:** Will we know how to preserve it?

# Las islas Galápagos
## ECUADOR

**Las islas Galápagos** están **localizadas** a 965 kilómetros (650 **millas**) de la costa del Ecuador. Las islas Galápagos **emergieron** del Océano Pacífico hace unos 6 millones de años **como resultado de erupciones volcánicas submarinas**. Las **edades más antiguas** de las islas están al **sureste**, mientras que las **edades más recientes** están al **noroeste**, donde también se encuentra toda la actividad volcánica, con ocho volcanes activos, **seis de los cuales** están **unidos formando** la isla Isabela, uno en la isla Fernandina y otro en la isla Marchena, **estas islas tienen una edad** de tres a cinco millones de años.

El **archipiélago fue descubierto** en 1535 por el **Obispo** Fray Tomás de Berlanga, quien le **dio** el nombre de "Islas de los Galápagos" por la **semejanza** de los **caparazones** de las **tortugas** Galápagos con la **montura** o **silla** para **cabalgar de mujeres** de la época. Los piratas **fueron los primeros** en **frecuentar** las islas por 200 años pues este archipiélago **era un lugar excelente** para **recuperarse** de las **heridas** después de los combates, **arreglar** sus **naves** y **buscar agua** y comida para sus nuevos combates.

En el año 1832 el Ecuador **toma posesión** del archipiélago de Galápagos por **derecho geográfico e histórico**.

En el año 1835 llegó Charles Darwin para hacer investigaciones **para sus escritos** de la teoría del "Origen de las Especies" ya que las islas Galápagos eran el **escenario perfecto** para **comprender** los **cambios evolutivos** de las especies. Las islas Galápagos fueron declaradas Parque Nacional por **el gobierno** de Ecuador en 1936 para preservar la flora y la fauna de las trece islas más grandes, seis islas menores y más de cuarenta islas pequeñas **que conforman** el archipiélago.

En 1959 **se crea** la Fundación Charles Darwin para las islas Galápagos, **creada bajo los auspicios** de la UNESCO y de la Unión Mundial para Conservación esta fundación está dedicada a la conservación de los ecosistemas de Galápagos. La flora y la fauna **únicas** de las islas Galápagos **se deben a** diferentes factores como: el origen volcánico, la distancia **hacia el continente**, la dirección de los **vientos** y la **confluencia de** las **corrientes marinas** en donde se produce un **curioso fenómeno**: las aguas del norte son más calientes que la del sur (unos cinco grados centígrados) por lo que hace que en el norte **haya más vida marina**.

La fauna que se puede encontrar en estas islas es **la siguiente**: iguanas marinas, **leones marinos**, pingüinos, **cormoranes**, **garzas**, tortugas marinas, tortugas galápagos, iguanas terrestres, **pinzones**, **gaviotas**, flamencos, pelícanos, **focas**, albatros y **tiburónes ballena** que son **inofensivos para el hombre** ya que **sólo comen peces pequeños**. La flora que se puede encontrar en las islas es la siguiente: **manglare**, **cactus endémicos**, vegetación húmeda, **guaco** y desiertos con cactus.

También se encuentran **paisajes** únicos como **playas blancas**, **radiantes rocas basálticas** obscuras y sólidas, túnel de lava hacia el volcán Scalesiastewarth, que es un cráter, diferentes volcanes, **formaciones de lava y lagunas**.

---

**para sus escritos:** for his writings
**escenario perfecto:** perfect setting
**comprender:** to understand
**cambios evolutivos:** evolutionary changes
**el gobierno:** the government
**que conforman/conformar:** that make up; form/to make up; form
**se crea/crear:** is created/to create
**creada bajo:** created under
**los auspicios:** the auspices (guiding sponsorship)
**únicas:** unique
**se deben a/deber:** are due to/to owe
**hacia el continente:** location of the continent
**vientos:** winds
**confluencia de/confluir:** gathering/to come together
**corrientes marinas:** sea currents
**curioso fenómeno:** peculiar phenomenon
**haya más vida marina:** there is more marine life
**la siguiente:** the following
**leones marinos:** sea lions
**cormoranes:** cormorants (coastal bird similiar to the pelican)
**garzas:** heron
**pinzones:** finch
**gaviotas:** seagulls
**focas:** seals
**tiburónes ballena:** whale sharks
**inofensivos para el hombre:** harmless to man
**sólo comen peces pequeños:** only eat small fish
**manglare:** mangrove
**cactus endémicos:** native cactus
**guaco:** guaco, tropical plant
**paisajes:** landscape
**playas blancas:** white beaches
**radiantes rocas basálticas:** radiating basaltic rock
**formaciones de lava y lagunas:** formations of lava and lagoons

**diversidad genética:** genetic diversity

**en peligro:** in danger

**mecanismo:** mechanism

**ha sido/ser:** it has been/to be

**proceso evolutivo:** evolutionary process

**últimos:** last

**se ha transformado/ transformar:** it has been transformed/to transform

**principal:** main

**amenaza:** threat

**actualmente:** nowadays

**estiman/estimar:** they estimate/ to estimate

**desaparece:** disappears

**lengua nativa:** native language

**precolombina:** pre-Columbian

**oso hormiguero gigante:** giant anteater

**bosques espinosos:** pine forests

**morador:** dweller

**medir:** to measure

**lengua:** tongue

**larga:** long

**fina:** thin

**pegajosa:** sticky

**atrapar:** to catch

**hormigas:** ants

**termitas:** termites

**deglutirlos/deglutir:** swallow them/to swallow

**estrategia de supervivencia:** survival strategy

**valiosa:** valuable

**controlados/controlar:** controlled/to control

**no se vuelven plagas:** they don't become a plague

**aunque:** although

**podría parecer:** it could seem

**suma importancia:** extremely important

**dañinas:** damaging

**transforma/transformar:** it transforms/to transform

**suelos:** lands, grounds

**desarrollo futuro:** future development

# El jurumí

PARAGUAY

La **diversidad genética** de las especies de nuestro planeta se encuentra **en peligro**. Si bien este **mecanismo ha sido,** y es, parte del **proceso evolutivo**, en los **últimos** 300 años es el hombre el que **se ha transformado** en la **principal amenaza**. **Actualmente**, algunos especialistas **estiman** que cada 15 minutos **desaparece** una especie**.**

"Jurumí" es el nombre en guaraní, la **lengua nativa precolombina**, del **oso hormiguero gigante**. Frecuentemente se encuentra en los **bosques espinosos** del Chaco paraguayo. Este típico **morador** de los bosques del Paraguay es un animal que puede llegar a **medir** hasta dos metros de largo y a pesar 40 kilos. Una de sus características más curiosas es su **lengua larga, fina** y **pegajosa,** que puede medir hasta 60 centímetros. Gracias a ella, le es posible **atrapar** todo tipo de insectos, fundamentalmente **hormigas** y **termitas,** y **deglutirlos** inmediatamente. Esta **estrategia de supervivencia** es muy **valiosa** para el ecosistema ya que así estos invertebrados están **controlados** y **no se vuelven plagas** para la región. **Aunque** esto **podría parecer** una cuestión menor, es de **suma importancia** ya que las termitas son **dañinas** en las zonas rurales. Su paso **transforma** los **suelos** y afecta el **desarrollo futuro** de la vegetación.

Por otra parte, este oso hormiguero **se caracteriza** por su **escasa** visión y **audición**. **Sin embargo**, su **sentido del olfato** está **altamente** desarrollado y es el que **le permite conseguir** sus mejores **presas** y **subsistir a lo largo del** día.

El jurumí es un animal de **hábitos diurnos**. Por la noche, **duerme** al **aire libre** en **zonas descampadas**. Si bien **se le reconoce** como un animal **sumamente pacífico**, puede llegar a ser peligroso si es **atacado,** ya que cuenta con **garras afiladas** y **antebrazos fuertes**. Aunque es un animal solitario, se le puede ver en pareja durante el **período de cortejo**. La **hembra** del jurumí tiene una sola **cría** por año y el período de gestación es de 190 días. La cría nace en la **primavera** y es frecuente **verla montada** en la **espalda** de su madre. El **recién nacido** es **amamantado** durante seis meses y no estará en condiciones de subsistir independientemente hasta cumplir los 2 años. Si el **cachorro crece** en su ambiente natural suele llegar a vivir 14 años pero, si se desarrolla en **cautiverio**, puede **alcanzar** los 25 años.

Los enemigos naturales del jurumí son el jaguar y el puma. Sin embargo, entre las principales causas que **lo amenazan** hoy se encuentran la destrucción de su hábitat y la **cacería**. Esta última es una práctica tradicional en el Paraguay y en toda Suramérica. Por eso, si bien los **pobladores rurales destacan** la importancia de esta especie y la protegen, son los **cazadores furtivos** los que la ponen en peligro. Afortunadamente, tanto el **gobierno** del Paraguay como diversas organizaciones ecologistas locales **han emprendido** valiosas acciones para protegerla.

**se caracteriza:** it is characterized
**escasa:** poor
**audición:** hearing
**sin embargo:** however
**sentido del olfato:** sense of smell
**altamente:** highly
**le permite conseguir:** it allows it to obtain
**presas:** prey
**subsistir:** to live
**a lo largo del:** throughout
**hábitos diurnos:** daytime habits
**duerme/dormir:** it sleeps/to sleep
**aire libre:** outdoors
**zonas descampadas:** open areas
**se le reconoce/reconocer:** it is recognized/to recognize
**sumamente:** extremely
**pacífico:** peaceful
**atacado/atacar:** attacked/ to attack
**garras afiladas:** sharp claws
**antebrazos fuertes:** strong forearms
**período de cortejo:** courtship period
**hembra:** female
**cría:** baby animal
**primavera:** spring
**verla/ver:** see it/to see
**montada/montar:** riding/to ride
**espalda:** back
**recién nacido:** newborn
**amamantado:** breast-fed
**cachorro:** baby, cub
**crece/crecer:** it grows up/to grow
**cautiverio:** captivity
**alcanzar:** to reach
**lo amenazan/amenazar:** they threaten it/to threaten
**cacería:** hunting
**pobladores rurales:** country dwellers
**destacan/destacar:** they emphasize/to emphasize
**cazadores:** hunters
**furtivos:** furtive
**gobierno:** government
**han emprendido/emprender:** they have undertaken/to undertake

| | |
|---|---|
| **departamento:** department (state) | |
| **impresionante:** impressive | |
| **llamado/llamar:** called/to call | |
| **lo hace único:** it makes it unique | |
| **cuencas hidrográficas:** water basins | |
| **compuesta por:** composed of | |
| **aves:** birds | |
| **mamíferos:** mammals | |
| **anfibios:** amphibians | |
| **peces:** fish | |
| **silvestre:** wild | |
| **muy variada:** very diverse | |
| **está formada por/estar formado por:** it is made up of/ to be made up of | |
| **bosques húmedos:** rain forests | |
| **inundados/inundar:** flooded/to flood | |
| **secos:** dry | |
| **fue declarado/declarar:** was declared/ to declare | |
| **Patrimonio Mundial de la Humanidad:** World Heritage Site | |
| **Organización de las Naciones Unidas:** United Nations | |
| **sobre el nivel del mar:** above sea level | |
| **sede del gobierno central:** central seat of the Government | |
| **se divide/dividirse:** it is divided/to be divided | |
| **zonas geográficas diferentes:** different geographic zones | |
| **zona subandina:** the area under the Andes | |
| **zona amazónica:** the area around the Amazon River | |
| **la capital más alta del mundo:** the highest capital city in the world | |
| **alberga/albergar:** it harbors/to harbor | |
| **se considera/considerar:** it is considered/to consider | |
| **sitio arqueológico:** archaeological site | |
| **habilidad artesanal:** craft skills, artistry | |
| **conocimiento de la medicina tradicional:** knowledge of traditional medicine | |
| **montañoso:** mountainous | |
| **conviven/convivir:** they coexist/ to coexist | |
| **artesanía:** handicrafts | |
| **fabrican/fabricar:** they make/to make | |

# Paisajes diversos
## BOLIVIA

SANTA CRUZ  Santa Cruz es un **departamento** muy importante en Bolivia porque tiene un reservorio natural **impresionante llamado** Noel Kempff Mercado.  El  parque tiene una gran diversidad que **lo hace único**, con ecosistemas naturales y **cuencas hidrográficas** y una fauna rica **compuesta por aves**, reptiles, **mamíferos**, **anfibios**, **peces** e insectos. Su flora **silvestre** es también **muy variada** y **está formada por bosques húmedos**, bosques **inundados**, bosques **secos** y sabanas. El reservorio de Noel Kempff Mercado **fue declarado Patrimonio Mundial de la Humanidad** por la **Organización de las Naciones Unidas** en el año 2000.

LA  PAZ  La Paz está situada al noroeste de Bolivia, a 3.649 metros **sobre el nivel del mar**, y es **sede del gobierno central**. La capital de Bolivia **se divide** en tres **zonas geográficas diferentes**. La zona del Altiplano,  donde se encuentra el lago Titicaca, es la región más húmeda. La **zona subandina** es muy húmeda y tiene una vegetación exuberante. La **zona amazónica** también tiene una vegetación exuberante. La Paz es **la capital más alta del mundo** y **alberga** el centro ceremonial Tiahuanaco, que **se considera** el **sitio arqueológico** más importante de Bolivia. El grupo étnico mayoritario en esta zona son los aymaras y los quechuas, que se caracterizan por su **habilidad artesanal** y su **conocimiento de la medicina tradicional**.

COCHABAMBA  Es esencialmente **montañoso** y se encuentra a 2.550 metros sobre el nivel del mar. En este departamento **conviven** diversos grupos étnicos como los cotas, los chius, los collas y los quechuas, quienes actualmente se dedican a la **artesanía** que **fabrican** con materiales de la región. Una de sus atracciones turísticas más importantes es una inmensa estatua de Jesús más alta que el Cristo del Corcovado de Río de Janeiro en Brasil.

Ofrece una **vista panorámica** de la ciudad increíble. Cochabamba es un departamento **agrícola**. Sus productos más importantes son: el **maíz**, el **trigo**, la **cebada**, el **lino**, la **avena**, la **papa**, las **hortalizas**, la **oca** y la fruta.

**LAGO** TITICACA   El lago Titicaca es el más grande de Sudamérica y tiene, además, la extensión de agua navegable más alta del mundo. Este lago, **compartido** por Bolivia y Perú, es semisalado y sus aguas tienen un **color azul muy particular**. Tiene 36 islas, varias penínsulas, **cabos** y el **estrecho** de Tiquina. En el lago se encuentran las islas del **sol** y la de la **luna**, famosa por su **leyenda** incaica y por sus importantes ruinas arquitectónicas. **De acuerdo** con la leyenda inca, por **mandato** del Dios Sol, Inti, de sus aguas **surgieron** Manco Kapac y Mama Ocllo, los **fundadores** del Imperio inca. Desde la Isla del Sol, que es muy pequeña, **se puede apreciar** una magnífica vista del lago y se puede ver el **monte** Illimani, donde están el Templo del sol y el Palacio Picolcayna. La Isla de la Luna tiene **playas desiertas** y ruinas incaicas, además de dos lagos. Huatajata es el lago **menor** y el Copacabana que es el **mayor**. Copacabana es muy interesante porque fue un centro ceremonial y de observaciones astronómicas. La fauna del lugar es variada y se encuentran **patos salvajes** y **truchas**.

SORATA   Es un pueblo pequeño **cerca** de La Paz que alberga **cuevas** y **grutas** con **aguas subterráneas calientes** (termas de aguas medicinales) y tiene un clima **templado** y **paisajes maravillosos** como las vistas de la Cordillera Real que están en las montañas Illampu.

TUPIZA   Tupiza está a unos cien kilómetros de la **frontera** con Argentina y al **sureste** de Potosí. Es un lugar muy atractivo con una flora y fauna únicas en Bolivia. La fauna que se encuentra es de aves, **perdices**, patos salvajes, alpacas, **vicuñas** y llamas. La flora del área está formada por **bosques de cactus**, muchos enormes con **flores rojas**, **sauces**, **álamos** y **matorrales**.

---

**vista panorámica:** panoramic view
**agrícola:** agricultural
**maíz:** corn
**trigo:** wheat
**cebada:** barley
**lino:** flax
**avena:** oats
**papa:** potato
**hortalizas:** vegetables
**oca:** Andean root vegetable
**lago:** lake
**compartido/compartir:** shared/ to share
**color azul muy particular:** particular blue color
**cabos:** cape
**estrecho:** strait
**sol:** sun
**luna:** moon
**leyenda:** legend
**de acuerdo:** according to
**mandato:** mandate
**surgieron/surgir:** they arose/to arise
**fundadores:** founders
**se puede apreciar:** it can be appreciated
**monte:** hill; small mountain
**playas desiertas:** deserted beaches
**menor:** smaller
**mayor:** greater
**patos salvajes:** wild ducks
**truchas:** trout
**cerca:** near
**cuevas:** coves
**grutas:** caves
**aguas subterráneas calientes:** hot subterranean waters
**templado:** mild
**paisajes maravillosos:** wonderful lanscapes
**frontera:** border
**sureste:** southeast
**perdices/perdiz:** partridge
**vicuñas:** vicuna; a relative of the camel that lives in the Andes
**bosques de cactus:** cactus forests
**flores rojas:** red flowers
**sauces:** willow
**álamos:** poplars
**matorrales:** bushes

# Paisajes, flora y fauna
## VENEZUELA

Venezuela está en la **costa noroeste** de **Sudamérica**. Sus **países limítrofes** son Guyana al **este**, Brasil al **sur**, Colombia al **oeste** y al **norte** el **Mar Caribe**. La **superficie** del país es de 900,000 **kilómetros cuadrados** y está **dividida** en 23 **estados**. Venezuela tiene un **clima poco variado** debido a que está **cerca** del **ecuador.**

### EL SALTO DEL ANGEL

El Salto del Angel está situado en el estado de Bolívar y es la **cascada más alta del mundo. Fue descubierta** por un **piloto norteamericano** alrededor del año 1920 **cuyo** nombre era Jimy Angel y **se dice que él mismo le puso el nombre.** La **altura** del salto o cascada es de unos 900 **metros, superando** así a la de Tugala en Sudáfrica, que tiene 948 metros. Alrededor del salto **se puede encontrar** una abundante flora como **orquídeas**, palmeras y **lianas.**

**LA GRAN SABANA** La gran sabana está **dentro** del parque nacional Camaima al sur de Venezuela en el estado de Bolívar. En la gran sabana hay ríos y cascadas. También se encuentra una montaña que tiene una **cima plana y paredes verticales llamada** "Tepuy" que son **formaciones de piedras areniscas formadas** por la erosión.

LOS ROQUES  Es un archipiélago situado en el mar Caribe a unos 168 kilómetros del puerto de Caracas (la capital de Venezuela); por su **belleza** e importancia ecológica fue declarado parque nacional en 1972. Está formado por cincuenta islas diferentes. La más importante es el Gran Roque, el cual es un lugar muy interesante porque tiene una gran extensión de **mar tranquilo**. También hay lagunas, **cayos**, **playas con arenas blancas** y **aguas cristalinas**. Una de las atracciones turísticas de esta área es la variedad de su fauna marina, como **pulpos**, **tiburones**, **langostas**, **gaviotas** y **garzas**.  En el sur está la **fundación científica** "Los Roques" que es una estación biológica dedicada a la preservación de la **tortuga verde**. También se puede encontrar una **extensa variedad de aves** y reptiles como iguanas, camaleones y salamandras.

MARGARITA  Es una isla **situada** en el mar Caribe al noroeste de Caracas. Se encuentran playas  **con o sin olas**, grandes o pequeñas, **profundas o llanas**, **tibias o calientes**, con **viento** o sin viento. La isla fue descubierta por Cristóbal Colón, **quien le dio el nombre** Margarita. El área marina está formada por una **extensa barranca** de arena y un **conjunto** de lagunas **costeras** con formaciones de manglar. Un atractivo turístico de esta isla es que se pueden practicar todos los **deportes acuáticos**.

LOS LLANOS  Los **llanos** se encuentran en el sur de Venezuela. Son extensas **sabanas** donde la vegetación y la fauna es muy variada.

El atractivo turístico más popular y **más visitado** es la **Cueva** del **Guácharo**, una formación natural donde están los guácharos y **pájaros** de **plumaje oscuro**.  Allí se puede apreciar una galería de figuras de animales y **santos**, altares. La vegetación que caracteriza a esta zona es las sabanas, los **palmares**, los **bosques secos** y los bosques de galerías. Esta **zona se caracteriza** por la **cantidad** de animales que se pueden observar, como el **chigüire**,  la **rana platanera**, el **venado**, la **baba**, el **pavón**,  **culebras**, anacondas, tortugas, **zorros** y armadillos.

---

**belleza:** beauty

**mar tranquilo:** calm sea

**cayos:** coves

**playas con arenas blancas:** beaches with white sand

**aguas cristalinas:** crystalline waters

**pulpos:** octopus

**tiburones:** sharks

**langostas:** lobsters

**gaviotas:** gulls

**garzas:** herons

**fundación científica:** scientific foundation

**tortuga verde:** green turtle

**extensa variedad de aves:** extensive variety of birds

**situada/situar:** situated/to situate

**con o sin olas:** with or without waves

**profundas o llanas:** deep or flat

**tibias o calientes:** lukewarm, hot

**viento:** wind

**quien le dio el nombre:** who gave it the name

**extensa barranca:** extensive hill

**conjunto:** set

**costeras:** coastal

**deportes acuáticos:**  aquatic sports

**llanos:** flat ground

**sabanas:**  savanna; grassland

**más visitado:** most popular

**cueva:** cave

**guácharo:** oil bird

**pájaros:** birds

**plumaje oscuro:** dark plumage

**santos:** saints

**palmares:** palm groves

**bosques secos:** dry forests

**zona se caracteriza:** the zone is characterized

**cantidad:** amount

**chigüire:** rodent native to Venezuela

**rana platanera:** banana-tree frog

**venado:** deer

**baba:** small alligator

**pavón:** peacock

**culebras:** snakes

**zorros:** foxes

# Las ballenas de Valdez
## ARGENTINA

La Península de Valdez, **bañada** por el océano Atlántico, es uno de los santuarios ecológicos más importantes del mundo. Con 4.000 **kilómetros cuadrados** de **superficie** total, 110 kilómetros de costas a **mar abierto** y 150 kilómetros de costas a los golfos Nuevo y San José, **alberga** seis reservas naturales. Con **clima seco**, tiene **veranos** con **días calurosos** y **noches frescas**, e **inviernos** fríos con **pocas lluvias**.

El Istmo Carlos Ameghino es la **estrecha franja de tierra** que conecta la península con el continente, **a través de** la que se puede ver la fuerza de las **olas** del océano Atlántico **romper** contra los **acantilados** de la costa. Toda esta zona es muy rica en fauna marina: **delfines, lobos y elefantes marinos,** toninos y orcas son algunas de las **tantas especies** que pueden encontrarse. La familia de las **aves** también es **destacable**: desde **pingüinos** y **gaviotas**, hasta albatros y **palomas** antárticas.

Pero el **espectáculo mayor** que **ofrece** la naturaleza **gratuitamente**, año a año, es la reproducción y el **alumbramiento** de la ballena franca. De julio a diciembre, este **mamífero** llega en grupos a esta agua para **parir** sus **ballenatos**. En Puerto Pirámides, una pequeña **villa balnearia**, pueden verse desde la costa, pero para estar a muy pocos metros de ellas es necesario (¡y recomendable!) **tomar** una de las excursiones en **lancha** con las que cientos de turistas **se adentran** en las **aguas cristalinas**. Todos con cámara fotográfica **en mano quieren verlas saltar a pesar de** sus **toneladas** de peso. Ver el **chorro** por donde **expulsan** su **largo aliento. Escuchar** sus **alaridos.** Y ver su **gran aleta dorsal** y su **cola**. Algo que quizás vieron **alguna vez** en un libro, foto o video pero imposible de ver en un zoológico. La **única manera** de ver a la ballena franca **austral** es **en vivo y en directo** y Argentina ofrece esa oportunidad única.

# La Reserva de El Vizcaíno
## MÉXICO

A **primera vista** el **desierto** de la Península de Baja California **parece ser** uno de los lugares mas **desolados** y solitarios del mundo. **Sin embargo**, lo que **aparenta** ser un **lugar inhospitalario** es **en realidad** un **santuario biológico** para un gran número de plantas y animales. **Compuesta de** aproximadamente 2,540,000 hectáreas, La Reserva de la Biosfera El Vizcaíno es considerada la área protegida más grande de LatinoAmérica. La reserva **se encuentra** en la parte norte del estado de Baja California Sur, México. Esta área **inmensa contiene** más de cuatrocientas especies de vegetales y más de trescientas especies de animales, **incluyendo mamíferos**, **aves**, reptiles y anfibios.

A pesar del **clima seco** y **árido** en el desierto, hay una variedad de plantas que **sobreviven abundantemente** en este ambiente. Entre ellas se encuentra el mesquite, **usado** por los nativos para hacer **fogatas**. También esta la pitaya con su **fruta deliciosa** y similar a la **tuna del nopal**. Otras plantas de esta zona incluyen el maguey que es un ingrediente importante del tequila, la biznaga y la savila con sus **propiedades curativas** y una variedad de otros cactus como la cholla y el cardón. **Algunos** de los animales en este desierto incluyen el coyote, la víbora de cascabel, el nurciélago, varios tipos de venado y lagartijas **al igual que** el conejo silvestre, la ardilla, el borrego cimarróne con sus **cuernos enroscados**, el gato montes o puma, y el zorrillo. Entre los **pájaros** de esta área están la chupa rosa, el cardenal, el pájaro carpintero, la paloma serrana, el gavilán, el aguila y el zopilote.

Aunque un lugar **caluroso** y con **poca agua**, el desierto de Baja California Sur es **hogar** para un gran número de diversas plantas y animales bien **adaptados** para vivir en este **ambiente duro**. **Gracias a** la reserva biológica **podrán seguir viviendo sin miedo** de la intervención humana.

**primera vista:** at first sight
**desierto:** desert
**parece ser/parecer:** it seems to be/ to seem
**desolados:** desolated
**sin embargo:** alhough, nevertheless
**aparenta/aparentar:** it looks like/ to look
**lugar inhospitalario:** inhospitable place
**en realidad:** in fact
**santuario biológico:** biological sanctuary
**compuesta de:** integrated by
**se encuentra/encontrarse:** it is located/to be located
**inmensa:** immense, huge
**contiene/contener:** it contains/ to contain
**incluyendo/incluir:** including/ to include
**mamíferos:** mammals
**aves:** birds
**clima seco:** dry climate
**árido:** arid
**sobreviven/sobrevivir:** they survive/ to survive
**abundantemente:** abundantly
**usado/usar:** used/to use
**fogatas:** bonfires
**fruta deliciosa:** delicious fruit
**tuna del nopal:** prickly pear fruits
**propiedades curativas:** healing properties
**algunos:** some
**al igual que:** just like
**cuernos enroscados:** curled horns, antlers
**pájaros:** birds
**caluroso:** hot
**poca agua:** little water
**hogar:** home
**adaptados:** adapted
**ambiente duro:** hard (severe) environment
**gracias a:** thanks to
**podrán seguir viviendo:** they'll be able to go on living
**sin miedo:** without fear

| | |
|---|---|
| **maravilloso:** wonderful | |

**maravilloso:** wonderful
**tiene lugar:** it takes place
**a lo largo:** along
**costa oeste:** west coast
**espectáculo:** show
**empieza/empezar:** it begins/to begin
**invierno:** winter
**ballenas grises:** gray whales
**comienzan/comenzar:** they start/ to start
**viaje migratorio:** migratory trip
**templadas:** warm
**recorren/recorrer:** they cover/to cover, to travel
**millas:** miles
**científicos:** scientists
**abordan/abordar:** they board/to board
**barcos:** boats
**cerca:** near
**meta final:** the finish line
**lagunas:** small lakes
**calientes:** hot
**dan a luz:** they give birth (literally: to give to the light)
**crías:** young
**recién nacidas:** newborn
**miden/medir:** they measure/ to measure
**alrededor de:** about
**pesan/pesar:** they weigh/to weigh
**libras:** pounds
**mamás:** mothers
**proveerán/proveer:** they will provide/ to provide
**galones de leche por día:** gallons of milk per day
**contenido de grasa:** fat content
**aumenten/aumentar:** they increase/ to increase
**gordura:** fat
**sobrevivir:** to survive
**heladas:** frozen
**verano:** summer

# La laguna de San Ignacio
## MÉXICO

Cada año hay un evento de la naturaleza **maravilloso** que **tiene lugar a lo largo** de la **costa oeste** de Norteamérica. Este **espectáculo empieza** en **invierno**, aproximadamente entre octubre y febrero. Las **ballenas grises comienzan** un **viaje migratorio** desde las aguas frías de Alaska y Canadá hasta las aguas **templadas** de México. Durante este viaje las ballenas **recorren** casi 5.000 **millas** y pueden ser observadas desde la costa. Muchos curiosos, y especialmente los **científicos**, **abordan barcos** para ver las ballenas desde más **cerca**.

La **meta final** de esta gran migración son las **lagunas** de Baja California en México. Allí, en aguas más **calientes**, las ballenas **dan a luz** a sus **crías**. Las ballenas **recién nacidas miden alrededor de** 15 pies de largo y **pesan** unas 2.000 **libras**. Durante los primeros seis meses, las **mamás proveerán** hasta 50 **galones de leche por día** con un **contenido de grasa** del 56 por ciento, lo que hará que las crías **aumenten** de peso entre 60 y 70 libras al día. Esta **gordura** es necesaria para que las ballenas puedan **sobrevivir** en las aguas **heladas** del norte durante el **verano**.

Una de las lagunas más populares para las ballenas es la de San Ignacio. Esta laguna es muy importante para los científicos porque **ha tenido** poco **impacto humano** y **está protegida** por el gobierno de México como reserva natural.

En esta laguna se ha observado un fenómeno tan increíble que ni los científicos pueden explicarlo. Normalmente, cuando un animal **salvaje es seguido** por un humano, **se retira** y muchas veces **huye**. **Lo mismo** pasa con las ballenas grises en el mar. Pero en la laguna, por alguna **razón** que no comprendemos todavía, **parece** ser que estas ballenas no tienen miedo de la gente. Es más, **se acercan** a las **lanchas** y **dejan** que las personas **las toquen**. Es realmente un **acto sorprendente** y **único**, algo que **cambia** la vida de cualquier persona que **lo haya experimentado**.

Las ballenas grises son un gran **tesoro** de la Laguna de San Ignacio y **vale la pena** proteger estas magníficas criaturas y su laguna maravillosa para que puedan seguir **criando, creciendo** y viviendo como parte de nuestro gran sistema ecológico.

**ha tenido/tener:** it has had/to have
**impacto humano:** human impact
**está protegida/proteger:** it is protected/to protect
**salvaje:** wild
**es seguido/seguir:** it is followed/to follow
**se retira/retirarse:** it withdraws/to withdraw
**huye/huir:** it runs away/to run away
**lo mismo:** the same
**razón:** reason
**parece/parecer:** it seems/to seem
**se acercan/acercarse:** they get close/to get close
**lanchas:** motorboat
**dejan/dejar:** they let /to let
**las toquen/tocar:** they touch them/to touch
**acto sorprendente:** surprising act
**único:** unique
**cambia/cambiar:** it changes/to change
**lo haya experimentado/experimentar:** (any person who) has experienced it/to experience
**tesoro:** treasure
**vale la pena/valer la pena:** it is worth it/to be worth it
**criando/criar:** breeding/to breed
**creciendo/crecer:** growing up/to grow

# Examina tu comprensión

## Parque Nacional Darién, page 166

**1.** The Darién national park is a good example of our complex ecosystem. What organization honored the park?

**2.** Describe the people and traditions that make up the ethno-cultural diversity of the park.

**3.** How is the diversity of this region being preserved?

## Las islas Galápagos, page 168

**1.** What natural event resulted in the creation of the Galapagos islands?

**2.** Pirates were the first to frequent the island because it was an excellent place for what?

**3.** What Englishman studied the Galapagos and wrote a book about evolution? What was the name of the book?

## El jurumí, page 170

**1.** What is *El Jurumí*?

**2.** What is the *Jurumí's* "best feature" and what purpose does it serve (for itself and the environment)?

**3.** What is the *Jurumí's* best sense and why is it important?

**4.** What are the *Jurumí's* enemies that may contribute to its extinction?

## Paisajes diversos, page 172

**1.** What makes the Noel Kempff Mercado natural reserve unique?

**2.** Describe the three zones of *La Paz*.

**3.** What is the tourist attraction you will find in *Cochabamba*?

**4.** In addition to the vegetation, what else makes *Copacabana* interesting?

# Test your comprehension

## Paisajes, flora y fauna, page 174

**1.** What are the famous waterfalls of Venezuela and how were they named?

**2.** What are "*Tepuyes*"?

**3.** What is the most important island in *Los Roques* and why?

**4.** In the south of *Los Roques* you will find a scientific foundation. What is it dedicated to?

## Las ballenas de Valdez, page 176

**1.** What is the name of the stretch of land that connects the peninsula with the continent?

**2.** What is the "greatest show" you will see here?

**3.** What parts of the whale might you see and what might you see them do?

## La Reserva de El Vizcaíno, page 177

**1.** What is the climate like in *La Reserva de la Biosfera El Vizcaíno*?

**2.** What are the uses of *mesquite* and *maguey* plants?

## La laguna de San Ignacio, page 178

**1.** When do the gray whales begin their trip and how many miles of coastline are covered?

**2.** Why do gray whales migrate to Mexico?

**3.** The high fat content in the mother's milk is necessary for what?

**4.** What is the incredible experience you can be a part of and why is it unusual?

El amor es tan importante como la comida.
Pero no alimenta.

Gabriel García Márquez

# Gastronomía

**cuando era niña:** when I was a little girl

**solía:** used to

**cortar:** to cut

**tallos:** stems

**árbol de la lechosa:** papaya tree

**limpiaba/limpiar:** used to clean, would clean/to clean

**me los daba:** give them to me

**vaso:** glass

**lleno de:** filled with

**jabón:** soap

**balcón:** porch

**soplar burbujas:** blow bubbles

**pasatiempos:** pastimes

**monda/mondar:** peel/to peel

**luego se corta:** then is cut

**pedazos finos:** thin pieces

**se hierven/hervir:** it is boiled/to boil

**mientras:** while

**se les añade:** (sugar) is added

**azúcar:** sugar

**canela:** cinnamon

**lista:** ready

**se pone/poner:** it is put/to put

**nevera:** refrigerator

**la mejor manera:** the best way

**acompañada:** along with

**queso blanco:** white cheese

**leche de cabra:** goat milk

**aún se disfruta/disfrutar:** is still enjoyed/to enjoy

**hogares:** homes

**prueben/probar:** try/to try

**postre:** dessert

**tendrán/tener:** have/to have

**pedazo:** piece

# El dulce de papaya
## PUERTO RICO

**Cuando era niña,** mi abuelo **solía cortar** los **tallos** del **árbol de la lechosa.** Los **limpiaba** y **me los daba** junto a un **vaso lleno de** agua con **jabón.** Yo me iba con mis tallos al **balcón** para **soplar burbujas** al aire. Este era uno de mis **pasatiempos** favoritos.

La lechosa es una fruta exquisita. El "dulce de lechosa" es muy popular en Puerto Rico. La fruta verde se **monda** y **luego se corta** en **pedazos finos.** Los pedazos **se hierven** y, **mientras** lo hacen, **se les añade azúcar** negra y **canela** hasta que la fruta esté suave. Cuando ya está **lista, se pone** en la **nevera.**

**La mejor manera** de comerla es **acompañada** con **queso blanco** de **leche de cabra.** Ésta es una receta de los abuelos que **aún se disfruta** en la mayoría de los **hogares** puertorriqueños así como en muchos de nuestros restaurantes típicos.

**Prueben** este delicioso **postre** y **tendrán** un **pedazo** de Puerto Rico en sus hogares.

# El mate
## ARGENTINA

**El mate** es una infusión muy popular **entre** los argentinos. **Para prepararlo no se necesita más que yerba mate**, **bombilla**, un mate y agua. **Sin embargo**, **en realidad**, el mate es **más que eso**. Es un ritual, una tradición y una costumbre con un particular **significado que hacen** de esta **bebida algo** muy especial.

**Hay distintas** y **variadas** formas de **tomarlo**: con **azúcar** o **amargo**, muy caliente o frío con **jugo de naranja**, con **una cucharadita de café** o con **yuyos.** Pero **nunca debe hacerse** con **agua hervida** porque **se lava**.

Se toma **solo** o en **compañía**. O con la sola compañía del mate. Cuando **se pasa de mano en mano** debe **respetarse** la **ronda**, y **no decir** "gracias" hasta **llegar al punto** de **no querer más**. La yerba es lo único que hay siempre en todas las casas argentinas. Y **si un día** uno **se quedara sin yerba**, un **vecino amablemente le dará**.

El mate es **compañerismo**, es generosidad. Es la hospitalidad de la invitación. La **alegría** de la **charla compartida** o el **alivio** de **nunca sentirse** del **todo solo**. El mate **iguala**, **une** y **ayuda** a **sanar** los **corazones heridos**.

**el mate:** tealike beverage consumed mainly in Argentina, Uruguay, Paraguay and southern Brazil
**entre:** among
**para prepararlo:** to prepare it
**no se necesita:** you do not need
**más que:** more than
**yerba mate:** maté herb
**bombilla:** straw used to sip the mate
**sin embargo:** nevertheless
**en realidad:** in fact, actually
**más que eso:** more than this
**significado:** meaning
**que hacen/hacer:** that makes/to make
**bebida:** drink
**algo:** something
**hay:** there are
**distintas:** different
**variadas:** varied, assorted
**tomarlo/tomar:** drink it/to drink
**azúcar:** sugar
**amargo:** bitter
**jugo de naranja:** orange juice
**una cucharadita de café:** a teaspoon of coffee
**yuyos:** medicinal herbs
**nunca debe hacerse:** it must never be made
**aqua hervida:** boiled water
**se lava/lavar:** it is washed/to wash
**solo:** alone
**compañía:** company
**se pasa de mano en mano:** it is passed from hand to hand
**respetarse:** to respect
**ronda:** round
**no decir:** do not say
**llegar al punto:** to reach the point
**no querer más:** not wanting more
**si un dia:** if one day
**se quedara sin yerba:** you ran out of yerba
**vecino:** neighbor
**amablemente:** kindly
**le dará:** he will give it to you
**compañerismo:** companionship
**alegría:** happiness
**charla compartida:** shared conversation
**alivio:** relief
**nunca sentirse:** never feeling
**todo solo:** all alone
**iguala/igualar:** it equals/to equal
**une/unir:** it unites/to unite
**ayuda/ayudar:** it helps/to help
**sanar:** to cure, to heal
**corazones heridos:** hurt (broken) hearts

| | |
|---|---|
| **sostienen/sostener:** they maintain/ to maintain | |

**sostienen/sostener:** they maintain/ to maintain

**nació/nacer:** it was born/to be born

**tierras:** lands

**no es bien conocido/conocer:** it is not well known/to know

**se disputan/disputarse:** they fight over/ to fight over

**paternidad:** paternity

**dulce:** cake, sweet

**alimentos:** foods

**arraigados:** deeply rooted

**rioplatenses:** from the region of the Rio de la Plata

**cualquier:** any

**postre:** dessert

**torta rellena:** filled cake

**convierte/convertir:** it turns/to turn

**vulgar:** simple, common

**receta:** recipe

**manjar:** a delicious food or dish

**dioses:** gods

**se come/comer:** it is eaten/to eat

**galletitas:** small cookies

**tostadas:** toast

**flanes:** caramel custards

**panqueques:** pancakes

**helados:** ice cream

**hecho en casa:** homemade

**cucharadita:** teaspoonful

**chaucha:** vanilla bean

**coloque/colocar:** put/to put

**recipiente:** container

**preferentemente:** preferably

**cobre:** copper

**a fuego fuerte:** over high heat

**rompa a hervir/romper a hervir:** it starts to boil/ to start boiling

**revuelva/revolver:** stir/to stir

**evitando/evitar:** avoiding/to avoid

**se derrame/derramarse:** it spills/ to spill

**deje/dejar:** let/to let

**tome/tomar:** it takes/to take

**espesar:** to thicken

**a menudo:** often

**cuchara de madera:** wooden spoon

# El dulce de leche
## ARGENTINA

Si bien muchos **sostienen** que el dulce de leche **nació** en **tierras** argentinas, su origen **no es bien conocido**. Chile, Perú y Uruguay **se disputan** también la **paternidad** de este **dulce**, uno de los **alimentos** más **arraigados** entre los **rioplatenses**. **Cualquier postre** o **torta rellena** con él **convierte** una **vulgar receta** en un **manjar** propio de **dioses**. **Se come** a cualquier hora, con **galletitas**, tortas, **tostadas, flanes**, con **panqueques** o, simplemente, a cucharadas. También se usa para la elaboración industrial de productos como **helados** y yogures.

Aunque es más fácil y rápido comprarlo en un supermercado, el dulce de leche **hecho en casa** es mucho más rico. Aquí va la receta:

Ingredientes:

    2 litros de leche
    1/2 kilo de azúcar
    ¼ **cucharadita** de bicarbonato de sodio
    1 **chaucha** de vainilla (opcional)

Preparación:

**Coloque** todos los ingredientes en un **recipiente** grande, **preferentemente** de **cobre** o aluminio, **a fuego fuerte** hasta que **rompa a hervir. Revuelva evitando** que **se derrame.** Con el fuego un poco más bajo, **deje** hervir durante unas horas hasta que **tome** un color marrón acaramelado y comience a **espesar**.

Baje el fuego al mínimo revolviendo **a menudo** con una **cuchara de madera**.

Para determinar **si está listo**, coloque un poquito de dulce en un plato y **fíjese** que **no se corra**. **Retire** del fuego y continúe revolviendo durante un rato hasta que **se entibie**.

## UN DULCE CON HISTORIA

Algunos cuentan que la leche condensada fue la **antecesora** del dulce de leche. En la Francia de 1700, Napoleón Bonaparte **necesitaba encontrar** la **manera** de transportar más **fácilmente** la leche (elemento esencial para sus hombres en las **campañas militares**) sin que **se cortase**. Así, nació la leche condensada, que se obtiene también de la concentración **por acción del calor** de la **mezcla** de leche e **hidratos de carbono** (azúcar).

Sin embargo, según la tradición oral **bonaerense** el dulce de leche se originó algún día del año 1800 en una **estancia** del interior, donde Juan Manuel de Rosas, jefe de la Fuerza Federal y su opositor, el Comandante del ejército Unitario Juan Lavalle, **se encontraban** por motivos políticos.

La leyenda cuenta que una **criada** de Rosas estaba haciendo la lechada (leche caliente azucarada) para servir a su patrón, cuando al llegar Lavalle, **cansado** por el viaje, **se acostó** en un **catre** en el que usualmente **descansaba** Rosas. La criada, al encontrar ocupado el lugar por el **jefe enemigo**, **dio aviso** a la guardia **olvidando** la leche que hervía en la **olla** y **cuyo contenido se transformó** en la **mezcla** que hoy **se conoce como** dulce de leche.

# La deliciosa papa
## PERÚ

¿**Quién no ha saboreado** un **puré de papas**, unas papas **al horno**, unas papas **fritas** o una **ensalada** de papa? Todos estos **platos** están preparados con el **tubérculo** más famoso del mundo, la papa o patata, que **apareció** en este planeta hace **miles** de años y que, además, **cuenta con** más de 3.000 **variedades** en el Perú, su país de origen.

**Según estudios** científicos, este vegetal **se cultivó** cerca del Lago Titicaca, entre los territorios del Perú y Bolivia, unos 10.000 años atrás. Las **muestras** más antiguas **datan** del período neolítico, es decir, 8.000 años ante de Cristo, y se **hallaron** en unas **cuevas** llamadas Tres **Ventanas**, en la localidad de Chilca, a 65 kilómetros al sur de Lima.

Esta planta **forma parte** de la historia peruana y, junto con el **maíz**, **se constituyó** en la base de la **alimentación** del **Imperio** incaico. Según una de las **leyendas** sobre la fundación de este **reino**, Manco Cápac, el primer Inca, junto con su **esposa** Mama Ocllo emergieron del Lago Titicaca para **enseñar** a los hombres el **cultivo** de este vegetal.

Este tubérculo **no era conocido** en Europa antes del **descubrimiento** de América. Los conquistadores españoles **lo llevaron** al viejo mundo en la segunda mitad del siglo XVI desde el Perú. España fue el primer país europeo donde **se introdujo** este alimento. Desde allí **pasó** a Italia, Francia, Alemania, Inglaterra y el resto de los países europeos.

**Al principio,** los europeos **se resistieron** a **comerla atribuyéndole** propiedades tóxicas. En Francia fue necesario que **el propio rey pusiera de moda** la flor de la papa en la corte, para **obligar** a los nobles a cultivarla en sus tierras.

Fue la **escasez** de alimentos en los años que precedieron a la Revolución Francesa, lo que **acabó imponiendo** su **consumo** en varios países europeos, **salvando** así a Europa de la **hambruna**.

## LA GASTRONOMÍA PERUANA

La patata es uno de los ingredientes fundamentales de la **fina** gastronomía peruana. Entre los platos más exquisitos **sobresalen** la papa a la huancaína (papas **sancochadas cubiertas** con una salsa hecha de **queso fresco, aceite, ají** y **galleta remojada** en leche) y la ocopa (papas sancochadas **acompañadas** de **crema de almendras, huacatay,** queso fresco y leche). También **destacan** la papa **rellena** (papa sancochada **amasada** y rellena con **carne picada,** cebolla y **pasas** fritas en aceite bien caliente) y la causa (papa sancochada y amasada con un poco de aceite, limón y ají, y rellenada con **verduras, pollo** o **pescado**).

Quizás para el común de los **pobladores** del mundo este alimento de los incas sea algo simple y hasta **soso,** pero si visita Perú **se encontrará** con toda una tradición al **degustar** este tubérculo andino **lleno de** historia y sabor.

---

**al principio:** at the beginning
**se resistieron/resistirse:** they were reluctant/to be reluctant
**comerla/comer:** eat it/to eat
**atribuyéndole/atribuir:** attributing to it/to attribute
**el propio rey:** the king himself
**pusiera de moda:** to make fashionable
**obligar:** to force
**escasez:** scarcity
**acabó/acabar:** it ended/to end
**imponiendo/imponer:** imposing/to impose
**consumo:** consumption
**salvando/salvar:** saving/to save
**hambruna:** starvation
**fina:** fine
**sobresalen/sobresalir:** they stand out/to stand out
**sancochadas:** boiled
**cubiertas:** covered
**queso fresco:** fresh cheese
**aceite:** oil
**ají:** chili, red pepper
**galleta:** cookie
**remojada:** soaked
**acompañadas:** together with
**crema de almendras:** thick almond soup
**huacatay:** a Peruvian mint
**destacan/destacar:** they stand out/to stand out
**rellena:** filled
**amasada:** mashed
**carne picada:** ground beef
**pasas:** raisins
**verduras:** vegetables
**pollo:** chicken
**pescado:** fish
**pobladores:** settlers
**soso:** tasteless
**se encontrará/encontrar:** one will find/to find
**degustar:** to taste
**lleno de:** filled with

papas: potatoes
cocidas: boiled
peladas: peeled
cebollas verdes: green onions
lavadas: washed
rebanadas: slices
huevo crudo: raw egg
cucharada: spoonful
perejil: parsley
finamente picado: finely chopped
taza: cup
queso: cheese
gratinado: grated
al gusto: to taste
pimienta negra: black pepper
haga/hacer: make/to make
puré: puree
añada/añadir: add/to add
forme/formar: make/to make
mezcla: mixture
caliente: heat up
fuego medio-alto: medium-high heat
deben/deber: they must/must
quedar bien doradas: to be well
    browned
quemadas/quemar: burnt/to burn


betabeles: beets
diente de ajo: garlic clove
cucharadita: teaspoonful
jugo: juice
mitad: half
macere/macerar: crush/to crush
molcajete: a Mexican mortar and
    pestle made from basalt rock
corte/cortar: cut/to cut
agregue/agregar: add/to add
los demás: the rest
déjelo/dejar: let it/to let
refrigerar: to cool, to refrigerate
servir: to serve
póngalo/poner: put it/to put

# Recetas con papas
## MÉXICO

## TORTA DE PAPA

Ingredientes:
2 ½ libras de **papas**, **cocidas** y **peladas**
2 **cebollas verdes**, **lavadas** y cortadas en **rebanadas**
1 **huevo crudo**
1 **cucharada** de **perejil finamente picado**
1 cucharada de aceite de olivo
1 **taza** de **queso gratinado**
Sal **al gusto**
**Pimienta negra** al gusto
Aceite de olivo para freír

Preparación:
**Haga** un **puré** con las papas. **Añada** el huevo, el perejil, la cebolla, el queso, la cucharada de aceite de olivo y la sal y la pimienta a su gusto. **Forme** la **mezcla** en cuatro hamburguesas. **Caliente** el aceite y fría la carne sobre **fuego medio-alto** en los dos lados. **Deben** de **quedar bien doradas** pero no **quemadas**.

## ENSALADA DE PAPA CON BETABEL

Ingredientes:
4 papas medianas, cocidas y peladas
4 **betabeles** medianos, cocidos y pelados
1 **diente de ajo**
½ **cucharadita** de sal
¼ de taza de aceite de olivo
El **jugo** de la **mitad** de un limón
Pimienta negra al gusto

Preparación:
**Macere** el ajo con la sal en un **molcajete**. **Corte** las papas y los betabeles en rebanadas. **Agregue los demás** ingredientes y **déjelo refrigerar** una hora antes de **servir**. **Póngalo** en un platón bonito.

# Ensalada de yuca
## CUBA

Ingredientes:

2 **libras** de yuca

2 **dicntcs** dc **ajo**

½ **cdta.** de sal

¾ **taza** de mayonesa

½ taza de cilantro **picadito**

7 **tomatines miniatura**

½ taza de **aceite de oliva**

3 **cdas.** de **jugo de naranja**

6 tazas de **lechugas**, **lavadas** y **bien secas**

Preparación:

**Sancoche** la yuca en agua con sal **hasta** que esté **blanda**. **Escurra** muy bien y **deje refrescar**. En una **vasija mezcle bien** la mayonesa con el **ajo machacado** y el jugo de naranja. **Al final**, se le **agrega el** aceite de oliva en chorrito y sal y pimienta **al gusto**. Esta salsa **se puede preparar** unas **horas antes**. Ahora **corte** la yuca en **trocitos** e incorporer en la salsa. Al final se le agrega el cilantro picadito. **Sirva sobre** las **hojas de lechuga** y **decore con** los tomatines.

**yuca:** yucca (manioc)
**libras:** pounds
**dientes:** cloves
**ajo:** garlic
**cdta.:** cucharadita (teaspoon)
**taza:** cup
**picadito:** chopped
**tomatines miniatura:** cherry tomatoes
**aceite de oliva:** olive oil
**cdas.:** cucharadas (tablespoons)
**jugo de naranja:** orange juice
**lechugas:** lettuce
**lavadas/lavar:** washed/to wash
**bien secas/secar:** well dried/to dry
**sancoche:** parboil
**hasta:** until
**blanda:** soft
**escurra/escurrir:** drain/to drain
**deje refrescar:** let cool
**vasija:** pot; dish
**mezcle bien/mezclar:** mix well/to mix
**ajo machacado:** crushed garlic
**al final:** finally
**agrega el/agregar:** add the/to add
**al gusto:** to taste
**se puede preparar:** can be prepared
**horas antes:** hours before
**corte:** cut
**trocitos:** small pieces
**sirva sobre:** serve on
**hojas de lechuga:** lettuce leaves
**decore con/decorar:** decorate with/ to decorate

## Vocabulario de la cocina

**cocer al horno:** bake
**rociando:** basting
**albardilla:** batter
**punto de ebullición:** boiling point
**escaldar:** scald
**caldo:** broth
**chorrito:** dash
**cortar en cuadritos:** dice
**guarnición:** garnish
**escurrir:** drain
**cuajar:** curdle
**hacer puré:** mash
**glasear:** glaze
**rallado:** grated

**molido, pulverizado:** ground
**hierba:** herb
**herbario:** herb garden
**jengibre:** ginger
**albahaca:** basil
**laurel:** bay leaf
**romero:** rosemary
**nuez moscada:** nutmeg
**jugoso:** juicy
**congelado:** frozen
**barbacoa/parrillada:** barbeque
**batir:** whisk
**migas de pan:** bread crumbs
**pedazo grande:** wedge

**apagar:** turn off
**saltear:** sauté
**sazonar:** season with salt
**estofado:** stew
**cortado en cuatro:** quartered
**taza para medir:** measuring cup
**cucharones:** ladles
**papel de aluminio:** aluminum foil
**fregadero:** kitchen sink
**comedor:** dining room
**escoba:** broom
**congelador:** freezer
**lavaplatos:** dishwasher
**gabinete:** cabinet

| | |
|---|---|
| **camarones:** shrimp | |

**camarones:** shrimp
**salsa blanca:** white sauce
**primera vez:** first time
**esposo:** husband
**recién casados:** just married
**me llevó/llevar:** he took me/to take
**se llamaba/llamar:** it was called/to call
**carta:** menu
**ese sigue/seguir:** it continues to be, it
   still is/to continue
**hoy en día:** nowadays
**cucharadita:** teaspoon
**harina blanca:** white flour
**mantequilla salada:** salted butter
**vino blanco seco:** dry white wine
**leche fría:** cold milk
**frasco mediano:** medium-sized bottle
**exprimido/exprimir:** squeezed/
   to squeeze
**cortado/cortar:** cut/to cut
**rajas:** pieces
**perejil:** parsley
**lavado/lavar:** washed/to wash
**sartén grande:** large frying pan
**derrita/derretir:** melt/to melt
**fuego medio-alto:** medium to high heat
**añada/añadir:** add/to add
**moviéndolo/mover:** stirring it/to stir
**espese/espesar:** it thickens/to thicken
**agregue/agregar:** add/to add
**siga removiendo/remover:**
   keep stirring/to stir
**así:** this way
**retírelo/retirar:** remove it/to remove
**sazone/sazonar:** season/to season
**mientras tanto:** in the meantime
**cuando hierva/hervir:** when it boils/
   to boil
**déjelos hervir:** let it boil
**quítelo/quitar:** remove it/to remove
**enjuague/enjuagar:** rinse/to rinse
**cáscara:** shell
**séquelos/secar:** dry them/to dry
**trapito de cocina:** dishcloth
**cacerola de vidrio:** glass saucepan
**ponga/poner:** put/to put
**adórnelo/adornar:** decorate it/
   to decorate
**métalo/meter:** put it inside/
   to put inside
**horno:** oven
**se puede/poder:** you can/can
**servir:** to serve
**pan tostado:** toast

# Camarones en salsa blanca
## MÉXICO

La **primera vez** que fui a México con mi **esposo** estábamos **recién casados** y era febrero.  El día de San Valentín **me llevó** a su restaurante favorito. **Se llamaba** El Rubí. ¡La **carta** era una delicia! ¡Camarones en salsa blanca! **Ese sigue** siendo **hoy en día** uno de mis platos favoritos.

Ingredientes:
12 camarones grandes sin pelar
½ **cucharadita** de sal
1 taza de agua
½ taza de **harina blanca**
8 onzas de **mantequilla salada**
½ taza de **vino blanco seco**
3 ¾ tazas de **leche fría**
1 **frasco mediano** de chile rojo dulce, **exprimido**,
**cortado** en **rajas**
½ taza de **perejil**, **lavado** y picado
Sal y pimienta negra al gusto

Preparación:
En una **sartén grande derrita** la mantequilla a **fuego medio-alto** y **añada** la harina, **moviéndolo** todo hasta que **espese**. **Agregue** el vino y la leche fría y **siga removiendo** con el fuego algo más bajo. Continúe **así** hasta que espese y **retírelo** del fuego. **Sazone** con sal y pimienta negra. **Mientras tanto**, caliente una taza de agua con media cucharadita de sal. **Cuando hierva**, añada los camarones y **déjelos hervir** durante un minuto. **Quítelo** del fuego y **enjuague** los camarones con agua fría.  Quite la **cáscara** y **séquelos** con un **trapito de cocina**. Caliente el horno a 400 grados F.  En una **cacerola de vidrio**, **ponga** la salsa blanca y los camarones, y **adórnelo** con las rajas de chile y el perejil. **Métalo** en el **horno** durante 10 minutos. **Se puede servir** con puntos de **pan tostado** y una ensalada.

# Carnitas
## MÉXICO

Los domingos es típico **salir temprano** a comprar carnitas. El **olor** de estos **pedacitos** de **carne de puerco**, hechos en grandes **ollas de cobre**, es incomparable. Sin embargo, ¡yo **prefiero hacerlos** en mi cocina!

Ingredientes:

5 **libras** de carne de puerco **cortada en cubos** de tres **pulgadas**

2 libras de **manteca vegetal**

1 **cucharada** de sal

1 **cucharadita** de **pimienta molida fresca**

5 **dientes de ajo**

1 **cebolla** grande, **pelada** y **en cuartos**

3 **trozos** de naranja sin pelar

1/3 de **taza** de leche

Para servir: Guacamole y tortillas frescas y **calientes**

Preparación:

**Ponga** sal y la pimienta a la carne **por todos lados**. En una **sartén** grande o una **cacerola** grande (preferiblemente de **hierro**), **dore** la carne **a fuego alto** en la manteca ya **derretida** durante unos 20 ó 30 minutos. Es necesario mover la carne **de vez en cuando**. **Añada** la cebolla, la naranja y el ajo. **Baje** el fuego hasta el mínimo posible y **déjelo cocer** una hora. Ponga entonces la leche y **mueva** bien todos los ingredientes. Después de media hora, **apáguelo** y **saque** los pedazos de carne. **Sirva** la carne en un **platón bonito acompañada del** guacamole y **cómala** como tacos con las tortillas calientes después de **deshebrar** la carne. ¡**Buen provecho**!

bebida: drink
verano: summer
seguramente: surely
usted ha visto: you have seen
tienda: store
embotellada: bottled
y si le gusta/gustar: and if you like/to like
prepararla/preparar: prepare it/to prepare
refrescante: refreshing
puede servirse: can be served
casi cualquier plato: almost any dish
comer: to have lunch
cenar: to have dinner
a pesar de: despite
orígenes humildes: humble origins
conocida en todo el mundo: known all around the world
vino tinto: red wine
azúcar: sugar
usted quiere/querer: you want/to want
también puede añadir: you can also add
ron: rum
se utiliza/utilizar: it is used/to use
incluso: even
receta: recipe
no es siempre la misma: is not always the same
podemos cambiar: we can change
cantidad: quantity
divertido: fun
nuestra propia: our own
botella: bottle
al gusto: as desired, to taste
rodajas finas: thin slices
naranja: orange
melocotón: peach
manzana: apple
cortados/cortar: cut/to cut
pequeños trozos: small pieces
gaseosa: bubbly water
mezclar: to mix
dejar reposar: let sit
frigorífico: refrigerator
mezcla: mixture
sabor adecuado: appropriate flavor
después de: after
agitar: to stir
sin sabor: flavorless
cuando bebamos/beber: when we drink/to drink
hielo: ice
servir lo más fría posible: to serve as cold as possible

# Sangría, la bebida del verano
## ESPAÑA

**Seguramente, usted ha visto** en la **tienda** o supermercado sangría **embotellada**. **Y si le gusta** la sangría, ¿por qué no **prepararla** en casa? Esta bebida es popular y **refrescante**, y **puede servirse** con **casi cualquier plato**, para **comer** o para **cenar**. **A pesar de** sus **orígenes humildes** en España, es ahora una bebida **conocida en todo el mundo**. Sus ingredientes básicos son: **vino tinto**, **azúcar** y frutas. Pero si **usted quiere**, **también puede añadir** brandy, **ron** o Bacardi. El vino es Rioja tinto, pero también **se utiliza** cualquier vino tinto, **incluso** vino blanco.

La **receta no es siempre la misma**. **Podemos cambiar** las frutas, las **cantidad** de azúcar, el tipo de vino e incluso añadir, si queremos, el licor. ¡Puede ser **divertido** crear **nuestra propia** Sangría!

Ingredientes:
Una **botella** de Rioja u otro vino tinto
Azúcar **al gusto**
Un limón en **rodajas finas**
Una **naranja** en rodajas finas
**Melocotón** y/o **manzana cortados** en **pequeños trozos**
**Gaseosa**
Licor: al gusto (opcional)

Preparación:
**Mezclar** todos los ingredientes y **dejar reposar** unas horas en el **frigorífico**. Es importante que la **mezcla** repose unas horas, para que la mezcla tenga el **sabor adecuado**.

**Después de** ese tiempo, **agitar** y añadir el azúcar, el licor y la gaseosa, que puede ser de limón o naranja, pero es mejor la gaseosa **sin sabor**.

**Cuando bebamos** la sangría, añadir **hielo** y **servir lo más fría posible**.

# La chicha
## ECUADOR

La chicha es una **bebida alcohólica** que las comunidades indígenas **toman** todos los días. El **significado** de la chicha es comida, bebida, **hospitalidad** y también la **fuerza**.

**Se prepara todos los días** para que **permanezca fresca**. **Muy temprano en la mañana** las mujeres se van a **la chacra** con los niños para **sacar** la **yuca madura**. **Mientras** ellas trabajan cantan **"anent"** para que los niños **aprendan la costumbre**. **Cuando llegan** a casa **meten los tubérculos** en **una olla** con un poco de agua **tapados** con **unas hojas** estén **cocinadas**.

Cuando están listas la mujer **saca** la olla de **la candela** y empieza a **aplastarlos** con el **"taink"**. Es mejor hacerlo cuando la yuca está caliente porque se **deshace fácilmente**. **Sin embargo**, el "alma" es la parte interna fibrosa; **hay que machacarla** muy bien. Cuando todo está machacado la mujer **vuelve a colocarla** en la olla y **la deja toda la noche fermentando**.

La mujer que la preparó también **la sirve en presencia de** su **marido**. Ella la mezcla bien con los dedos y es importante **no tocar** su mano **al coger** el **"pinink"**. **Rechazar** la chicha es **grave** porque significa **desprecio** o **desconfianza**.

¡**Acuérdense**, si usted visita el oriente, **prepárense para tomar** chica!

---

**bebida alcohólica:** alcoholic drink
**toman/tomar:** they drink/to drink
**significado:** meaning
**hospitalidad:** hospitality
**fuerza:** strength
**se prepara/preparar:** make, prepare/ to prepare
**todos los días:** every day
**permanezca fresca** stay fresh
**muy temprano en la mañana:** very early in the morning
**la chacra:** small farm
**sacar:** to take out
**yuca madura:** ripe yucca
**mientras:** meanwhile
**anent:** ceremonial song used during manioc planting
**aprendan la costumbre:** they learn the custom
**cuando llegan:** when they come back
**meten los tubérculos:** place the tuber (root)
**una olla:** a pot
**tapados/tapar:** covered/to cover
**unas hojas:** some leaves
**cocinadas/cocinar:** cooked/to cook
**saca:** take away or out
**la candela:** the fire
**aplastarlos:** to squash or flatten them
**taink:** stick used for mashing the yucca
**deshace facilmente:** it falls apart easily
**sin embargo:** however
**hay que machacarla/machacar:** it has to be to crushed/to crush
**vuelve a colocarla:** put it back, return it to it's place
**la deja/dejar:** leave it/to leave
**toda la noche fermentando:** the whole night fermenting
**la sirve/servir:** serve it/to serve
**en presencia de:** in the presence of
**marido:** husband
**no tocar:** do not touch
**al coger:** upon grabbing
**pinink:** bowl used to drink the chicha
**rechazar:** to refuse
**grave:** serious
**desprecio:** slight; snub
**desconfianza:** distrust; mistrust
**acuérdense:** remember
**prepárense para tomar:** prepare to drink

# El turrón
## ESPAÑA

**Aunque** el turrón **está disponible** todo el año, todos **lo comemos** en Navidad. **Digamos** que el turrón es **imprescindible** durante estas celebraciones. **Hay muchos tipos** de turrón: de **yema**, **coco**, chocolate, etc. Pero el turrón por excelencia es el turrón de almendra. Hay dos tipos de turrón de almedra: turrón de Alicante (**llamado también** "turrón **duro**") y turrón de Jijon (o"turrón **blando**"). **El primero** está **hecho con trozos** de almendras, y **el segundo** con almendras **molidas**.

Aproximadamente **un mes antes de Navidad**, todos los comercios tienen ya **a la venta** gran variedad de turrones. Pero este año **intentaremos** hacer **nuestro propio** turrón en casa.

**Seguidamente encontrarás** la receta del turrón de Alicante.

Ingredientes:
1 Kilo (2,20 **libras**) de **miel**
500 gramos (1,10 libras) de azúcar
2 **claras de huevo**
1,5 Kilos (3.30 libras) de almendras **tostadas** (Puedes tostarlas en el **horno**).
la **corteza de un limón**

Preparación:
Primero, **coceremos a fuego lento** la miel, en un **cazo**, **hasta que espese** (hasta que el agua **que contiene se evapore**). **A continuación** añadir el azúcar y **mezclar**. Se recomienda usar una **espátula de madera**.

**Batir** las claras de huevo **a punto de nieve** y **añadirlas** a la mezcla. **Remover con energía** durante **unos diez minutos** hasta que la mezlca **se oscurezca**. Añadir las almendras y la corteza de limón. Mezclar bien y cocer a fuego lento, **cuidando de** que **no se pegue**.

Seguidamente **verteremos** la mezcla en **moldes de madera forrados** con **papel vegetal**. Después de dos horas y media, el turrón estará listo. **Conservar** los trozos, cuando estén **completamente fríos**, en un **envase hermético**.

# Tradicional comida
## GUATEMALA

## ARROZ CON LECHE

Ingredientes:
2 **tazas** de **arroz**
4 tazas de **leche**
2 **huevos**
1 ½ tazas de **azúcar**
1 taza de **pasas sin semilla**
4 **ramas** de canela
Agua

Preparación:
**Lave** el arroz. **Cocínelo hasta suavizarlo**. Ponga al **fuego** la leche, el azúcar y la canela. **Retírelo del fuego** cuando la leche **tenga el sabor de la** canela. **Cuélelo. Mezcle** la leche con una **batidora eléctrica** y **añada** los huevos. Mezcle el arroz con leche, el azúcar y la canela. **Ponga** al fuego y añada las pasas, **revolviendo** constantemente. Se **sirve frío o caliente**, adornado con **canela en polvo**.

## LA FRITADA

Ingredientes:
1 Kg de **costilla de cerdo**
1/2 **taza de agua**
Sal
4 **dientes** de **ajo**
1 **cebolla blanca cortada en** 4 **trozos**
1 **ramita de apio**

Preparación:
En un **sartén grueso** poner todos los ingredientes, excepto la cebolla. **Cocinar** a **fuego alto**, dando **vueltas** a la **carne**, hasta que se **evapore toda el agua**. **Bajar** a llama media y **seguir friendo**, **aplastando** las **partes grasosas** de la carne, durante 25 a 35 minutos, **o hasta** que **se dore** en la **manteca que suelta**. **Añadir** el apio y la cebolla en los **últimos 15 minutos**. La fritada **debe estar muy dorada**, de color café. Típicamente se sirve con papas y **plátano maduro**.

---

**tazas:** cups
**arroz:** rice
**leche:** milk
**huevos:** eggs
**azúcar:** sugar
**pasas sin semilla:** seedless raisins
**ramas:** stalks (sticks)
**canela:** cinnamon
**lave/llavar:** wash/to wash
**cocínelo hasta suavizarlo:** cooking
    it until soft
**fuego:** heat
**retírelo del fuego:** remove from heat
**tenga el sabor de la:** tastes like, it has
    the flavor of
**cuélelo:** drain (sieve)
**mezcle/mezclar:** mix/to mix
**batidora eléctrica:** electric mixer
**añada/añadir:** add/to add
**ponga/poner:** put/to put
**revolviendo/revolver:** stiring/to stir
**sirve frío o caliente:** serve cold or hot
**canela en polvo:** ground cinnamon

**costilla de cerdo:** pork ribs
**taza de agua:** cup of water
**dientes de ajo:** garlic cloves
**cebolla blanca:** white onion
**cortada en/cortar:** cut in/to cut
**trozos:** pieces
**ramita de apio:** small stalk of celery
**sartén grueso:** heavy frying pan
**cocinar:** cook
**fuego alto:** high heat
**vueltas/vuelta:** turning/to turn
**carne:** meat
**evapore toda el agua:** all the water
    evaporates
**bajar:** lower
**seguir friendo:** continue frying
**aplastando/aplastar:** squashing/
    to squash, to flatten
**partes grasosas:** greasy parts
**o hasta:** or until
**se dore/dorar:** it is brown/to brown
**manteca que suelta:** fat that it gives off
**añadir:** add
**últimos 15 minutos:** last 15 minutes
**debe estar muy dorada:** must be very
    browned
**plátano maduro:** ripe plantains

# La "dieta mediterránea"
## ESPAÑA

El concepto de "Dieta Mediterránea"... **¡está poniéndose de moda! Actualmente**, los mejores "maitres" de la cocina española **hablan de este tipo de dieta. Podemos encontrar** muchas páginas web que hablan sobre esta cocina, pero, ¿Cuál es el origen de la dieta mediterránea? Y ¿cuáles son sus **principales** características?

Sobre su origen, **cuando se estudiaron las costumbres alimenticias** de los países mediterráneos, (Grecia, Italia, Francia, España, etc.), **descubrieron** que en general **los habitantes de estas zonas** tenían un **bajo nivel de colesterol, comparados con** los **consumidores anglosajones**, centroeuropeos o norteamericanos, que **consumían** dietas **con más calorías**, más carnes, **grasas**, dulces y mantequilla. **Al contrario**, la dieta mediterránea **se basa** en los cereales, verduras, frutas, vino, pescados y... ¡también, pero **en menor cantidad! Así**, la dieta mediterránea **se ha creado a lo largo de los siglos**. Por ejemplo: los romanos y los griegos **nos dieron** "los tres productos mediterráneos", esto es, pan, vino y aceite de oliva. Más tarde, la cultura árabe nos dio la **berenjena**, la **alcachofa**, y muchas otras **hortalizas**. Y la dieta mediterránea también está influenciada por el descubrimiento de América: de allí **llegaron** el tomate, el **pimiento**, la patata o el maíz.

**Ahora que ya sabemos** sobre el origen de la dieta mediterránea, ¿Cuáles son sus características? Primero, es una dieta **saludable** y beneficiosa que previene las **enfermedades vasculares**, ya que **reduce** el nivel de colesterol. Segundo, el uso de aceite de oliva es muy importante. Tercero, gran consumo de productos vegetales y frutas. Cuarto, consumo **diario** de productos **lácteos** (yoghurt, leche, queso etc.) Quinto, consumo **semanal** de pescados. Sexto, consumo **mensual moderado** de carnes. Podemos encontrar la dieta mediterránea en **varios países**, y cada uno de estos países tiene **su propia** gastronomía basada siempre en este tipo de dieta.

Y ahora una nota personal: **No penséis** que esta dieta es **pobre en sabor o variedad**. Yo, **como seguidora** de esta cocina, **he probado** platos realmente deliciosos!

# Un delicioso postre: flan de huevo
## LATINOAMÉRICA

Uno de los **postres** más populares de Latinoamérica es el **flan de huevo**, **aunque** también **puede** ser de vainilla, chocolate, etc... ¿Qué ingredientes **necesitamos** para esta receta?

Ingredientes:
1 **litro de leche**
7 **cucharadas grandes** de **azúcar**
1 **corteza de limón**
6 huevos
**canela** (**un trozo pequeño**)

Preparación:
Muy bien; **ahora**, **para preparar** el flan, **seguiremos los siguientes pasos**: **Colocar** la **bandeja del horno** a **altura media** y **precalentar** a 350ºF.

**Hervir** la leche con el azúcar, la canela y la corteza de limón. Mientras **se calienta** la leche con los demás ingredientes, **batir** los huevos en un recipiente.

**Mezclar** la leche caliente con los huevos batidos. **Antes de verter la mezcla** en las **flaneras**, verter en ellas un poco de caramelo líquido. Pero **si no tenemos**, **podemos hacerlo así**: Mezclar **una taza pequeña** de azúcar con 1/3 de agua y calentar **a fuego lento hasta que** el azúcar **se disuelva**. **Subir el fuego** y **no remover** la mezcla, **hasta que tome un color ámbar oscuro**. Verter el caramelo inmediatamente en las flaneras. (Nota: Personalmente, **yo utilizo** caramelo líquido; **podéis comprarlo** en **cualquier tienda** y es **más útil que hacerlo en casa**.)

Verter la mezcla caliente de leche, azúcar, canela y corteza de limón en las flaneras caramelizadas. (**No llenarlas hasta arriba.**)

Colocar las flaneras dentro de una **cacerola** con agua caliente. El agua caliente **debe llegar a media altura** de las flaneras. **Cocer** en el horno durante 30 minutos aproximadamente. **Para saber** cuándo está hecho el flan, introducir una **aguja de tejer** o un **tenedor**. **Si está limpio**, el flan está hecho.

Sólo **tenemos que esperar** a que los flanes **se enfríen**.

---

**postres:** dessert
**flan de huevo:** egg custard
**aunque:** though
**puede/poder:** it can/can
**necesitamos/necesitar:** we need/to need
**litro de leche:** liter of milk
**cucharadas grandes:** large tablespoons
**azúcar:** sugar
**corteza de limón:** lemon peel
**canela:** cinnamon
**un trozo pequeño:** a small piece, portion
**ahora:** now
**para preparar:** to prepare
**seguiremos los siguientes pasos:** we will follow the following steps
**colocar:** to place
**bandeja del horno:** oven tray
**altura media:** in center of oven
**precalentar:** to preheat
**hervir:** to simmer
**se calienta/calentarse:** it gets warm/to get warm
**batir:** to whisk
**mezclar:** to combine; mix
**antes de verter la mezcla:** before you pour the mixture
**flaneras:** bowls used to prepare flan
**si no tenemos:** we don't have
**podemos hacerlo así:** we can make it this way (or as follows)
**una taza pequeña:** a small cup
**a fuego lento:** over low heat
**hasta que:** until
**se disuelva/disolverse:** it dissolves/to dissolve
**subir el fuego:** to increase heat
**no remover:** do not stir
**hasta que tome un color ámbar oscuro:** until it turns a deep amber color
**yo utilizo/utilizar:** I use/to use
**podéis comprarlo:** you can buy it
**cualquier tienda:** any store
**más útil que hacerlo en casa:** more useful than making it at home
**no llenarlas hasta arriba/llenar:** do not fill them to the top/to fill
**cacerola:** saucepan
**debe llegar a media altura:** must come halfway up
**cocer:** to cook
**para saber:** to know
**aguja de tejer:** knitting needle
**tenedor:** fork
**si está limpio:** if it is clean
**tenemos que esperar:** we have to wait
**se enfríen/enfriar:** they cool down/to cool down

# Examina tu comprensión

## El dulce de papaya, page 184

**1.** Children in Puerto Rico use the stems of the papaya for what purpose?

**2.** What food is a good accompaniment with the papaya dessert featured in this article?

## El mate, page 185

**1.** Name some different ways *mate* is served.

**2.** In Argentina, if you run out of yerba for tea, what is the natural solution?

**3.** The custom of drinking *mate* with friends, over conversation unites people, and encourages companionship. What is another unexpected benefit to the heart?

## La deliciosa papa, page 188

**1.** How many varieties of potato originated in Peru?

**2.** Peruvians have found ways to make the usually simple and tasteless potato full of flavor and history. Describe the ingredients in a stuffed potato.

## Ensalada de yuca, page 191

**1.** How many pounds of *yuca* are used in a *yuca* salad?

**2.** What kind of juice is used in a *yuca* salad?

**3.** What vegetable is used to decorate the salad when it is finished?

## Camarones, page 192

**1.** What is the name of the restaurant where this recipe was made?

**2.** What type of liquor is used in this dish?

# Test your comprehension

## Carnitas, page 193

1. How many cloves of garlic are used in this recipe?

2. What type of meat is the main ingredient of this dish?

3. Carnitas are served on a plate, accompanied by what?

## Sangría, page 194

1. What is the main ingredient of this beverage?

2. What fruits are in this beverage?

3. After the wine and fruits are mixed, how long should you wait to assure the appropriate flavors intermingle.

## La chicha, page 195

1. What cultural meaning is associated with *la chicha*?

2. *La chicha* is an alcoholic beverage made of what?

## El turrón, page 196

1. How much honey is used to make this candy?

2. This candy is prepared about a month before what holiday?

3. What is this candy stored in?

## La dieta mediterranea, page 198

1. When nutritional customs were studied, what was discovered about those who ate a traditional Mediterranean diet?

2. Do those who eat a Mediterranan diet consume more or less calories than those who eat an Anglo-Saxon diet?

# Respuestas

**Cultura** **Vejigantes page 4** 1. Africa   2. Christians and Moors   3. coconut shell, the inside fruit is cut out and the shell is carved into a mask   **De Tapeo page 6** 1. to be with friends, talk non-stop, cheer, "cheer up one's soul"   2. Province of Cadiz   3. He covered the glass of wine with a piece of ham so that the sand wouldn't ruin the wine.   4. garlic mushrooms, pork sausages, stuffed olives, spicy potatoes, cuttlefish, stuffed mushrooms **La siesta en Argentina page 8** 1. The word *siesta* comes from the latin word "sixta" meaning the sixth hour of the day. corresponding with midday, the hours between 1-3 pm.   2. regain energy, relieve anxieties, clear the mind and stimulate creativity   3. relieves tension, prevents ageing, prolongs life   4. 15-30 minutes and never more than 40 minutes   **Pescando con "caballos" page 10** 1. rustic boats made of cane called "caballitos de totora"   2. more than 1,200 years   3. loss of interest by future generations, trawler boats are destroying the fish, and the urban growth **Los alebrijes page 12** 1. wood, cardboard, paper mache   2. copies of animals in bright and lively colors such as turtles, butterflies, scorpions and frogs   3. The legend of Pedro Linares: At the age of 30 he became ill and he was left unconscious in bed.   He dreamed of donkeys with wings, roosters with horns, lions with eagle heads and dogs with spider legs. A loud voice screamed the name 'alebrijes' and with that scream he woke up from his sickness. He recovered and he wanted his friends and family to know these animals that had saved him and he begin to create them. **La pollera page 14** 1. *pollera montuna* worn as everyday dress or to work; *pollera de encajes* worn for holidays or important occasions.   2. The flowers are made by hand and can be made from fine coiled wire, with fish scales and silk. 3. chapines, made from satin or velvet   4. The exact origin of the *pollera* is unknown however some believe it has Spanish roots.   **El Gaucho page 16** 1. an important folklore symbol that symbolizes liberty and individuality 2. serves as a weapon and work tool; two rounded stones united by a rope made of braided leather   3. wide leg pants, waist with a girdle or belt, made of fabric or leather and decorated with silver or other metals, handkerchief around the neck, widebrim hat, poncho as a coat, leather boots or when he is not on his horse he might be wearing espadrilles (canvas sandals)   **El Rodeo y los "Huasos" page 19** 1. the hard work of the farmers and the need to round up the cattle   2. capacity or ability, physical strength, skill

**Viaje** **Barrio Gótico page 24** 1. Roman city   2. Puente de los Suspiros – Bridge of Sighs   3. to wear comfortable footwear/shoes   **Colonia del Sacramento page 26** 1. wool and leather clothing, decorated coasters, boxes of cookies, earrings, handmade hats and gloves, wooden games/toys   2. Leave with your *mate* (tea) and stroll along the harbor with family and friends.   **Verano en enero y febrero page 28** 1. miniskirts and Bermuda shorts 2. In the daytime you can walk along the boulevard, sit beside the sea, watch the surfers.  At night you can go to a show or a café or go dancing.   3. Mar del Plata   4. Pinamar y Cariló, the beach and the forest, the yellow sand against the dark wood creates a magical feeling. **Mallorca y sus castillos page 30** 1. They are known for their beauty and they are located in the Mediterranean sea.   2. circular form; It was built for King Jaime I. He was sick and suffering from tuberculosis and needed a place to recover and rest   3. The castle was burnt to disinfect it from the plague, after this is was cleaned and painted.   **Un paraíso en el Caribe page 32** 1. mountains, semidesert, tropical forests, beaches   2. Casa de Campo, enjoy environment similar to cities south of France, the seashore 3. poisonous snakes   **Varadero, arenas blancas page 34** 1. the marine life   2. The famous Bay of Pigs 3. Cueva de Ambrosio you can find cave drawings.  La Casa de la Cultura; Cuban culture, local artists, theatre and dance classes.  Museo Municipal de Varadero; historical and cultural pieces.   **Turismo Rural page 37** 1. the environment, the absence of crowds, relaxaation, bicycle rides and farm visits   2. *casas rurales* and *hoteles rurales*; both are old village houses or castles reconstructed for lodging   3. search the internet   **San Miguel de Allende page 38** 1. US and Canada   2. Spanish and art   **Tulum page 39** 1. priests, mathematicians, engineers, astronomers; they were considered gifted beings

# Answers

**Tradición**  **Chichicastenango page 45** 1. Patron Saint Thomas  2. "Palo Volador"  3. The manuscript of Popol Vuh. It tells the history and the legends of the people that lived in that area. **Pachamama page 46** 1. *Pacha* means universe, world, place. *Mama* means mother. Paying tribute to 'Mother Earth', giving thanks for nature bringing them food (making seeds grow and fruits ripen)  2. corn cobs, coca leaves, cigarettes, wine and beer  3. chopped paper or confetti that symbolizes happiness, handmade crafts made with sheep wool that symbolize wishes and intentions  **Una Navidad en Paraguay page 49** 1. summer  2. manger, decorated with flowers, coconut tree  **La Gritería page 50** 1. fireworks  2. "Who causes so much joy?" "The conception of Mary" **Gaspar, Melchor, Baltasar page 52** 1. grass and water for the camels of the three wise men  2. He opens his doors and has music and food for the children to give hope and happiness.  **7 de Julio page 54** 1. Ernest Hemingway; *The Sun also Rises*  2. more than 400 years  3. commercial holiday featuring bull fighting, music, running of the bulls, fireworks  **Viva el novio! page 56** 1. They found their car full of balloons.  2. an old restored convent that was a cloister 3. waltz  **Castillos en el Aire  page 58** 1. They stand on one another's shoulders, forming the shape of a human tower.  2. intergenerational with grandparents, fathers, mothers, children and infants  3. no protection, white pants, a black sash/belt, a shirt a distinctive color of the group, red handkerchief on the head

**Celebración**  **La Mama Negra page 64** 1. honor to the Virgin of Merced for the protection from the volcano that erupted in 1742, and Independence day (September 23rd)  2. She is represented as a black doll, figure transported through the parade on the back of a horse  3. shamans that conduct exorcisms to cleanse the soul  4. Star = angel Gabriel; Moorish King = the arrival of the Spaniards in Ecuador; The Captain = war. **Día de los Muertos page 66** 1. life, joy, facing the fears of death  2. "To the dead the big box, to the living the big party."  3. skulls; made of sugar; bones made from bread dough  **Festeja su independencia page 68** 1. Fiestas Patrias  2. an entire week, starting on the 18th of September  3. entertainers on the rooftops, playing to attract purchasers/ buyers; street vendors with cakes, pies, set up outside buildings, garlands hanging from tree branches, dances – polkas and the South American handkerchief dance  4. "El palo ensebado" The pole is buried and greased, and the competitors try to climb up the pole.  **Menudo Tomate page 70** 1. A group of young people got involved in a fight and started throwing fruit and vegetables at one another, and others got involved.  2. 120 tons; 1 hour  3. gather for breakfast to get strength for the battle, and to bring in the loads of tomatoes;  **La Virgen de la Candelaria page 74** 1. February 2nd and lasts 15 days; to honor the Virgen de la Candelaria and Mother Earth – to give thanks  2. folklore capital of Peru; because this festival is full of artisitic displays of the cultures of Peru  3. in the  Enrique Torres Bellón Stadium;  music and dance contests, and concerts  **La Pascua y Semana Santa page 76** 1. Friday is remembering the crucifixion. Some people fast, or consider this a day of silence and reflection.  2. Saturday is dedicated to the lament of the death of Christ. **La Fiesta con más gracia  page 78** 1. the neighbors, neighborhoods; recycled objects, yogurt cups, egg boxes, cardboard boxes  2. the most original, the best lit up, the most ecological and the most beautiful;  the prize-winning streets get more visitors and so they sell more food and drinks **Carnaval de Cadiz page 80** 1. during the month of February  2. The city of Cadiz had one of the most important sea ports. They started the celebration as a copy of the carnival in Venice but over time they adopted their own customs.  3. the official contest of singing and dancing

# Respuestas

**Personas** **García Márquez page 88** 1. He studied law. 2. suspense novels 3. journalism 4. Kafka, Faulkner, Virginia Wolf, Hemingway **Diego Rivera page 90** 1. Frida Kahlo 2. murals, on buildings, with a social message 3. the history of Mexico 4. social revolution, resistance to foreign oppression, value of indigenous people, value of the people, value of the past and the future of the country **Frida Kahlo page 92** 1. she wasn't able to bear children; she had continual physical pain in her spine, legs, and her entire body 2. self portrait 3. Diego Rivera; together they worked to paint social murals **Celia Cruz page 94** 1. children; she adopted hundreds of godchildren 2. perform in Carnegie Hall 3. brain tumor **Rubén Diarío page 95** 1. a poet and writer **Che Guevera page 96** 1. He suffered from asthma. 2. He discovered the misery and oppression among the people and he was educated in Marxist ideology. He became politically active and began working with doctors in labor unions. 3. He was executed by Bolivian soldiers in Havana, Cuba. **Unamuno page 98** 1. dean; political views led to the job ending 2. memories of his love and his personal crisis about religion **Andrés Segovia page 100** 1. four years old; 16 years old 2. His guitar did not produce sufficient sound to fill the concert hall. He experimented with wood and different designs to naturally increase the amplification of the guitar. 3. His transcription of Bach's Chaconne **Eduardo Galeano page 102** 1. a trilogy that describes the history of the Americas through real and mythical characters; The first volume includes indigenous legends and myths about the arrival of Europeans. The second is the history during the 19th century. The third covers the events in detail of the 20th century. 2. walking along the boulevard, enjoying the fresh air and the sea, or in a café.

**Deportes** **Imitar a los pájaros page 108** 1. no special training needed 2. an old sacred viewpoint 3. Río Pintos **Acampando en San Felipe page 109** 1. Northern Baja Mexico 2. dry and hot desert land 3. the stars and the moon, as there are no city lights **Surfing en Costa Rica page 110** 1. warm waters, miles of coast, nice people and reasonable prices 2. December – April 3. Do not leave your watch, passport or other valuable items on the dashboard. **El Fútbol page 112** 1. soccer ball or a t-shirt with a team name 2. to go to the countryside and play a friendly game without serious rivalry 3. passion, goose bumps for the fans, and tension, joy, bitterness, crying, and shouts **Jai Alai page 114** 1. a Basque word that means fiesta alegre – happy party; Pelota Vasca 2. action and speed 3. the court has three walls; main wall made of granite, the other walls are cement 4. tennis **Sierra Nevada page 116** 1. all through winter and the beginning of spring 2. with colors 3. horseback riding and mountain biking **Senderismo en el Perú page 118** 1. warm coastline, mountain range, rivers and amazon jungle 2. grade of adventure, risk and emotion you wish to experience 3. the town was set up for walking; they didn't know the horse or the wheel so all of their travels were on foot 4. four days

**Música** **Bailando al son de merengue page 124** 1. African and European 2. guitar, accordion, tambourine 3. 1960's **Instrumentos musicales page 125** 1. conch shell and deer skull 2. palm leaf 3. avocado tree trunk **El arte flamenco page 126** 1. dance, song and guitar 2. Andalucia 3. started as song and then grew to include the guitar 4. accompaniment and for solos **El reguetón está "rankeao" page 128** 1. rap, hip hop and reggae with the influences of typical dances *la bomba* and *la plena*, sounds of the drum and a catchy rhythm 2. the realities of the street, social views and love and passion 3. *pichaera*: to ignore; *guerlas o gatas*: girls; *guillao*: pride; *flow*: style; *yales*: women; *gata fina*: a conservative girl; *corillo*: group of people; *perrear*: a term given by Puerto Ricans to the way reggaeton is danced **Tango page 130** 1. Spain, France, Germany, Poland 2. sailors, craftsmen, unskilled laborers 3. brothel-like environments 4. in the 1940's **Mariachi page 134** 1. Coco Indians; music 2. violins, trumpets and guitars of various types/sizes 3. A form of guitar with a short neck and a large belly on the back side. **Candombe page 136** 1. in neighborhoods around Montevideo, at dusk, during the summer weekends, on street corners 2. African origin; it helps maintain the African culture in Uruguay 3. paintings and musicals/ theatre **La música andina page 138** 1. happy, sad, solemn, festive, and war-like 2. nine flutes made of reed tied together 3. Paul Simon

# Answers

**Historia**   **Cinco de Mayo page 146** 1. Puebla   2. September 16th   3. triumph of the Mexicans over the French army   4. valor, determination and national patriotism   **Los hijos del sol page 148** 1. 16th century, invaders were the Spaniards   2. it was considered the center of the world   3. Civil War   **La Independencia de Colombia  page 152** 1. Morales presented a vase to decorate the table of Llorente, and Llorente reacted rudely, insulting the creoles. They began to fight, and the fight extended to the streets to the Plaza De Bolívar   2. nine years on August 7, 1819   3. Simon Bolivar   **Un símbolo de la nación page 154** 1. belonging and patriotism   2. three powers of the state; majesty, law, and strength   3. red = spilled blood, white = snow of the mountain range, blue = clean skies of the city   **Bandera de Mexico page 155** 1. green = independence and hope, white = purity of the nation's ideals, red = blood loss in war   2. an eagle on a *nopal* plant fighting with a serpent; the strength and history of Mexico   3. Aztec Indians arrived in a valley and saw a lake with a small island in the middle of it. They saw an eagle on a flowering *nopal* devouring a viper. They took this image as a sign of the gods and constructed what is now the capital city.   **San Juan page 156** 1. Juan Ponce de León; Caparra   2. Plaza de San José; the bronze statue of Juan Ponce de León   3. They organized an impromptu procession, walking the streets, carrying torches and ringing bells.   4. old fort now a park; a labyrinth of tunnels, dungeons and shacks and the famous sentry box   **Ruinas de Tiwanaku page 158** 1. because of the sophisticated systems of agriculture   2. great blocks of stone oriented towards astronomy, the perfection of mummification and astonishing feats in the field of medicine   3. to pay homage and give thanks to their ancestors   **Los Garifunas page 160** 1. formed by a mixture Spanish, Nigerians and native Kalipunas that over time became the Garifunas community   2. the Spanish; they took them to work as farmers and they served in the army   3. music, dance, language, religion and customs

**Geografía**   **Parque Nacional Darién page 166** 1. UNESCO   2. Indigenous pre-columbian people live at the foot of a sacred mountain, Cerro Tarcuna on the riverbanks. Also there is a population of African descent. 3. Scientists indicate it is essential to regulate and control farming and forestry and studying environmental impact. **Las Islas Galápagos page 168** 1. submarine volcanic eruptions   2. to recuperate from their combat wounds 3. Charles Darwin; 'The Origin of the species'   **El Jurumí page 170** 1. giant anteater   2. long, thin, sticky tongue; catches food and helps control insects in the environment   3. sense of smell; it allows it to smell prey   4. jaguar, puma, hunters and destruction of the environment   **Paisajes diversos page 172** 1. diverse ecosystem, water basins, wildlife 2 . altiplano zone where Lake Titicaca is, sub-andean zone where it is humid and there is lots of vegetation, Amazon zone surrounding the Amazon river   3. huge statue of Jesus   4. ceremonial center and astronomy observation center **Paisajes, flora y fauna page 174** 1. Angel Falls, named after a pilot Jimmy Angel   2. sandstone formations   3. Gran Roque, because of the calm sea, great sea life   4. the preservation of the green turtle   **Las ballenas de Valdez page 176** 1. Istmo Carlos Ameghino   2. whale migration, reproduction and  birth   3. watch them jump, spray water when they take a breath, screech, great dorsal fin and tail   **La Reserva de El Vizcaíno page 177** 1. dry, hot and arid 2. mesquite used to make bonfires, maguey an ingredient in tequila   **Laguna de San Ignacio page 178** 1. October and  February; 5000 miles   2. warm waters to give birth   3. The fat is necessary for the whales to survive in the winter. 4. You can touch the whales; this is rare because  most wild animals  retreat and run away from human contact.

**Gastronomía**   **Dulce de Papaya page 184** 1. as a bubble-blower   2. goat cheese   **El Mate page 185** 1. with sugar, hot, cold, with orange juice, with a teaspoon of coffee, with medicinal herbs   2. Ask your neighbor, who will gladly give it to you.   3. It may heal broken hearts.   **La deliciosa papa page 188** 1. 3,000   2. mashed potato mixed with ground beef, onions, raisins   **Ensalada de Yuca page 191** 1. two pounds   2. orange juice 3. cherry tomatoes   **Camarones en salsa blanca page 192** 1. El Rubí   2. dry white wine   **Carnitas page 193** 1. five   2. pork   3. guacamole and hot tortillas   **Sangría page 194** 1. red wine   2. lemon, orange, peach, apple 3. one hour   **La Chicha page 195** 1. food, drink, hospitality, and strength   2. ripe yucca   **El turrón page 196** 1. one kilo, approximately 2.2 pounds   2. Christmas   3. airtight container   **La Dieta Mediterránea page 198** 1. lower cholesterol levels   2. more

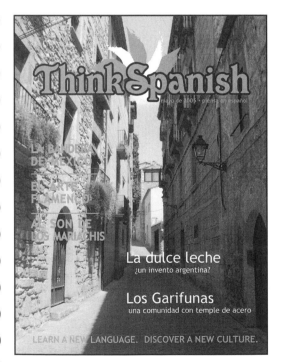